HIDDEN NATURE

HIDDEN NATURE

Wild Southern Caves

MICHAEL RAY TAYLOR

VANDERBILT UNIVERSITY PRESS
Nashville

© 2020 by Vanderbilt University Press
Nashville, Tennessee 37235
All rights reserved
First printing 2020

Library of Congress Cataloging-in-Publication Data

Names: Taylor, Michael Ray, 1959– author.
Title: Hidden nature : wild southern caves / Michael Ray Taylor.
Description: Nashville : Vanderbilt University Press, [2020] | Includes
    bibliographical references and index.
Identifiers: LCCN 2020004222 (print) | LCCN 2020004223 (ebook) | ISBN
    9780826501028 (paperback) | ISBN 9780826501035 (epub) | ISBN
    9780826501042 (pdf)
Subjects: LCSH: Caves—Tennessee. | Caving—Tennessee.
Classification: LCC GB605.T2 T39 2020 (print) | LCC GB605.T2 (ebook) |
    DDC 551.44/70976—dc23

LC record available at https://lccn.loc.gov/2020004222
LC ebook record available at https://lccn.loc.gov/2020004223

This book is dedicated to Marion O. Smith, one of America's greatest explorers, and to H. Lee Pearson, one of my greatest friends.

CONTENTS

As Jim Smith sets a bolt traverse above a cave pool, Frank Bogel provides belay.

I spent the weekend camping and caving in middle Tennessee and visited one of the project caves we are working on. A large passage was seen on the last trip which was on the opposite side of a 20 ft. deep pool of water. Joel Buckner, Hal Love, James Smith, Kyle Lassiter, Garrett Sexton, Marion O. Smith, Jason Lavender, Clinton Elmore, and I met at the cave Saturday morning to ferry climbing gear and provide support to those doing the traverse. Jim Smith did a 25 to 30 ft. long horizontal bolt traverse about 15 ft. above the pool which led to a virgin upper level passage. Kyle Lassiter came behind and cleaned the gear off the traverse. After rigging the drop, we joined Kyle and Jim and mapped about 200 feet of cave before it ended in a large breakdown collapse room. We ended up spending about 10 hours underground.

FRANK BOGLE | Facebook post, August 16, 2015

Chapter 1

NEAR SPENCER

I'm in a cave, lying on my side atop a bed of mud and sand washed in probably decades ago by some forgotten storm. Above me a pleasant fall afternoon warms a pastoral valley. Leaves have begun to turn beneath the spotless blue sky. Up there the Cumberland Plateau dominates the southern horizon, rearing like a green tsunami poised to crash over central Tennessee. In a sense the plateau is an ocean, if one long dead: its stacked sediments bristle with the fossilized remains of Carboniferous sea creatures. Beneath the plateau's hard sandstone cap, voids riddle the softer limestone—more caves per square mile than in any other location in the United States, according to data compiled by the National Speleological Society. These water-carved caverns send out tendrils beneath the plateau's edges. They can run on for miles, curling and coiling like a labyrinth Lovecraft might have imagined.

Several long caves reach this valley. I'm digging with hopes of breaking into a new one from a short, allegedly dead-end passage. The surrounding landscape is karst, a term derived from a German word describing the geology and topography of the Dinaric Alps, now applied to any limestone landscape featuring caves, sinkholes, and streams that vanish underground. I was sweating before I began this work because I

View of the Cumberland Plateau from the Sequatchie Valley, Cumberland County, Tennessee.

could not find the entrance, hiking an unnecessary hour through boulders, chest-high thorns, and cow pies before giving up, driving up to the ridge for a cell signal, and calling the landowner for more detailed directions. Then I drove straight to it, thorns scratching at my rented SUV, boulders and stobs threatening to gouge the pan. I geared up and crawled over the rough cobbles of the entrance to begin digging in a smooth-walled rotunda at the end of the known space.

Barely two hundred feet long, this little cave has been known to local residents for over a century. Proof is written on the white limestone ceiling in the form of a half-dozen blackened signatures and dates, scrawled in candle smoke by rural visitors during the late 1800s and early 1900s. Elsewhere in this valley are caves explored by much earlier settlers from early in the nineteenth century all the way back to Native Americans who lit their way with cane torches thousands of years ago.

People have always been drawn underground. The oldest human remains have been discovered in the caves of Africa, Europe, and Asia—some of them older than our most ancient common ancestor. A spate of studies of human mitochondrial DNA has pushed forward the date when a small band of African humans began to populate the rest of the world. As recently as sixty thousand years ago, or fewer than two thousand human generations, our common ancestors may have journeyed outward. Traces of their lives persist: caves serve as repositories for the earliest known examples of art, basketry, shoes, and clothing.

Humanity's more recent spread through the American South is also chronicled below ground. Less than an hour's drive away from the spot where I lie digging, I once followed bare footprints in soft, damp cave mud, noting bits of ash and mineral samples dropped by three walkers. Protected from casual obliteration by colored plastic flagging and extreme secrecy, these prints were made by the lined, leathered feet of explorers who traversed the passage more than four thousand years before me, according to the carbon dating of bits of river cane that fell from their flickering torches.

A big-eared bat chirps nearby. Ruffling leathery wings with a drumming sound, he objects to my intrusion into his normally silent chamber. Over the past decade much of the bat population of the eastern United States has been decimated by white-nose syndrome, a deadly plague spread by fungal spores, but the few individuals I can see appear robust and healthy. Their annual hibernation period will soon approach. For now the weather outside remains warm enough that I know they will exit at sunset, each consuming hundreds of insects before returning at dawn.

Except for bats and a few cave crickets, I'm alone in a passage perhaps twenty feet wide and twelve feet high at the center. The old signatures are spread over a comfortable alcove where the ceiling height is about six feet. Farther from the center of the chamber, the roof slopes downward to meet the floor, giving the room the appearance of a lens. At the edge where I've worked for the past hour, the white limestone ceiling sits no more than twenty inches above the dried mud on which I recline. I reach with a garden hoe into a still smaller space, barely wider than the hoe's blade: the spot where all present-day drainage vanishes. Water is rare here. The entrance sits on the high side of a sinkhole so that it only comes in during the largest floods.

Following a list of clues over the past few months, I have found reason to believe that somewhere beyond the reach of my hoe unexplored passages and chambers await, perhaps connecting to a hidden borehole winding northward from the plateau. I can't say that I'm here merely in the hope of scientific discovery. Other cavers far more accomplished than me have also been poking into sinks in this area, seeking a back door into a known subterranean system many miles long. I deeply admire these explorers: I once wrote a glowing profile of their cantankerous patriarch, Marion O. Smith, in *Sports Illustrated*, a publication not normally known for caver stories. Smith is by far the world's most experienced caver, with well-documented trips to over eight thousand separate caves in his seventy-seven years. Each of these caves is meticulously recorded in a shelf of journals going back over sixty years, yet he calls the "most experienced" title "hogwash."

"True," Smith recently wrote me, "I've been to a lot of holes, primarily short, blind-bottomed pits or 50 to 100 foot-long duds. But I have no technical skill of any kind." He doesn't set rigging bolts, draft cave maps, camp underground for weeks on long expeditions, or take on other advanced technical skills commonly applied to modern caving. "I'm lazy," he says, preferring to call in friends with technical skills to help explore his finds that are *not* duds. Yet over the decades many young, strong, technically skilled cavers have struggled to keep up with Smith underground. At some of his discoveries—like the fifteen-mile-long system running beneath a nearby valley—he spent many months in secret survey of deep pits and massive rooms never before seen by humans, modern or ancient. As an outsider from Arkansas, I look with awe upon Smith's accomplishments, yet I would be thrilled to scoop him here all the same.

To cavers, *scoop* as a verb can mean a couple of things, both marginally scandalous. The lesser offense refers to excitedly rushing through virgin passage without mapping as one proceeds, which caving ethics demand. The greater offense is to quietly slip into an area where one person or team has been digging or otherwise searching for some hidden cave, then to pluck the jewel from under the noses of those who have labored diligently to find it. I sense such a jewel may hide within this overlooked and disregarded passage.

A faint breath exhales from the narrow drainage path, brushing my face, driving me to work harder. I push the hoe inward to its full length and pull back moist soil, which I shove into a growing pile beside me. I study a handful of the stuff. It is reddish brown from clay content. Bits of leaf and rotting wood from the surface indicate that this particular handful has likely been underground no more than a decade. I pull it close to my face and sniff, inhaling a musky smell familiar to most gardeners. This signature aroma of southern caves and gardens is actually the smell of actinomycetes. Biology textbooks refer to these filamentous organisms as "transitional forms" between bacteria and fungi, sometimes calling them "higher bacteria." They constitute a sort of missing link between single-celled organisms, like E. coli, and multicellular life like us.

Actinomycetes sit atop a vast hidden ecosystem of subterranean microorganisms. Some keep busy breaking down organic material brought in from above, as here. They also interact with countless other microbial species that feed off minerals brought up from below. In other words, some microbes eat rocks. Their excretions may be involved in producing colorful mineral formations like stalactites and stalagmites, and in excavating the very voids that form caves. Some bacterial colonies process elemental sulfur into tiny drops of sulfuric acid that eat through limestone like gasoline poured on a Styrofoam cup. Picture the acidic saliva dripping from the creatures in the *Alien* films at a teeny-tiny scale, constantly removing grains of rock.

Scientists working with NASA believe similar microorganisms may exist today beneath the rock and ice of Mars and other worlds within our solar system. Sunlight and oxygen don't figure into the list of "minimum requirements for life" with such organisms. All they need are minerals and liquid water, which may be abundant below ground on other worlds. Researchers have put a great deal of energy into studying this dark life, virtually unknown a quarter-century ago. I recently collected a swab of native petroleum that lay in a black pool at the bottom of a Tennessee cave stream. Biology students working with a colleague at my university found the drop to hold hundreds of unique species, including some previously found only in the black smokers of deep-sea hydrothermal vents. How did they get from an ocean into the middle of North America? The answer to that question lies deep underground.

Biology, however, is a task for another day. I drop my handful of soil and rake out some more with my hoe. After several pulls I turn the tool around, using its wooden handle to probe the depth of the channel not yet enlarged. It is always deeper than the length of my hoe. The odds of me breaking through into larger passage today are slim. But they are not nonexistent. Such knowledge keeps me digging. Understanding why I'm driven to lie alone in muddy darkness on such a beautiful fall day requires that I dig into my own past.

The suburban neighborhood where I grew up straddled a spit of sand separating the Atlantic Ocean from the Intracoastal Waterway of Florida's east coast. It was a pleasant enough place for childhood—ranch houses surrounded by palm trees, sunshine, and salt air, with much swimming and boating—but it contained no hills, rocks, or streams. The geography presented no variety to strike the imagination of a boy addicted to adventure books. Luckily, at least once a year my parents loaded my younger sister and me into the family car for an escape. We would strike out for southern Illinois, one thousand miles away, where my parents were born. On these trips to rolling farm country we crossed actual mountains in Tennessee, winding over dizzying two-lane highways that offered occasional glimpses of the new interstate system then under construction.

The earliest of these excursions I can recall occurred the summer after I finished first grade, which would have been 1966. I was reading above grade level, eagerly consuming anything printed. I noticed gigantic words on barns: "See Rock City," and "See Ruby Falls." I puzzled these words out and read them aloud to the car. As we encountered more barns I began to recite them with a frequency beyond the point of irritation.

I asked my father what the words meant.

"Tourist traps," he muttered.

I asked my mother the same question.

"I think one is a rock formation and the other one is a cave," she answered.

Both were things I had previously encountered only in stories. I began to follow each barn reading with "Can we go?" I enlisted my sister in this effort.

For reasons I have never understood, my father, who traveled as cheaply as humanly possible, gave in as we approached Chattanooga on

Caves hide marvels. Beyond the chance for discovery, they offer an opportunity for increased human understanding of biology, paleontology, history, geology, and the environmental health of the surface world above. Although few cavers realize it at the start, gaining underground skill means becoming an expert in and ultimately an advocate for safety and conservation, as well as least an armchair geologist and paleontologist. What began as a childhood fantasy and a college pastime grew into a significant part of my life, much of which has been occupied with describing caves and cavers to the general public, accurately sharing the scientific, environmental, and archeological secrets they hide. That word, *hide*, applies not only to the caves, but to the people who explore them.

Cavers have kept many great discoveries of the past fifty years secret for a variety of (mostly) good reasons. Caves present dangerous environments, where unprepared explorers can become the subject of massive rescue attempts (or in the worst case, body recoveries). These can last hours or days, costing hundreds of thousands of dollars, often giving everyone involved—from the injured person to the landowner to local authorities—terrible press, even when the outcome is happy. A careless touch can shatter delicate mineral formations or obliterate ancient artifacts. The passing of a single human can forever change a complex ecosystem, as when a caver inadvertently transports the fungus that causes white-nose syndrome from one place to another. Because of their close link to safe groundwater, caves can become political hot potatoes, the subject of acrimonious legislative hearings and regulations.

Yet while some cavers remain convinced that all press is bad press, others work to educate the public on the need for conservation and protection. In 2017, Chuck Sutherland, a groundwater specialist and consultant living in Nashville, decided to create a visual representation of the TAG region, adding in the state of Kentucky to show that all of these caves are distributed within a related geologic unit. He called this super-region "KTAG," and plotted thousands of entrance locations as recorded in the electronic (and not generally accessible) databases of all four state cave survey associations. The Tennessee Cave Survey alone lists over ten thousand known caves, each appearing as a tiny dot on Sutherland's map. They depict regional clusters centered over Mammoth to the north and Chattanooga to the south, with the two largest groupings occupying the central Cumberland Plateau and the Ridge and Valley topography that stretches into Alabama and the corner of Georgia. But the red-hot center of cave distribution in the Southeast— the densest known location of entrances anywhere within the United States—stretches across a forty-mile swath of middle Tennessee, where there are, on average, four known caves per square mile.

The one where I have chosen to dig today lies smack in the middle of this swath.

Barring clumsy spelunkers, earthquakes, or environmental disasters, caves tend to change imperceptibly on human time scales. Many that I first saw forty years ago look the same now, with maybe a few more boot prints. They will likely look the same for at least several centuries into the future. But I have changed. As I revisit my TAG favorites or follow young experts into strange new places, my accounts of these visits can't help but straddle a line between personal reflection and objective reporting. To fully share what I've learned about Southern caves, as I hope to do in this book, requires that I wander first on one side of that ridge and then on the other. Some chapters recount my long relationship with a few outstanding caves and cavers, while others describe recent trips investigating spelean biology, archeology, history, conservation, and similar scientific matters. If you go deep enough, everything is connected.

In *Cave Passages*, published in 1996, I wrote that I was fortunate to have begun caving in an era of great discovery. A quarter of a century later, that golden age persists, even as its luminaries have begun to die off or become too old for the intense physical work of caving. I wrote in that book of my caving buddy Lee Pearson, who took me into a wild Tennessee cave in 1980 when I was twenty and he was twenty-five. Lee and I, and our spouses, have been friends ever since. Life-related interruptions have slowed the frequency of our excursions, but together we have seen wondrous things. My view of TAG caves, their value to the environment, and the challenges presented in exploring and protecting them, has become inextricably intertwined with my own story of aging, friendship, and occasional subterranean triumph. As witness to a golden age of caving, I found a sort of philosophy of caving practiced by devotees the world over, most especially here in the South.

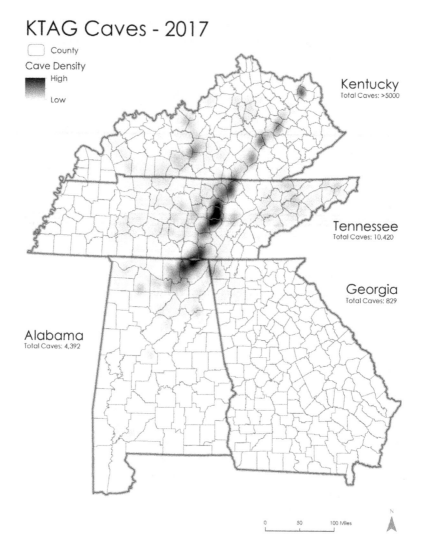

KTAG Caves - 2017

County

Cave Density

High

Low

Kentucky
Total Caves: >5000

Tennessee
Total Caves: 10,420

Georgia
Total Caves: 829

Alabama
Total Caves: 4,392

0   50   100 Miles

N

Despite a general policy of secrecy, cavers and cave scientists some-times lead me to their favorite hidden spaces knowing full well that I'm a writer. These explorers recognize what humankind has always known: Beyond mere fact, caves hold an unlimited capacity for story. No matter how objectively I might try to report the science and culture of caving, whenever I follow others underground what emerges is a tale of the journey, mine mixed with theirs. Like the ancients, we leave our familiar surface lives for hidden realms of fable, seeking places where story changes understanding. Whatever we might say upon our return is more than mere trip report: it becomes a message about what it means to be human. Caves move me. They moved our most ancient ancestors. I hope they will move you.

Cavers, of course, tend to be scientific, analytical, and skeptical—not the least bit shamanistic. Whenever they mention mystical places they've been, they tend to grin to let you know they're kidding. But after forty years I've grown to realize they aren't kidding, at least not always. I first felt that force of enlightenment in a Florida cave on February 2, 1980. I have a photograph. I feel it now in the kiss of a breeze rising from blackness.

As I pull the hoe toward me, I see that I am rolling a small cylindrical object: an antique bottle. The deep cobalt color suggests it held the nineteenth-century whitening compound commonly called "bluing." Its location here in my digging area supports my theory that this was once an open tunnel that became filled with modern storm detritus. I dig some more. Eventually I stop for the day and return to a nearby rental cabin furnished with Wi-Fi and ready access to the surface world. I see reminders of the force that drives me underground in the Facebook posts of Tennessee cavers. As with many specialized pursuits, much is shared on social media.

Evidence: A 73-year-old man says as a teen he explored "at least a mile" beyond the mud plug in the cave now, and to me the deposit looks ancient. Still,
when I crawled in today with a hoe and shovel for a test dig, I pulled out this
little beauty, with part of its rusty top. Lee Pearson, we need to recruit some
diggers and take a trip sometime.

MICHAEL TAYLOR | Facebook post, October 11, 2015

Chapter 2

FLORIDA-GEORGIA LINE

Thanks to the magic of CLEP tests, which once allowed students to skip basic courses, I earned an AA degree in three semesters at what was then called Daytona Beach Community College. I entered Florida State University as a junior for the start of the winter term in January 1979. Rather than live in a dorm, I received housing from a nonprofit foundation that bought up old houses around campus and provided rent-free rooms to students with good grades. We paid only for utilities and a basic food supply, sharing housework and cooking duties (which is how I learned to cook for large groups, a skill that later came in handy at caver gatherings, not to mention within my own family). Collectively, these houses, some for men and some for women, became a sort of low-rent fraternity and sorority system, a de facto dating field for nerds.

The nerds in the room next to mine were Tim Glover, a wiry chemistry major from Sebring, and Ed Hill, a tall, somewhat intense film major. Ed had grown up in Lakeland, but his mother came from Trinidad, likely the source of his sharp cheekbones and the subtle musical lilt in his voice. The three of us bonded over our shared ability to recite *Monty Python* sketches from memory, as well as an interest in hiking, canoeing, and other outdoor pursuits. Two blocks away my sister, who had preceded me to FSU, lived in a similar house for women. Tim and Ed sometimes accompanied me on visits to my sister—after all, a dozen women lived in her house. There Ed met and soon began dating an English lit. major and College Bowl quiz star named Terri Olson.

The four of us, often accompanied by Terri's aging Labrador retriever, began to regularly canoe area streams, visit local springs, and camp at nearby parks. Despite our heavy course loads, we tried to schedule these wilderness weekends once or twice per month. It was in this manner that we all became cavers on the same day in the early summer of 1979. Like most beginners I have encountered in the years since, we did nearly everything wrong.

In college I was ripe for attraction to caving, not only because of a fondness for fantasy novels and memories of Ruby Falls, but from a long habit of escaping into nature. I had grown to love Florida's streams and rivers, which were far more familiar to me than the mountains or caves I occasionally experienced on family vacations. A family album shows me as a baby perched in my mother's arms. She sits on the bow of my father's StarCraft aluminum runabout, wearing a one-piece swimsuit. The boat floats on opalescent water. I wear a diaper, my mouth and eyes both open in evident delight. I have an early memory of my Aunt Violet and my mother skiing behind that boat, effortlessly slaloming across one another's wake.

Aunt Violet chain-smoked Kools, and for nearly a year she saved coupons from cigarette cartons to surprise me with a promotional sailboat for my thirteenth birthday. It had a Styrofoam hull, a green-and-white nylon sail bearing the Kool logo, and just enough room for me and a passenger. In junior high I would set out from the rickety wooden dock of my family's home on the Halifax River—actually a brackish lagoon of the Intracoastal Waterway—and pick up a schoolmate who lived on the other side. We explored sandbars and oyster bars, surfed the wakes of large motor yachts cruising the East Coast between winter and summer berths, and wove among schools of cavorting dolphins, which swam up the Halifax each year to give birth and nurse their young.

A couple of years later, I doubled my fleet with an open fishing boat powered by an iffy outboard Mercury. This greatly extended my nautical range. With a full tank of gas I could strike south toward Ponce de Leon Inlet, once more aptly—if less invitingly to tourism—called Mosquito Inlet. It appears by that name in Stephen Crane's great sea story "The Open Boat." The inlet and its old lighthouse look, at least from the sea, much the same today as Crane described them in 1897. Or I would set off north toward the Tomoka Basin and into the Tomoka River, winding through swamps and mangroves to anchor at sugar plantations abandoned during the First Seminole War of 1816–19 or the derelict set of a Johnny Weissmuller *Tarzan* film shot in 1932. At the furthest navigable reaches of the Tomoka it approached civilization, and I could sometimes hear the roar of the Daytona Speedway.

My first date, early in high school, was an afternoon cruise in the sailboat, which I promptly capsized. It was the only time I ever did so, and the last time I went out with that particular girl. For my second date, I asked a different girl to join me in the fishing boat. We at least managed to stay dry through an awkward picnic at Tomoka. Even as I became increasingly expert at navigating the shifting sands of saltwater estuaries (if not high school romance), I began to venture onto more distant fresh water. From earliest childhood, one or two weekends each summer my family left the boat at home, packing a picnic lunch to drive an hour or so inland for a day of swimming at one of the blue springs dotting central Florida: Alexander, Juniper, Salt, De Leon, Ichetucknee, and others. Regardless of season or weather, the water remained a cool seventy-two degrees.

As a teenager, I returned to these springs to snorkel and occasionally spearfish, testing my swimming strength against the powerful boil that emanated from the base of each clear pool. My friends and I would rent canoes or inner tubes and float the cool, narrow rivers that flowed from these sources, following them through forests of pine and palmetto. Dragonflies lighted on our elbows as great blue herons soared and plashed.

In a theoretical sort of way, I knew that these streams emerged from flooded caverns, if only because so many scuba divers drowned in them. Signs at each spring's parking area would warn against entering the water's source, listing the number of divers known to have perished there. Local newspapers carried accounts of these fatalities. Knowing that I liked to snorkel just outside such dangerous places, my mother always pointed these out to me. In truth, I did enjoy holding my breath and swimming down to the submerged entrance, where I could peer at the darkness and read one final, dire warning sign placed underwater.

Sometimes the divers died in the caves alone, sometimes in parties of three or four at a time. Their story was generally the same: Water so clear as to impart the sense of flying when they had entered became an enveloping, disorienting cloud as they disturbed layers of thick silt with their fins. Untrained cave divers would lose their bearings, run out of air, and drown with great regularity. I stayed out of the caves.

For Tim, Ed, Terri, and me, caving began with a typical weekend camping trip to Florida Caverns State Park in Marianna, about seventy miles west of Tallahassee. We piled the usual gear into Tim's Volkswagen Squareback and camped near the spring-fed Chipola River. The park sat atop a relatively high ridge. Many caves there had once been part of Florida's vast limestone aquifer but had drained and could now be entered on foot. Until that day, I had not realized that the state contained dry caves at all, other than perhaps Tom Sawyer's Cave at Disney World. (Later I would learn that clusters of dry caves dot several elevated regions scattered across Florida.)

The main draw of the state park was a well-decorated tourist cavern. We adventurers had no interest in taking a guided tour, however—especially since ticket prices were higher than poor college students were willing to pay. Instead we set off down a hiking trail that wound past limestone rock formations and passed directly through a couple of short caves. We could see other entrances in the woods, inviting us to leave the trail. With two flashlights between us, we eagerly explored each new hole, at first stoop-walking, then on hands and knees, then on our bellies.

We became certain we were entering chambers that all others had missed. Who else would be willing to lie in mud and wriggle into a room so small you could barely sit up? At some point we stumbled upon the most inviting entrance yet, a horizontal blackness six feet in diameter, opening within the flat limestone. With our flashlights, we could barely make out a large walking passage at least 15 feet below. Frustratingly, the park had blocked this vertical drop with a metal grate. Ed, the skinniest, tried to squeeze through the bars, hoping maybe he could find us another way in. They proved too tight even for his narrow frame.

After noting the location we discussed coming back another weekend, armed with tools that might help us bypass this bureaucratic impediment. We decided we needed more flashlights and extra batteries; by day's end we were down to a single dim light between us. One of the plastic flashlights had burst to pieces against a rock, so we planned to acquire some heavy-duty models from a military surplus store in Tallahassee. Around the campfire that night, we compared our adventures to those of Bilbo Baggins.

The following week, I searched the university library for a book on Florida's caves. I found a few on famous locations in the US and Mexico and a short one on cave exploration methods, which seemed mildly interesting, but there was nothing specific to the state. I had hoped to find listings of additional locations near the park that we could explore. The reference librarian I asked for help suggested that I talk to someone in the university cave club.

A cave club? At Florida State? I practically ran to the student union, where I was given a telephone number for Karen Witte, the club's president. I called her that night and introduced myself.

"My friends and I have been spelunking in pretty much all of the caves near the hiking trails at Florida Caverns," I explained. "We're hoping to get more entrance locations. Do you have a list?"

She paused a moment before answering. "Um, you probably need to come to one of our meetings for that." Her voice contained an odd hint of amusement.

It was my turn to pause. We four adventurers were not really *joiners*. We had no interest in any sort of official club. But if this were the way to get new locations . . . "When do you meet?" I asked.

She told me the next meeting was the following Sunday night at seven in the student union.

"That will work," I said. "We have a Marianna trip planned, but we can probably be back by seven."

We arrived at the meeting with army surplus flashlights dangling off our belts, our jeans and t-shirts torn. Mud clung from our wet, disheveled hair to our squishy tennis shoes, which leaked like sponges as we walked. Terri's black lab had eagerly joined us in the caves this time, and the dog painted blobs on the wall with his muddy tail as we approached the meeting room. We had discussed cleaning ourselves up on the drive back to Tallahassee, but we were running late. Plus, we felt our condition would demonstrate that we were serious spelunkers, so the club would open its secret files to us. The fifteen or so people in the room smiled as we entered, many of them stooping to pet the wet, smelly dog, who loved everyone.

The Florida State Cave Club, or FSCC, was not only a student organization but an official "grotto," or chapter, of the National Speleological Society. President Karen Witte looked like an average college student dressed in jeans and t-shirt, as did one or two others, but most of those present appeared older. All were fairly lean and fit, if more than a little scruffy. They looked as though they had just returned from Woodstock or maybe a Depression-era hobo camp. The single exception was a quiet, clean-cut man in his late twenties, dressed in a khaki shirt and pressed jeans, who resembled a cartoon game warden. I later learned his name was Allen Mosler and that he actually worked for the state's department of natural resources.

Several of the group stood around a folding table as we entered, studying at a sheet of paper about three feet wide and eight or ten feet long. I realized I was looking at one end of a scroll bearing the details of a winding passage—most of the map was hidden at the end of the table like an economy-sized roll of holiday wrapping paper. One caver quickly returned the exposed portion back into the scroll as we approached. Nearly everyone in the room would have a profound effect on my life from that point forward.

From them I learned one of the most important lessons college can offer, which is that great mistakes can be made when people don't know what they don't know. There was much I didn't know about caving. Over the next hour I learned that "spelunker" was a term of derision. *Cavers* had been *caving* for decades by the time a New England Boy Scout leader coined "spelunking" for a 1930s expedition that popularized it in the press. A bumper sticker sold at caving conventions summed up the difference: "Cavers Rescue Spelunkers." (Years later, a few seasoned TAG cavers tried to combat such elitism by taking what they ironically described as "spelunking" trips to extremely difficult locations. Despite this effort, saying "I'm a spelunker" generally equates with saying "I am a rank amateur with no earthly idea what I'm doing.")

I learned that in addition to "spelunker," another term for a clueless beginner was "flashlight caver." This was because the single most common callout for a rescue began when a group entered a cave by flashlight. A few hours into the trip, batteries would fail, and one by one lights would flicker and die, leaving the group to sit in the dark until hours later when, typically, someone who knew their destination called the authorities, and the authorities called qualified cavers to launch a rescue. Depending on the time of the call, the remoteness of the area, and whether the caller actually knew which cave the group had planned to enter, usually late that night or the next day rescuers would locate the spelunkers. Cold, thirsty, convinced they would die, members of the stranded group would rejoice at the approaching glow of cavers who would lead them back to sunshine. They would stand blinking and numb before local TV cameras, telling their adventurous story, and in a living room somewhere a mother would turn to her child and admonish, "You are never, ever going into a cave."

Experienced cavers, I learned, each carried a small rugged flashlight or two for backup and to spotlight interesting formations, but their primary light source, at least in the late 1970s, was an antique carbide miner's lamp. Someone at the meeting—it may have been a caver named Chuck Machovec—presented one to demonstrate. The brass lamp's upper chamber held water, which would slowly drip into a screw-on base. The base held pea-sized chunks of calcium carbide. Chuck produced a plastic baby bottle and shook a few of the gray rocks into our hands. He explained that water produced a chemical reaction with these that released acetylene, which fueled the lamp. Its flame, amplified by a chrome reflector, could light your path for several hours, and when the carbide was spent, you would collect the powdery residue—he produced another baby bottle about half full of the stuff—then recharge your lamp with fresh carbide.

He charged the base of an empty lamp at the meeting, set the water drip, and placed his tongue in front of the nozzle as though to lick it.

"You can taste the stream of acetylene coming out if you've done right and don't have any leaks," he said. "Then you cover the reflector with your hand to collect some gas so that you can fire it."

I hadn't noticed, but there was a tiny metal wheel and flint embedded in one side of the reflector, similar to a Zippo lighter. Chuck covered the reflector a few seconds with his right hand, then rapidly pulled his palm over this wheel, giving spark to the gas—the lamp popped with a noise that made us jump. He turned out the room's overhead lights, and we could clearly see by a cone of yellow light from the steady half-inch flame at the center of the reflector. Antiques were preferred, he explained, because the newer lamps were shoddy and tended to explode on your helmet. No decent carbide lamps had been manufactured since the last coal mines had switched to electric in the 1950s. The club would let us borrow helmets and lamps for our first few outings, we were told, but eventually we would have to buy our own.

Like many cavers, I would come to spend hours frequenting rural flea markets and antique shops to pick up the most-sought-after lamp models. In coming decades, as lighting technology improved, efficient electrics that could last for days on a single charge gradually replaced traditional carbides. Lamp collections like mine were relegated to display shelves. While dependable and easy to recharge, carbide lamps could also be fussy. They could repeatedly slow a trip as one person after another paused for field repairs. They produced waste that could pollute the cave if not diligently removed (in some well-traveled and abused southern caves you can find mounds of spent carbide over seventy years old). They also stank—with Chuck's short demonstration, an odd chemical odor wafted through the meeting room. Yet some cavers grew to love that smell and even today remain nostalgic for it.

Whether carbide or electric, our primary lamp, club members explained, should always be mounted on a helmet with a secure chin strap. This was because the second most common sort of cave rescue after "lost with no light" was "head injury from a ceiling bump or fall." Besides walking directly into low-hanging rocks, spelunkers were prone to slip on inclines in part because one hand was occupied with the business of holding the flashlight. Cavers needed two hands to navigate the three-dimensional complexity of underground mazes. Almost always, going forward meant a great deal of going "over," "under," or "around." While we had easily walked over the flat, sandy trails running through a couple of small caves in Florida Caverns State Park, such passages were uncommon.

Another reason for slip-and-fall injuries was, we were told, athletic shoes. While great for cross-training or jogging, these did not offer the ankle support, traction, and secure attachment required for caving. One person at the meeting asked how many of us had stepped out of our shoes at some point that day. We sheepishly admitted that the thick mud had left two of us briefly unshod. We were instructed that most cavers (at least at that time) wore inexpensive army-surplus jungle boots, manufactured in the millions for Vietnam.

"Don't spend a fortune on good hiking boots," Karen Witte advised. "You'll ruin them on the first trip."

Another caver pointed out that Allen Mosler had expensive hiking boots—was in fact wearing them at the meeting—and they looked perfectly clean.

"Yeah, but Allen's weird," another responded, to general nods.

"He stays clean the whole time he's underground," added a third.

Allen smiled sheepishly, as though he had heard this before.

Perhaps because we were so muddy, raw, and enthusiastic, the cavers shared additional tips to the point of bombardment, most of which began with "never" or "always": Never enter a cave without three sources of light per person. Always carry a small, rugged pack with water, extra carbide and batteries, a candle and matches, and some waterproof food. Never leave your pack behind while "checking out" a tight crawlway or lead. Always tell someone not on the trip which caves you planned to enter and what time you planned to return. Never bring a rope underground until you have been certified in the grotto's vertical training course. Always pack a large garbage bag in the liner of your helmet to use as an emergency blanket or as a rain poncho on the hike back to the car; it could also come in handy for collecting discarded batteries and candy wrappers left behind by spelunkers. Always map virgin passage as you explore it. Always glance over your shoulder at intersections, because they will look different going out than they looked going in. Always bring a complete change of clothing, including shoes and underwear, for after the cave, and always bring extra trash bags for your muddy clothes and boots. And finally, they delivered a mantra I would hear many times in many places: *Take nothing but pictures. Leave nothing but footprints. Kill nothing but time.*

The thing that kept me nodding along with all these rules and regulations was not so much a desire to become a "proper" caver as that tantalizing glimpse I had caught of the map when we first entered. It clearly depicted something much larger and more complex than any cave we had seen in Marianna. Eventually the safety orientation petered out and club members resumed the meeting's agenda. They discussed mapping new passages in Climax Cave, about forty miles north of Tallahassee in southern Georgia.

The map we had seen earlier depicted one branch of Climax, which was known to be over seven miles long. Although the group was interested in a single section, for the benefit of us newbies they unrolled the entire scroll across the floor. It stretched from one corner of the room out the door and into the hall. One of the principal cartographers took evident pride in pointing out spots on the map depicting big chambers, small crawlways, chimneys to upper levels, formations, fossils, and all sorts of features beyond anything we had seen thus far.

The cavers had hooked us, and they knew it. If this was a cult, we were ready to sign up.

Over the next year, our core group—Tim, Ed, Terri, me, and sometimes the dog (at least for the shorter trips)—continued to explore together, but most often we went along with other members of the club. Starting with the FSCC official "novice" trip to Malloy's Waterfall Cave, also in southern Georgia, we worked our way up to more difficult to excursions into Climax and Glory Hole (cavers get to name their finds—caving, I learned, is nothing if not Freudian). Part of the entrance system at Climax included a climb of about eighteen feet down a "chimney," where cavers used opposing pressure from feet and back to stay wedged within a vertical space, gradually working their way up or down while taking advantage of small handholds and footholds.

The first time in the entrance chimney was scary for everyone—it seemed you were about to flush yourself down a chute. But as more experienced cavers pointed out the smooth side to place your back and the rough side to place your feet, you began to learn the steps and remembered them next time. Near the bottom, the chimney intersected a passage in what appeared to be a dangerous five-foot drop to the floor, but if someone below guided your feet, you could step down the wall on a series of protruding rocks not visible from above. Once you knew where these were, you began to feel a certain mastery in moving effortlessly up or down a chute that had exhausted you the first time. The same was true of crawlways that worked best when approached at a certain angle, or bypass tunnels that allowed you to avoid upcoming obstacles if you knew where to leave the main trail.

Gradually we learned details of the complex route and could thus move much more quickly through it to areas of "interesting" features or new exploration. This sort of competence produced a euphoric feeling akin to a runner's high. The very aspect of caving that made it so difficult became pleasurable. It required a mixture of grace and brute force. Watching Climax veterans like Karen or Chuck move through a rocky tunnel was like watching a ballet and a perfectly executed football play rolled into one. I began to understand what cavers meant by the allure of "project" caves—complex systems that an individual might devote years or decades to, getting to know every twist and turn like the lines on a lover's face.

After a few trips, we became adept at stripping off muddy clothes on the side of country lanes and dressing in dry jeans and t-shirts before any passing farmer might call the sheriff to report naked hippies on the highway. When your every bodily surface and crevice is caked with mud, matters of appearance such as haircut, clothing style, or body type begin to seem trivial. With enough mud, even gender becomes indistinct. Standing filthy and naked on a highway at midnight makes you less self-conscious about appearance than typical college students, more focused on the solid than the transitory. We were learning secrets and turning into cavers.

Sometimes, from necessity, we stripped out of our muddy clothing *during* the trip in order to keep mud out of a delicate formation area or clean subterranean pool. The passage everyone had been studying at that first meeting included "The Pool of Naked FROGs." FROG was an acronym for the Fort Rucker-Ozark Grotto, an NSS club based in

Glory Hole Cave in South Georgia, a gated cave mapped and monitored by the Florida State Cave Club and in more recent years by its successor, the Flint River Grotto.

Fort Rucker, Alabama, about two hours away. A group of FROGs had found and mapped a previously unknown pool in Climax. As was the custom, they had removed their muddy clothing and gear—except for helmets and lamps—to swim to the far side of the deep, pristine pool and measure its size. Hence the body of water's name. Word was they continued to skinny dip a while after, just for funsies.

The FROGs' sketch had noted a couple of leads near the pool, so our gang of four joined a later grotto trip to push those leads. We brought extra trash bags so that if we found dry passage on the far side, we could keep our clothes and gear relatively dry, floating them across the pool to reassemble on the other shore. This is what we did, surveying a few new crawls and rooms near water level. There was nothing terribly remarkable about these finds but this: we were almost certainly the first humans there. And that felt remarkable indeed.

Jim Smith, Kristen Bobo, Marion Smith, Frank Bogle, and Gerald Moni set off on a 2015 trip to a project cave in Tennessee. Moni and Bobo planned to photograph a formation area while the others pushed a vertical lead.

We surveyed 1400 feet of river passage. We wore floatation while we surveyed in swimming passage. We wore wetsuits under our cave suits. Lots of blind fish and crawfish. Our cave is about 8,000 feet long surveyed. Our trip was 11 ½ hours. Rained while were in cave. Noticed a barometric shift as the wind in the cave stalled then gusted. We hiked back with 60-pound packs. We ate chili and drank beer at 1:30 am. Finally crashed at 3 a.m. Great friends, great adventure, great memories, and we surveyed. We are up to 16 miles of surveyed cave in our project area.

JAMES SMITH | Facebook post, August 30, 2015

Chapter 3

BAT SEASON

On a Saturday morning in late February 2018 I drove southeast on Interstate 24, descending the treacherous Monteagle grade in the general direction of Chattanooga. Torrential rains the week before had given way to sunshine and wildflowers. Temporary but spectacular waterfalls crashed over roadcuts in the limestone, throwing up clouds of mist. The tiny drops assaulting my windshield had emerged from surrounding springs only minutes earlier. Beside me eighteen-wheelers downshifted through the switchbacks.

In his 1989 song "Monteagle Mountain," Johnny Cash accurately noted that this stretch of highway has "claimed many a trucker's life." A permanent smell of hot brake pads wafts over the road. Along the eastbound lanes, two runaway truck ramps veer off to the left, several miles apart. The wise motorist glances periodically at the rearview to check for speeding vehicles in need of them.

When I was a child and this portion of interstate was still under construction, I remember my parents' fear and agitation each time we traveled old US 41 on family vacations. I recall wrecked trucks lying on their sides near tight curves and flagmen directing cars around boxes of spilled goods. These days the road is considerably safer, yet its 6 percent

View from Signal Point, near Chattanooga on the Cumberland Trail.

grade remains the steepest of any encountered throughout the interstate highway system. As the highway finally comes off the plateau and levels out, the first exits are crowded with truck stops, fast food restaurants, and fireworks stores. The truck stops fortify drivers heading up and reward those who make it safely down, while the fireworks stores cater mostly to Georgia residents crossing into Tennessee to stock up for Fourth of July and New Year's. A few miles short of the Georgia line I pulled into the large parking lot of a truck stop just beyond a fireworks warehouse.

I was looking for a group of strangers I was to meet for a bat count. Late February marks the height of the annual period researchers informally call "bat season." Throughout the country, small teams head underground to survey bat colonies that have survived winter hibernation. The bats counts—along with occasional banding, tracking, experimental treatments, and tests of new monitoring methods—are part of a coordinated national effort run by the US Fish and Wildlife Service. Dozens of state and federal agencies participate, along with private conservation organizations, universities, and individual volunteers—most of whom are cavers like me. Their shared goal: saving America's bats.

A tri-colored bat displaying signs of WNS, held and photographed by Dustin Thames during a survey of a Tennessee cave.

Here at the start of the 2018 season, it seemed a losing battle.

In 2006, the disease white-nose syndrome (or WNS) was first detected in a single bat in a commercial cavern located in Schoharie County, New York. Since then the fungal pathogen *Pseudogymonascus destructans*, commonly called Pd among researchers, had endlessly cloned itself, spreading across the eastern United States and Canada, killing more than seven million bats along the way. Some infected colonies experience a 95 percent mortality rate. In one sense the disease mimics the spread of American chestnut blight in the early twentieth century, in that it is carried by a fungus spreading south and west from

New England. The fungus appears to have originated in Asia and spread to Europe. Exactly how it reached the US remains a hotly debated topic. One theory is that it was unwittingly carried into that New York cave by someone who had come into contact with it in Europe. Another is that it may have traveled to a US port aboard a container ship.

What is clear are the economic implications. Bats eat insects that damage crops, saving farmers billions of dollars every year on pest control, according to the United States Geological Survey. And the disease continues to spread.

I was spending a few weeks in Sewanee, Tennessee, near the campus of the University of the South, when I had learned of an upcoming bat count from an email exchange with Dr. Amy Turner, an ecologist directing the university's Office of Environmental Stewardship and Sustainability. She had invited me to join a team led by Cory Holliday, a cave and karst expert with the Tennessee chapter of the Nature Conservancy. The team also included bat researchers from the Tennessee Wildlife Resources Agency and from the environmental office of nearby Arnold Air Force Base, along with a couple of student researchers.

As I pulled into the parking lot I spotted six or seven scruffily dressed men and women of various ages. They stood amid a small cluster of government-issue pick-up trucks, chatting and shifting boxes of gear. I parked and approached Holliday, a cheerful, burly fellow with a full red beard. He looked very familiar. We agreed it was likely we had met at some previous caving convention—we stood in the heart of prime caving country. Two or three regional or national caver gatherings were hosted nearby each year, and we had both attended several without ever having been formally introduced.

As he began detailing the day's plan, Holliday made a request I had grown to expect from bat researchers: He asked that I promise not to identify in public the specific location we were about to visit. Institutional secrecy has always been a component of cave conservation, for a variety of good reasons. Caves are low-energy environments, meaning that the life inhabiting them tends to be small, highly specialized populations, vulnerable to disturbance. Caves also house unique and fragile mineral formations, cultural artifacts, and water resources—not to mention dangerous pitfalls that can kill or maim the unprepared visitor. But the spread of WNS has ramped up the institutional practice of secrecy regarding Southern caves.

The one we were to enter housed a vulnerable bat population, already devastated by WNS, its rag-tag band of survivors under long-term study. Even though the entrance was gated, Holliday explained, unauthorized visitation spurred by publicity could have profoundly dire consequences. It could alter the results of base-level information being gathered on how the disease was progressing in Tennessee. Not to mention the site was privately owned, and the landowner had allowed researchers access with the understanding that they would discourage casual trespass.

Holliday told me that in 2014 Tennessee had been designated an "endemic zone" for WNS. "This means that Pd and WNS are presumed ubiquitous throughout the state."

Because of this, everyone present would follow WNS-positive caving standards established by the National Response Team. Our gear had to be clean before entering the cave and had to be decontaminated to government-defined standards after exiting. Even so, we were to avoid ever taking any of it, from boots to helmet to pack, into a region that the disease had not yet touched.

As we stood in the parking lot, the southern front of the advancing epidemic lay less than one hundred miles away in northern Georgia. It had not reached southern Georgia and the many caves I had explored there decades earlier with the Florida State Cave Club. Recent research had suggested that bats—and not humans—most commonly carried the disease from place to place, but that did not mean human transmission never happened. We followed the WNS protocols in hopes that none of us on today's trip would become personally responsible for introducing the deadly fungus to colonies elsewhere.

Like many other cavers and some leading experts, I was beginning to doubt that the disease could be slowed or reversed though human action. The night before, I had seen an animation on the website of the national response team depicting tendrils of WNS spreading across a US map, from the first case in New York to the most recent discoveries. The progress reminded me of maps that would be displayed in an early scene of most zombie movies, usually shown to a group of worried generals gathered in a bunker. The steady advance of WNS seemed unstoppable. Over the course of twelve years, the thickest concentrations had moved down the Appalachian Mountains and westward into Missouri and northern Arkansas. A ring of infestation circled the Great Lakes in southeastern Canada and the northern US. A few outlier cases had been found in Texas and Alabama. Except for one small, largely inexplicable appearance in Washington state in 2016, most of the American West was at that time clear of the disease. (Within months, however, it would be identified for the first time in South Dakota, Wyoming, and other western locations.)

Just two weeks earlier, the celebrated bat researcher Merlin Tuttle and the top two officers of the National Speleological Society had written a letter to the US secretaries of the interior and agriculture calling for an end to the national WNS response. "It is time to acknowledge that WNS is going to run its course," they wrote, arguing that "survey and research efforts in the bats' hibernation caves is causing far more harm than good. WNS kills infected bats by waking them up too early from hibernation, forcing them to waste limited fat reserves, and research activities increased such sleep interruptions." Clearly the group I had joined disagreed with these conclusions, as did many recreational cavers I knew. But evidence of any positive results from research or the widespread closure of caves on public lands was scarce.

With WNS endemic in Tennessee, our job for the day was not to look for the disease per se, but to monitor the health of survivors in a tri-colored bat colony infected about five years earlier. Recent warm weather had likely ended hibernation earlier than normal. This meant we wouldn't be waking individuals that couldn't find food that evening.

I knew the species well, since it was common to north Florida and South Georgia. Not long after I began caving, one of them flew up my pant leg in a tight, sandy crawlway of Climax. I had been heading toward the entrance sinkhole after a long day pushing distant passages. As the sun fell on the surface, hundreds of bats dodged the cavers strung along the crawlway, heading out, as they did nightly, to eat thousands of mosquitos and moths. I got the little guy out of my pants only by undoing my belt and crawling forward, rolling the pants to my ankles. I gently pulled the bat from my thigh. It seemed a little dazed, but shook

Dustin Thames searches a crevice for
bats during a survey.

its head and flew off with others. We all lay still for another ten minutes or so as they zipped by, the chirps of their echolocation bouncing
around us. Most echolocation is ultrasound, above human hearing. But
they are noisy little critters in the audible range as well.

Experienced cavers in the club told me the species was the "eastern
pipistrelle." I encountered them at many places in TAG over the years.
It turned out that this common name (along with the related "western pipistrelle" of the Pacific coast) was a misnomer. The rise of DNA
testing in the twenty-first century had proven what biologists had long
suspected: although similar in appearance to actual pipistrelles, these
American bats differed from their namesake, an old world species ranging through Europe, North Africa, and parts of Asia. The new name,
"tri-colored," came into vogue around 2010, suggested because each hair
of the eastern American species contains three colors: black at the base,
yellow in the middle, and brown at the tip.

Not all bat species are adversely affected by WNS. The Indiana
bat, a critically endangered species since 1967, appears somewhat less

susceptible to effects of the disease than tri-colored bats. The Mexican free-tailed bat resists WNS because it does not hibernate for extended periods. Tourists watch this migrating species, named for its warm winter residence, exit by the millions each summer night from Austin's Congress Avenue Bridge and New Mexico's Carlsbad Caverns. The gray bat, also federally endangered, seems more resistant to the disease because of its larger size.

The more vulnerable species, such as the tri-colored, tend to be smaller in size and more likely to succumb during hibernation. For the previous three years, Dustin Thames, a young researcher with the Tennessee Wildlife Resources Agency, had banded infected bats in the cave we were visiting. He hoped to collect some of these tagged individuals today in order to see how well they had survived with the disease.

Because parking was limited, not to mention plainly visible from a nearby state highway, we consolidated the group into fewer vehicles. One goal outside the cave was not to be noticed going into it. I moved my caving gear to Holliday's truck and rode with him the few miles to the entrance. The moment we parked, I knew that we were headed to a spot I had visited before. Featured in many convention guidebooks of the 1970s and 80s, it was considered an "easy horizontal trip." Its pleasant stream passage, about the diameter of a subway tunnel, meandered for several thousand feet under the surrounding hillside.

I recalled spending a couple of hours there with my school friends Tim Glover, Ed Hill, and Terri Olson while attending my first caver gathering, the 1980 SERA Summer Cave Carnival (SERA is an acronym for the Southeastern Regional Association of the NSS), held at Russell Cave National Monument in Alabama. The stream emerges from an arched entrance to join a rocky surface creek. We had come out of the cave that hot summer day thoroughly caked with mud, accumulated from checking out several side leads and slick climbs along the way. Once outside we had walked downstream to a wooded area with a deep pool. We took off our filthy clothing in the cool water, scrubbing the outer layers of mud onto rocks in the stream before putting them into plastic bags. We donned shorts, flip-flops and T-shirts for the ride back to camp. I couldn't remember many bats, but evidently a robust colony had occupied the cave at the time.

Following Holliday and the others down the short trail to the entrance, I saw a large steel gate that had not been there in 1980.

"Is that a Kristen Bobo?" I asked, nodding toward the gate.

"It sure is," said Holliday. "She's the best."

Bobo, a caver based in Cookeville, is well known throughout TAG for her skill in designing and welding cave gates that are difficult for vandals to breach but allow bats unfettered access. Her gate designs are as distinctive as a painting by Mondrian or a house by Frank Lloyd Wright. As with others she had built, this gate was sealed by an interior padlock that was difficult to reach from outside. Hiding the lock in an awkward enclosure made it virtually impossible to remove with a saw, crowbar, or bolt-cutters. But it meant that the person holding the key had to be somewhat dexterous, feeling around to fit it into the lock with one hand. The key-holder usually kept it attached to a wrist cord to avoid accidentally dropping it beyond the gate. Eventually Holliday popped it open and we entered a large room just beyond the entrance. As was the custom, once everyone was inside, he locked the gate behind us.

The cave opened into a larger chamber with several short side passages and balconies bordering the main stream. We split into two groups, with one sloshing upstream in the ankle-deep water while the other checked for bats in the various cubbies and fissures on either side. I started out with the second group, which itself split into Thames and another volunteer on the left, and researcher Amy Turner and I on the right. We very quickly spotted solitary tri-colored bats on the walls and ceiling. They appeared somewhat torpid but not sleeping. Turner explained that it was common for WNS-positive tri-colored bats to roost near entrances, presumably so that they could be close to food sources, although no one knew the actual reason.

Each bat we spotted would be counted in a survey book as well as being examined for positive signs of WNS and for previous banding. Nearly all were visibly WNS positive, the namesake fuzz of white fungus surrounding their snouts. Whenever we spotted a banded bat, we would call across to Thames who would examine it and determine the year it had been banded. One that had been banded in 2015 was WNS positive, but otherwise appeared healthy, as though it had learned to live with the disease. He also tagged several previously unbanded bats.

When the cave narrowed to a point where our two teams were closer, I walked over to better observe the process.

He plucked the bat from the limestone wall as though picking a ripe fruit, then held the protesting animal gently in his left hand. The volunteer assisting him handed Thames a small numbered brass band from a plastic bag, which he crimped onto the leading edge of the bat's wing using a modified pair of stainless steel needle-nosed pliers. As he worked, he described the bat's sex, size, and general health, and the assistant wrote this information beside the number of the tag that was being attached. When he released the bat, it wheeled angrily away, much like the bat I had released from my trousers all those years ago.

In this manner we worked our way toward the back of the cave, usually working in pairs but with team members regrouping and splitting as dictated by the winding passages. After a couple of hours we reached the terminus, turned, and headed back to the gate. By the trip's end we had counted sixty-four bats, just five down from the previous February, in a place that in years past had housed as many as 1,400 bats.

Two days later and 150 miles to the east, I stepped aside as four scientists in Tyvek suits and rubber boots carried an aluminum fishing boat toward an opening in a granite rock face. Mist cascaded from surrounding north Georgia mountains, curling over swollen streams, obscuring county signs for Broke Axle Trail and Warwoman Road. This was *Deliverance* country—the 1972 film had been shot nearby—and I recalled stories of the remote production that James Dickey, my former writing professor, had always enjoyed telling. On the last day of an unusually warm February, green shoots bristled in the forest floor. I heard no banjo music.

Along with a half-dozen researchers, I stood in the rain as the white-clad figures entered Black Diamond Tunnel, a segment of never-completed railway begun in the 1850s. They set the boat beside a makeshift landing, climbed aboard, switched on helmet lamps, and set off down a black river.

Christopher Cornelison, a research assistant professor and principal investigator at the BioInnovation Laboratory at Kennesaw State University, watched his colleagues recede into stygian blackness. The previous year they had sprayed an antifungal agent in the tunnel to see if it would protect the bats that live there from WNS. Now they were back to see the results.

"It's taken me years to get to this point," he said. "We've learned a lot, but there's never enough time."

While the survey I had joined was the most common sort of bat season activity, a few researchers had been trying out high-tech strategies to actually slow or stop the progress of Pd. Black Diamond Tunnel's tri-colored bat population had numbered over 5,000 in 2013 but was down to 152 individuals by 2017. I watched as Pete Pattavina, a bat biologist and UFSWSF's WNS Southeast Coordinator, expertly piloted the crowded boat to learn if a long-term treatment project there showed any signs of success.

Because the tunnel was man-made and contained few other species, it provided a perfect testing ground for an antifungal chemical called B23, derived from an unlikely source: a microbe found within the tissues of wild Bolivian pineapples. Used as a flavoring and in veterinary medicine, B23 was already certified as harmless to wildlife. With a commercial mosquito fogger bolted to a remote controlled boat—which Cornelison's team christened "Batilda"—researchers had sprayed several applications of the drug during the previous year.

"If the numbers are too low today, we may have to abandon the project," Pattavina had confided during our drive to the site. "It's hard to justify the continued expense if we only have a few survivors."

Elsewhere in the country, researchers were testing various stratagems that might increase resistance to the disease including vaccine development and treatments based on oils found on certain bat wings, ultraviolet light, and "cocktails" that mixed several natural products. Kelly Lutsch, a first-year graduate student of Cornelison, had begun a study of concrete culverts along Interstates 75 and 95 through Georgia's coastal plains. She believed that infected bats using them here, where there were no caves, could be carrying the pathogen south into cave-rich zones near the Florida panhandle. One Georgia cave near the Florida border hosts a robust colony of over 90,000 southeastern myotis bats, a species recently confirmed to be susceptible to WNS. The bats were counted using modified missile-tracking algorithms developed by the Defense Department.

Emily Ferrall, a wildlife technician with the Georgia Department of Natural Resources, had entered a South Georgia cave a week earlier to swab healthy-looking bats for lab tests confirming that the disease had not arrived there—at least, not yet. In eastern Texas, a researcher named Melissa Meierhofer had shown me the state's largest known colony of tri-color bats. They lived in culverts beneath a busy interstate highway an hour from Houston, somehow healthy and beyond the reach of WNS thus far, unlike the same species here in Black Diamond.

The tunnel's ceiling sloped toward deepening water, lights on the distant boat becoming stars in a field of black to those of us onshore. Occasional meteoric flashes reached us from spotlights swung to detect bats clinging to damp walls. After an hour, the team slowly paddled back to share their results: 178 bats, up by 26 from the last count.

Cornelison cautioned against interpreting this as B23 success, since other factors could affect the count. Still, he was "ecstatic" that the number was higher, not lower.

"I don't think we will ever know the full ecological effect of WNS," Pattavina said as the team began to disassemble and decontaminate gear on the rainy hillside. "We only realize the value of biodiversity when catastrophe happens."

SOCIAL INTERLUDE

In about 15 minutes, I'll be leaving for a secret spot in North Georgia to help dig open what we hope to be a new cave. I've been there a number of times already.

We make an average of maybe five feet of progress each time. All day long, moving rocks using a bucket to carry them out of the hole. Blasting rock with boom. Digging dirt. Moving salamanders out of the way. Wash, rinse, repeat.

It's fun. Not sarcastic fun, actual fun. Getting up early, driving over two hours, likely ruining whatever clothes I wear, getting home as late as 9–10 p.m., hiking a mile in the early morning cold carrying heavy digging equipment, using up a $40 tank of gas to get there and back . . . none of these things even cross my mind. On this trip, I'll have to carry a chainsaw I spent last night getting ready so I can cut up some huge trees that have fallen across the abandoned road so we'll have better access. I don't care, I'm happy to do it. I want to see what the next 1, 2, 3, or 20 feet of this project has in store. Anything folks would find annoying in order to make this happen, I don't even notice.

I'm part of a small team doing this, people who do it often. We do not know what we will find. We may find out today that the cave doesn't go anywhere and have to abandon the project. It's happened before. Or, we may find the deepest cave in North America (possible, given the geography and geology of the area).

This is exploration. What I'll see later today is something no human who has ever existed has ever seen. Each trip is like that.

SAM MOORE | Facebook post, November 25, 2019

Chapter 4

FINDING CAVES

After my college friends and I joined the grotto, we also began to map and explore new leads near Florida Caverns. On one of these excursions, I learned that a member of our club was one of the volunteers who helped install the gate we had so recently hoped to vandalize. (Luckily for us, we had found the club before we managed to find a hydraulic jack and hacksaw, probably avoiding arrest.) On another club trip to the Marianna area, we four friends were scheduled to spend a day ridge-walking—a universal code word for cave hunting—in a little-explored area near Bumpnose Road, while others were to assist with the survey of a short cave near the park's visitor center. It was February 2, 1980. I was twenty years old.

The new location had been discovered by Dr. Paul Boyer, a FROG member and geology professor at a nearby community college. On his only previous visit there, Boyer had found the partial skeleton of an ice-age relative of a llama, probably dragged inside by a saber-toothed cat or similar predator. At some point much later—perhaps two centuries ago—a live oak began growing over the entrance, eventually obscuring it and protecting the tunnel throughout the arrival of civilization and state parks. A recent storm had blown the old tree down, exposing an entrance between its thick roots.

Boyer estimated the entire cave to be only ninety feet long, all of it crawling passage. It had to be a small survey crew, both in numbers and in waistline, to map not only the tunnel itself but the precise location and arrangement of the prehistoric bones. As the tiniest cavers in the club, Karen and Marianne agreed to lead the survey. Others would hang in the parking lot, switching out as needed. I hoped to be able to go in later to take some photographs of the skeletal remains.

Our Bumpnose Road crew returned to check on their efforts that afternoon. We had found only a few small holes ourselves, none worthy of survey. An excited caver met us in the visitor center parking lot. He told us that Marianne and Karen had "poked around" halfway down the crawlway while Dr. Boyer was sketching the skeleton near the end of the passage. Karen had noticed a small hole leading downward, but it proved too tight even for her, so she and Marianne began digging at the loose dirt to enlarge it. With difficulty, Karen wormed her way through, slid down a slope, and announced from below that she was "standing up." In Florida caves, these were magic words. The group began digging at the loose silt near where Karen had slid through, enlarging the hole so others, including Dr. Boyer, his sketch of bones laid aside, could also get in and survey.

"How big is it?" I asked.

"So far we've mapped about 750 feet," the caver said, deadpan as he could manage. "You pretty much have to see this for yourself. We decided no more than four should go in at a time, to protect the, um, features. The first survey team just came out, so I can take three of you in."

Even without the survey footage, "features" and "first" would have been clue enough. We were practically bouncing with excitement. Terri stayed outside to watch her dog, with the promise of a later trip inside. I grabbed my new camera pack—a waterproof army surplus ammo case—and followed Tim, Ed, and our leader into the hands-and-knees crawl. When we reached the "little hole," Tim and I debated whether anyone had actually enlarged the spot bigger than Karen size, but by leading with one arm forward and one arm trailing to reduce our shoulder width, we each managed to struggle through.

Once through, we slid about eight feet down a sandy slope to a limestone floor. The room in which we landed was perhaps the size of a suburban bedroom. This alone was reason for excitement in Florida, where new finds tended to be small. But one side of the room—beyond which the passage clearly continued—was draped with a large calcite formation, perhaps eight feet wide and five feet tall, resembling a dragon's open mouth. The space beyond this mouth appeared larger still.

Following a narrow trail marked with orange flagging, we carefully dodged the dragon's stalactite and stalagmite "teeth." Beyond the mouth lay a room perhaps 120 feet by 30 feet, its ceiling reaching more than 20 feet above our heads. The chamber was festooned with tall, narrow stalagmites. Each grew up from the floor beneath a discreet water droplet that hung from a narrow "soda straw" formation. The tallest of these totems stood some nine feet tall, yet no larger in diameter than a baseball bat. It balanced precariously atop the overhanging edge of a loose boulder about three feet wide. Clearly the slightest bump might send it crashing down, or even into other nearby stalagmites, creating a horrible domino effect. Behind the tall formation, a mound of white flowstone stretched from the ceiling down and across the floor like a great snowdrift.

"They've designated a path to keep everyone away from the more delicate stuff," our guide explained.

I could see flagging marking the route, which already bore the footprints of the first cavers to enter. The soil on either side of the path remained undisturbed. It seemed to somehow sparkle. The general rule of thumb I had been taught was that formations grew at a rate of about one inch per century, which meant that the tallest stalagmite must have begun growing on the edge of that boulder more than ten thousand years ago—perhaps about the same time a hungry saber-tooth cat dragged its prey into the tunnel behind us.

I had only recently begun experimenting with cave photography, advised by Allen Mosler, who had been doing it for years. I pulled out my tripod and flashes and snapped what remains one of my most prized photographs. Tim Glover stands in blue coveralls aiming a flashlight at the nine-foot column, with many other formations in the room clearly visible behind him, and an inviting blackness beyond that.

Tim Glover in Boyer's Discovery, photographed by the author on February 2, 1980.

It was a busy spring for the club. In addition to continued mapping in the new cave and in Climax, some members joined distant expeditions. At one meeting, Karen reported on her recent excursion to "yo-yo" deep pits in Mexico—the sort of trip where vertical cavers become the toy on a string, bouncing down and back up again before heading off to the next site. The most impressive pit she described was Sótano de las Golondrinas, which offered a "freefall" rappel, where on the high side the rope did not touch surrounding walls for nearly 1,200 feet. As she spoke, I wondered aloud at the point of rappelling into a vertical shaft with no extensive passage at its base. Karen answered by grabbing a piece of chalk and walking to a blackboard in the meeting room. She drew an elongated gourd-like outline, skinny at the top and broad at the bottom. She added a tiny cliff projecting over the top of the gourd and a tiny tree spouting behind it. Then she drew a line demonstrating a rope going from the tree to the lip and down the center of the gourd to its bottom. Finally she added a little stick figure with a smiling face, right in the center of the rope.

"That's me," she said, tapping the stick figure with her chalk. "When you are here, you are in the middle of some of the most amazing cave passage you've ever seen. Gravity flies you through it, and then your own legs and skill take you back out." She drew arrows pointing up, down, and around. "Being here *is* the point."

Listening to Karen's report spurred me to sign up for one of the club's vertical training classes, dreaming of far-off lands. Frank Hutchison, an eccentric music graduate student who favored old tuxedo pants for caving in Climax, taught Tim, Ed, Terri, and me how to tie Prusik knots. I already knew bowlines and butterflies from sailing, but could use the refresher. While mechanical, ratchet-like ascenders called Jumars and Gibbs had become popular among serious TAG cavers, we were taught the old-fashioned method of Prusiking first. If you knew how to tie Prusik knots, you could always climb a rope out of a cave. We climbed and rappelled on a practice rope attached to a pulley that hung from a massive oak outside Frank's attic apartment. We learned how to stop in midair to switch from rappel to climb and vice versa.

Allen began helping me work a promising dig he had spotted at the bottom of a sinkhole in South Georgia. He led several trips to the Marianna area and planned a Tennessee visit to photograph a major new discovery there that a friend had described. He hinted that he might give the grotto a "pretty amazing" future slide show—about as superlative as Allen ever got about anything. The entire club worked to support a complicated weekend diving push in Climax, where three separate teams of experienced cave divers from around Florida entered known pools to map and connect some of the underwater passages.

Yet some of the grotto's hardest work that spring took place aboveground. The members took on a major conservation effort, one I realized that I was in a unique position to assist. A year earlier, Karen had partnered with a friend in law school to try to start an effort toward creating a Florida cave protection act. While the caves on state park property were well insulated from vandalism, there was little or no legal recourse available to stop anyone who wanted to remove formations or spray-paint the walls of caves on private land. A couple years earlier the club had helped the elderly owner of Georgia's Glory Hole prosecute three teenagers for trespassing, after they broke through the gate and spray-painted their names in an upper passage (making it fairly easy to find and prosecute them). Luckily the teens never reached the chamber containing the cave's superb, fairy-like helictite formations. The judge hearing their misdemeanor case sentenced them to clean off the spray paint under the supervision of the cave club, which they did, all while getting lessons in conservation and safety.

A few cave-rich states in the South had passed legislation specifically designed to protect underground resources, and I decided I could help do it in Florida. The previous fall I had taken a part-time job at the state capitol within walking distance of my scholarship house. I had started out on the night janitor crew in the Florida House of Representatives, but eventually moved to a day job there as doorkeeper. Several other college students and I wore blue blazers, opening the big ceremonial doors to the House chamber for legislators. We ceremonially stood sentry in front of them whenever the speaker called a closed-door vote.

In this position, I got to see how the sausage was made. I met a Sierra Club lobbyist in, well, the lobby, who said he was willing to help me with a cave protection law. Moreover, I knew that one of my housemates was the son of a state senator. By taking summer courses (more so I could keep caving with the club than for any love of learning) I was finishing a double major in business and English in a year and a half since I had left the community college. I was accepted to start law school at FSU that fall, with the vague idea of becoming an environmental lawyer. In truth I felt more interest in caving and in a young woman I had begun dating than in any study of jurisprudence. But as a first-year law student, I took the research that Karen's friend had done and drafted a model bill matching the language of other states. With the help of the lobbyist and the senator's son, we soon found sponsors for the cave protection act in both chambers. Using other connections with the speaker's office, we were able to get it assigned to committee that April.

I soon realized there was much work involved in getting a bill passed into law—and it hit at the same time I trying to pass my last set of final exams as an undergraduate. Dr. Boyer agreed to testify about the need for cave protection before an upcoming senate committee meeting, by chance scheduled a few days before exam week. We knew he would be a more respectable speaker than our motley assortment of students. The survey of his new cave had just passed 1,500 feet, and he wrote to a friend, "All my life I've considered attaching my name to some discovery, only to have it fizzle in a dung-covered crevice. This time it goes." At the May 2 committee hearing, he successfully answered tough questions from a Tampa lawyer concerned that the law would impede new housing developments spreading across the state like wildfire at the time. Boyer passionately described the fossils, Native American artifacts, and other scientific and cultural treasures the state's caves possessed and argued the need to preserve them in a way that did not unnecessarily block development. The committee chair eventually shut down the lawyer, and the committee moved the bill on to the full senate.

On the Saturday in May when I might have invited my family to drive hundreds of miles to wait in a gigantic crowd for me to collect my diploma, I skipped graduation in favor of a Climax trip. That summer, between caving and occasional canoe runs every weekend, we ushered our bill back and forth between legislative chambers as various representatives and senators tacked on amendments for unrelated projects, forcing additional votes. I didn't know at the time that Dr. Boyer was dying of stomach cancer. Something no one knew back then was that the Marianna caves bore unusually high levels of radon—a known carcinogen that may have played a role in triggering his disease.

At a Sunday grotto meeting Allen finally delivered his Tennessee slide show, which proved more than pretty amazing. With Lee Pearson, another Florida caver who was then attending college in Cookeville, Allen had taken photos of large rooms in Xanadu, a newly discovered system hidden beneath rugged terrain at the northern edge of the Cumberland Plateau. Cavers had first entered the system in 1977, and by the summer of 1980 they had mapped over fifteen miles of virgin cave, with survey trips continuing to make new discoveries.

In keeping with the theme of the Coleridge poem for which the cave was named, surveyors had christened a major trunk passage Kublai Khan's Camel Raceway. Although the flat ceiling rose over one hundred feet above the tunnel floor, a series of fifteen "sand dunes"—really collapsed piles of rock and sandy cave soil—filled parts of the Camel Raceway. At the peaks of the tallest such hills, Allen said you could reach up and brush your fingers against the roof. Using large, old-fashioned flash bulbs and multiple exposures, he had captured his friend Lee climbing up and down these hills, creating images that resembled a candlelit

49

Cavers ascend one of the fifteen sand hills in Xanadu's Camel Raceway.

medieval procession through some great limestone cathedral. Allen suggested a full grotto trip to Xanadu, and I agreed to go in a heartbeat.

That summer the Florida State Cave Club received the Victor A. Schmidt Conservation Award from the National Speleological Society at its annual convention, held that year in White Bear Lake, Minnesota. On August 14, Dr. Paul Boyer died at the age of forty. Two months later, Florida Section 810.13, concerning cave vandalism and related offenses, informally known as the Florida Cave Protection Act, finally passed both houses with the same wording and was signed into law by Gov. Bob Graham. The park officially named his find Boyer's New Discovery Cave. Five years later, Frank Hutchison would die of a similar cancer, and five years after that the Florida Cavern State Park developed guidelines for maximum weekly exposure to radon-laced cave air.

Although not open to the general public, after Paul Boyer's death the park occasionally allowed guided educational trips to enter his discovery. On one of these, a teenage boy strayed off the flagged path to get a closer look at the nine-foot-tall stalagmite that balanced atop a rounded boulder. He stumbled and caught himself on the rock on which the totem balanced, causing it to wobble. The formation fell and shattered across the white flowstone floor.

Today the cave is closed.

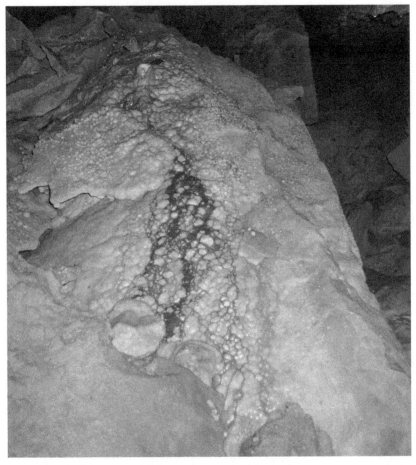

MICHAEL TAYLOR: Has anyone sampled this for bacteria yet? Clearly biological, and if it could be isolated perhaps something new.

JOEL BUCKNER: No, but perhaps we can find someone to do so.

MICHAEL TAYLOR: I may have such a person in mind—will try to email tomorrow.

JOEL BUCKNER | Facebook post, March 23, 2017

FROM: TAYLOR, MICHAEL   Fri, May 5, 2017, at 9:25 AM
TO: cavitater
SUBJECT: cave microbes

Hi Joel,

Re my comment the other day on your Facebook image of "redstone": Any time I see bright colors in flowstone I get excited about the possibility of bacterially influenced mineralization. I suspect I should have recognized the entrance from my Tennessee caving days, but I did not. In what cave (or if the cave name is undisclosed, in what county) is this located? Is the owner private or public, and what would be the permitting process (if any) for microbial sampling? How remote from the surface and/or human traffic is the location? I have a couple thoughts on how this might be properly investigated.

Best wishes,
Mike

FROM: cavitater   Fri, May 5, 2017, at 12:33 PM
TO: MICHAEL TAYLOR
SUBJECT: Re: cave microbes

It's ███████████ Cave in Cannon County. Access is via another artificial gated entrance, private owner but we have permission. Location is approximately a half mile in cave, mostly walking over breakdown, some crawling and easy climbing. No permit needed as far as I know. There are a number of other places in the cave with red, orange or yellow formations as well as naturally occurring oil globules in a stretch of passage with a long pool.
        Be glad to get it checked whatever way you can arrange.
        If you're FB friends w/ Bob Biddix, check out his Secret Squirrel Cave album for more photos.

Thanks,
Joel

FROM: TAYLOR, MICHAEL   Fri, May 5, 2017, at 1:07 PM
TO: cavitater
SUBJECT: Re: cave microbes

The oil and colored formations have me excited. That is the same situation
as Lower Kane Cave in Wyoming, which has become a center for study of
petroleum-eating bugs that seem to play a role in some types of speleogenesis.
    I will talk with a couple of biologists about this and email you and/or Bob
later about getting out there in May or June.

Thanks!
Mike

Chapter 5

SECRET SQUIRREL & THE DEEP BIOSPHERE

It looked like someone had butchered a chicken on a boulder. Blood-red liquid flowed around raised pebbles, centered in what appeared to be the yellowish remnants of past mayhem. Yet I knew at a glance that this colorful liquid did not indicate the ghoulish rituals of some underground cult—or anything else done by human hands. It was not even a liquid. Solid calcite had bled across the rock, doubtlessly spreading over a period of decades rather than seconds. It shimmered in the camera's flash, my past experience suggested, only because a tiny film of clear water clung to the crimson surface. This water served an unseen ecosystem in a place far from daylight and chickens. What I saw might be the tip of a living iceberg.

From the moment I stumbled upon the photo on Facebook, I knew I had to go there. And I knew I had to bring a microbial sampling kit when I did. Something strange, at least for a Tennessee cave, was growing in the dark, bleeding red and yellow over white limestone. I recognized a clue to a hidden universe, a connection to an idea that with the arrival of the twenty-first century had shattered many previous notions of the nature of life on Earth. In the 1990s I had become obsessed with hunting cave bugs—not to disparage subterranean insects, which are plentiful in many locations and are themselves fascinating subjects of study, but "bugs" in the slang I picked up from microbiologists.

Before the final decades of the twentieth century few people paid attention to them, but microbial colonies large enough to be seen with the naked eye thrive in many caves. Surviving far from sunlight and, in some cases, in the total absence of nutrients from the surface world, these alien creatures sustain themselves through chemistry, converting rocks and minerals into energy, leaving behind unusual formations and odd compounds. Certain caves, scientists were beginning to understand, had probably been excavated from solid rock by the slow metabolic action of these organisms—an idea that did not sit well with geologists, who had accumulated a century of evidence that limestone caves were formed by nonbiological chemical reactions involving flowing water.

The existence of rock-eating microbes caught the attention of NASA scientists, because it greatly increased the possibility of life elsewhere in our solar system. How? The prevailing theory of the origin of life on Earth began with Charles Darwin, who speculated in a letter to his friend Joseph Hooker about a "warm little pond" in which the first molecules of life could have formed. Although the idea was too controversial for Darwin to publish it in his lifetime, a slightly more sophisticated version of it nonetheless became an accepted part of the scientific canon. Proteins, amino acids, and other random gunk in the little pool were somehow nudged—perhaps via a bolt of lightning—into the first living things. So long as a planet had water, sunlight, and minerals, the theory held, life would eventually flourish. The inhospitable surfaces of Mars, the moons of Jupiter and Saturn, and most of the thousands of exoplanets beyond our solar system that astronomers began to catalog in 1992 could not support liquid water; therefore, the thinking went, these worlds could not support life.

But microbes found in caves, mines, and deep-sea ocean vents, as well as beneath glaciers and polar ice caps, challenged basic assumptions. They appeared to be far older than any surface life, suggesting that the first organisms on this planet may have emerged somewhere inside it. Neither surface water nor sunlight was required to sustain deep microorganisms—only subsurface liquid and mineral-based chemistry.

When first collected, deep microbes were regarded as little more than a fringe curiosity, but the development of DNA classification methods would soon elevate their status.

By the time I saw the "redstone" image on Facebook, thousands of scientists had begun to understand that these creatures—not the animals, the insects, the fish, the birds, or any other living thing that children commonly study in school—constitute the greatest mass of life on Earth and have always done so. Not us. Both ancient fossils and the young science of DNA support the notion that a deep biosphere appeared very soon after our planet cooled from a rotating disk of hot debris surrounding a young star. Such organisms were possible in the warmer depths far below the frozen, airless plains of other planets and moons. But this new understanding took thirty years to become accepted canon.

In 1990, Carl Woese, a microbiologist at the University of Illinois, proposed a new classification system for all life, replacing the Five Kingdoms taught in high school biology classes—Prokaryotae, Protoctista, Fungi, Plantae, and Animalia—with three "domains," all of which were microscopic at their roots: Archaea, Bacteria, and Eucarya. Whereas the old kingdoms had been established through the careful observation and categorization of organisms based on their physical similarities by generations of scientists, the new domains were based on cellular chemistry rather than physical characteristics. The invention of genetic testing revealed familial relationships that eventually became accepted as solid evidence in both courtrooms and biology labs.

Woese, using genetic techniques originated in his lab, similar to those employed in kits that now tell you what percentage of your ancestry is Italian, proved that the Archaea were unrelated to all other bacteria, more distant from them on the tree of life than those other bacteria were from giraffes. In fact, giraffes, your cat, the yeast in your beer, the salmon you ate at lunch, and the petunias in your garden are all much, much more closely related to one another within the Eukarya domain than they are related to the Archaea.

Under the new classification system, all fungi, plants, and animals (including us) were relegated to the domain of Eucarya, defined as

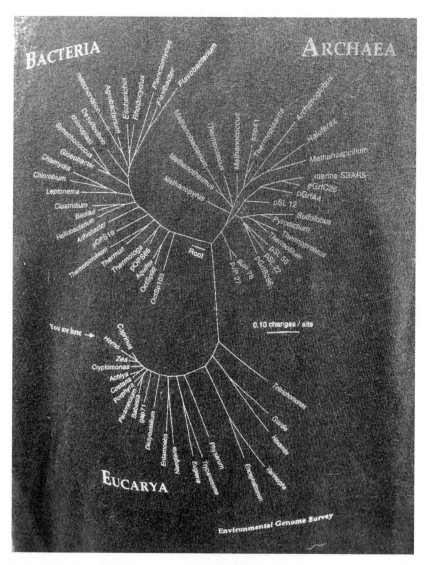

The author's Pace Lab T-Shirt, circa 1998, modeled in 2019 by Chris Taylor.

organisms with a cell nucleus. The old system had lumped all single-celled life with no cellular nucleus into the Prokaryotae. This was generally understood to mean bacteria, although there was a very strange type of prokaryotic life first sampled in the boiling hot springs of Yellowstone National Park. Originally called *Archaebacteria*, these organisms thrived at high temperatures and other harsh conditions that would kill most bacteria. They survived under great pressure, high salinity, and in both acidic and alkaline environments. "Black smokers" rising from deep-sea hydrothermal vents, first discovered in 1977 by scientists aboard the submarine Alvin, were loaded with these bugs. They also produced methane in the guts of cows and termites, and in oil wells.

Woess's student Norm Pace was a gifted microbiologist and coincidentally a celebrated caver, having received the Lew Bicking Award, the highest honor for cave exploration given by the NSS. (I once heard Pace say that this was more than chance, that caving demands a sort of self-reliant approach to problem-solving ideal for sparking innovative scientific inquiry and casting aside old ideas.) First with Woese and later in his own lab, Pace developed phylogenetic classification of the Universal Tree, becoming in the process an advocate for eliminating the term *Prokarya* from scientific nomenclature.

In 1997, he published in the journal *Science* "A Molecular View of Microbial Diversity and the Biosphere," immediately regarded as the seminal paper defining modern molecular-phylogenetic study. Shortly after the paper appeared, I wore a T-shirt depicting the Pace Lab's Tree of Life into New Mexico's Lechuguilla Cave in Carlsbad Caverns National Park. I was a Sherpa on a microbial collection team. The tree had a little arrow pointing near the tip of the Eukarya indicating "You are here." The shirt and that trip redefined my own view of life.

Although its ninety-foot entrance shaft had been known for decades, cavers first dug their way into the main passage of Lechuguilla on May 26, 1986. A frenzy of exploration after the breakthrough revealed miles of virgin leads and spectacular decorations. The cave became the fourth longest known in the United States. It was briefly the deepest as well, although it was later relegated to sixth place by deeper lava tubes on the Big Island of Hawaii and a deeper limestone system in Montana. As of January 2020, Lechuguilla contained over 150 miles of known passage, with expeditions each year finding new tunnels and chambers. When I had first entered Lech, as cavers call it, with a mapping team in 1988, it was a stunning visual experience unlike anything I had encountered before. I described a 1991 expedition there in my first book, *Cave Passages*:

> We passed a few nuisance crawls and climbs just beyond the entrance crawl, including a descent over a sparkling slope of flowstone. But Lechuguilla's unique personality wasn't revealed until Boulder Falls, a 150-foot pit well into the cave. The name refers to loose rocks that rain down whenever you rappel off the crumbling cliff at the end of the entrance passage.
>
> Once beyond the lip, Lechuguilla ceased to be ordinary. I landed in a chamber much larger than the weak beam of my carbide lamp could define. I waited under a protective ledge while the others descended. . . . Finally, Garry Petrie led us through twin columns called the Pearly Gates in Glacier Bay, a vast hollow fjord lined with gypsum blocks of megalithic size.
>
> The tilted white surface looked for all the world like the fissured top of a flowing glacier. Freestanding gypsum bergs had broken from the mass. They seemed to float toward the distant darkness. The white mineral used to make plaster of Paris is found in many caves but in minute amounts. Lee Pearson and I once traveled for hours in a Tennessee cavern to see a single gypsum flower three inches in diameter. The *smallest* of blocks now before me was the size of an upended school bus.

Scientists such as Diana Northup of the University of New Mexico began to study microorganisms in Lechuguilla in the early 1990s using a variety of methods, including scanning electron microscopes and mRNA-based genetic analysis, to classify them within the Universal Tree of Life. In a cave with no natural connection to the surface and no plainly visible biology, she found Bacteria, Eukarya, and Archaea surviving on hydrogen sulfide, carbon monoxide, and formaldehyde, among other gases. She

Microbiologist Hazel Barton collects a substance cavers call "gorilla shit," actually a microbially induced deposit of manganese oxide, from the walls of Lechuguilla Cave during a 2007 expedition with Diana Northup and other scientists.

believed the body chemistry of some of these organisms secreted acid that dissolved new passages, thereby slowly increasing their habitat.

The cave's massive gypsum deposits seemed a remnant of its microbial origins, a residue left over from untold centuries of, for want of a better term, bug shit. Lechuguilla became a crucial piece of evidence for a then-controversial theory called hypogene speleogenesis, meaning it had been created not by slightly acidic rainwater flowing from above, as is the case with most limestone caves, but by the metabolic action of microbial organisms rising from the deep subsurface. Large amounts of gypsum, sulfur, and manganese in Lechuguilla attested not only to microbial colonization, but also to the cave's actual formation by strange life from below.

I jumped at a chance to spend several days in Lechuguilla on one of Northup's microbial research teams. After a crash course in sterile collections methods, I helped her gather evidence of this hidden biosphere, which became the genesis of my second book, *Dark Life*. The title was an intentional play on *dark matter*, an astronomical puzzle that makes up the unseen mass of the physical universe: here was a living sort of dark matter that similarly made up the unseen mass of life on Earth. While I had seen Lechuguilla previously through the eyes of an explorer, Northup taught me to see its stunning decorations, along with those in other microbe-rich caves, through the eyes of a naturalist entering a new habitat. This was a revelation—it felt as though I had been given a chance to explore the Galapagos with Darwin.

On that first collection trip, Northup pointed out hidden habitats everywhere: Fuzzy white gypsum snowballs lay scattered across floors like exploded snowmen. Tangled knots of gypsum helictites rose from walls like crystalline, spontaneously generated ramen noodles. Sprays of sharp white crystal hung from the ceilings like chandeliers in Superman's Fortress of Solitude. Brownish-black crusts called rusticles draped the walls as on the rotting sides of the Titanic on the ocean floor. Totem-like formations called hoodoos, made by countless thin wafers of gypsum dropping to the bottom of some long-lost pool, stood sentinel in what was now a dry tunnel.

Odd bacterial shapes found in a meteorite from Mars that same year sparked a firestorm of scientific debate over the possibility that the Red Planet might also harbor rock-eating bacteria in a deep, wet subsurface. I accompanied several NASA scientists and university microbiologists into caves (and occasionally volcanos and glaciers) on Earth that appeared to bear out this hypothesis. Assisting the NASA planetary scientist then in charge of the Apollo moon rocks, Mars meteorites, and other off-planet material stored by the agency, I was able to place sterile glass slides into underground hot springs thirty miles north of my university office, inside tunnels beneath the tourist bustle of Hot Springs National Park. I retrieved them a couple of months later, by which time they were covered with a white mineral film. Under a scanning electron microscope at the Johnson Space Center in Houston, my slides revealed tubular microbial remains embedded in calcite that were nearly identical to the shapes in the much-debated Martian meteorite, which had been photographed with the same microscope.

I stuck my hand into a crack in the wall and pulled out a black, shimmering, gelatinous fistful of living matter on an NSS biology field trip to Lower Kane Cave in Wyoming. Reminiscent of the titular creature in the classic horror film *The Blob*, this black ooze was only one of a dozen types of bacterial colonies visible to the naked eye at Lower Kane. This was the place that had first inspired the idea of hypogene speleogenesis in the early 1970s. The pattern of its passages suggested that they had been slowly dissolved by rising sulfuric acid, rather than by carbonic acid contained in rainwater, and the cave's unusual biology suggested a relationship to its geology.

In Lower Kane I saw translucent microbial films resembling lily pads that floated on a subterranean pool. From the bottom of each pad, a central stem connected it to nutrients on the pool's bottom. Here was an otherworldly analog of Darwin's "warm little pond." The visible structures comprised hundreds, perhaps thousands, of separate bacterial and fungal species, each of them a microbial city with trillions of tiny inhabitants, all hovering in silence too far from sunlight to involve the plant life they visually resembled. Technically called biofilm, Northup referred to such substances, with great enthusiasm, as "slime." She and microbiologist Penny Boston organized a group of like-minded microbiologists into the SLIME team, an acronym for Subsurface Life in Mineral Environments. While touring Lower Kane with several members of this team, I walked alongside a mineral rich stream that stank of petroleum. Bands of bright red and yellow bordered the water. They reminded me of the microbial bands ringing the hot springs of Yellowstone National Park, where the Archaea were first cataloged.

Working under a NASA grant, Annette Summers Engel, a geochemist now at the University of Tennessee, proved that the color changes bordering this particular stream were tied to something she termed "redox-based biogeochemical nutrient cycles." This meant that the cave provided a transitional zone between organisms from a deep, oxygen-free habitat far below to organisms comfortable in the oxygen-rich zones of the surface world. As one chemical nutrient would be used up by a particular rock-eating organism, the food chain based on that organism would gradually change chemical composition and character. The different-colored mineral deposits left behind by these changes slowly accumulated into quantities visible to the naked eye.

At Villa Luz (literally the "House of Light") in the Mexican state of Tabasco, I saw wiggly, spaghetti-like formations called "snottites." These microbial colonies dripped bacterially produced acid as powerful as the creature's spit in the movie *Alien*. The air in the chamber where the snottites lived was so poisonous that we had to wear powerful breathing filters and air-quality monitors made for coal miners. We could safely stay in the room for only a few minutes at a time. Elsewhere in the cave I donned a Tyvek suit to join the geomicrobiologist Louise Hose in sampling hair-like, nearly invisible microbial strands that crisscrossed a crawlway, capable of stinging exposed skin a like a spiderweb made of acid.

In the late 1990s and early 2000s, biologists like Northup, Engel, and Hose had been routinely dismissed by geologists who studied caves, due to long-held beliefs that chemical reactions explained everything happening underground in nonliving terms, with no microbes required. Whenever little bugs happened to be found on a wall, the party line went, these were opportunists that had drifted in from the surface—and most definitely not the original excavators of the cave or creators of any mineral formation. Caves and the colorful formations that lured tourists in to look at them could be explained by simple formulas that could be recreated in a chemistry lab. End of discussion.

As with terrestrial geologists and cave microbiologists, planetary geologists tended to have the upper hand whenever biologists affiliated with NASA claimed they had detected signs of possible microbial life from space rocks or in the presence of methane within the Martian atmosphere. Evidence of methane or microscopic chains of magnetite could be explained with simple, abiotic chemistry, and what was more likely to be their cause: ordinary chemical reactions or little green bugs from space? Occam's razor was repeatedly cited as refutation of a growing shelf of scientific papers touting evidence of extraterrestrial microbes.

A snottite cluster in Villa Luz cave.

Never mind that field microbiologists had observed that such life was ubiquitous within extreme environments on Earth, including some nearly as harsh as Mars. Job titles like geomicrobiologist or exobiologist were more science fiction than fact. As late as 2007, my older son's middle school science book listed the traditional Five Kingdoms of life with no mention of the three domains. (When Alex raised his hand and suggested the textbook was wrong, the teacher, to his credit, went home and did some reading on science websites. The next day he told the class Alex was right, that their textbook was in fact out of date.)

Educational change was happening elsewhere. Within the first two decades of the twenty-first century, entire schools of geomicrobiology and exobiology cropped up at major universities, where they now conduct (literally) groundbreaking science. Evidence continues to mount that a deep, chemically based biosphere represents both the oldest and the largest presence of life on this planet and is likely evidence that microbial life exists on many worlds. Widespread news reports in late 2018 described the mass of microbial life between Earth's surface and its core as weighing between three hundred and four hundred times more than all life known to inhabit Earth's surface or its oceans. This astounding number was obtained by the Deep Carbon Observatory group, comprising more than one thousand scientists from fifty-two countries. They had spent the previous decade sharing data from myriad sources: caves, mines, wells, glaciers, volcanos, deep ocean rifts—basically any window that allowed humans to see the unknown universe beneath our feet.

Many of the Archaea found in deep environments are methanogens, meaning they consume naturally produced methane gas. A 2018 study by Kelly Wrighton of Ohio State University showed that US fracking wells harbor methane-producing bacteria thousands of feet below the surface. Cal-Tech marine biologist Victoria Orphan had found similar microbes eating the methane that bubbled from seeps spread throughout the world's oceans. Using a new technology called secondary-ion mass spectrometry (SIMS), Orphan discovered a symbiotic relationship between different microbial species, methane producers and methane eaters. This exchange, she had come to believe, was central to the global ecosystem.

Plants and trees consume carbon dioxide and release oxygen, allowing animal life (i.e., us) to consume oxygen and release CO_2. In the same way, this hidden life mixes methane and carbon dioxide in oxygen-free depths. Methane is a potent greenhouse gas, with twenty-five times the warming potential of CO_2. It seems possible that humans increasingly penetrating their realm through fracking, oil and brine extraction, and the global reduction of glaciers from CO_2 emissions, might upset the delicate balance between our ecosystems.

One thing that hypogenically produced caves like Lechuguilla, Lower Kane, and Villa Luz all seemed to have in common is that they lie within regions of oil production. All are positioned in regions containing much deeper pools of crude oil that may somehow provide fuel for their hidden life. Before seeing Joel Buckner's Facebook post, I had not heard of evidence of this sort of mineral-based Archaea in caves east of the Mississippi. I knew there were a few producing oil wells in extreme northeastern Tennessee, as famously discovered by Jed Clampett in the 1960s sitcom *The Beverly Hillbillies*. But those were located over a hundred miles from the place where Joel took his photos.

Through an exchange of emails I learned that Joel, Hal Love, David Parr, and Trey Caplenor had spent part of the previous decade mapping a complex system to a length approaching fifteen miles. After major discoveries, they invited Bob Biddix to photograph large rooms and unique formations. The cave lay in an unpopulated area about sixty miles southeast of Nashville. As with many active "project caves" in middle Tennessee, the process involved a fair amount of secrecy. The real name and exact location were listed among the ten thousand caves recorded in the Tennessee Cave Survey, but few cavers were aware that this particular known entrance led to so much newfound passage. Reports of lengthy exploration trips and photographs of formations shared publicly in grotto meetings or on Facebook failed to mention the cave's actual name. That identification would probably not be made public until the survey was considered complete, a detailed map drafted and published—which was a slow process.

Instead of using the cave's real name, Biddix nicknamed it "Secret Squirrel" after a character in a 1960s Saturday morning cartoon. He engaged in some good-natured taunting of other cavers by printing up

Secret Squirrel T-shirts and patches. Survey team members would conspicuously wear these to caver gatherings, dropping hints about recently discovered boreholes, vertical pitches, and formations. As explorers pushed new discoveries to distances requiring trips that lasted twenty hours, they began seeking a new entrance to more easily access remote finds. Using a radio-location tool, they learned that a particular crawlway in the new area rose to within a few feet of a forested overhead ravine. After several weekends of excavation and the installation of manhole-like gate, they created an easier path to virgin territory and new discoveries. By any name, these new passages were loaded with striking and unusual mineral formations, which Biddix shared on his Secret Squirrel album.

When I saw his professional-quality photos, along with a few additional shots Joel had taken, I was immediately reminded of formations I had seen in Lechuguilla. The rooms were not as large, nor were the formations as rich in number or size, but there was unquestionably a Lech resemblance most odd for Tennessee. I hypothesized that the photos might depict methanogens associated not with subsurface petroleum deposits, but perhaps with some sort of pollution from an abandoned factory or oil-storage facility.

When Joel sent me a map depicting known passages placed beneath a topographic overlay, I realized that surface pollution was unlikely. The area above the cave was hilly, rocky, undeveloped forestland. A few old farm houses dotted the county road where cavers would park before hiking a half mile up a wooded streambed to the artificial entrance. The only other evidence of civilization on the map was a commercial shooting range several miles to the west of the cave and a craft whiskey distillery several miles to the east. While these two establishments expressed Tennessee cave country in a nutshell, neither seemed a likely source for subsurface oil or methane. Something else was going on.

As I talked with Joel on the phone, trying to arrange a collection trip, he casually mentioned that the "redstone" formation was near the "tarball pool."

"Tarballs?" I asked, recalling the black goo in Lower Kane Cave.

"Yes," he said. "About the size of black marbles, floating on the surface of a pool with a strong methane smell."

Allowing a known writer into a passage that had thus far been seen by only a dozen or so original explorers—even in the name of science—took some time. It turned out that the route to the oddest formations was complex and not easy to locate. At least two or three original explorers would have to give up a Saturday in order to lead curious scientists to that part of the cave, a Saturday that might be better spent exploring someplace new. Because Joel and I had worked together earlier in central Tennessee, he vouched for me with the others. Our first planned dates had to be rescheduled due to bad weather, a work conflict with one of the guides, and other issues, but finally we settled on meeting in Murfreesboro on the first weekend in December—more than six months after I saw the first Facebook photo.

My Henderson colleague James Engman—Jamie to his friends—had first become interested in cave microbiology as a graduate student sharing an office with Serban M. Sârbu, a Romanian scientist made famous by his work in Movile Cave, home to one of the most bizarre ecosystems on Earth. Reachable only through a dangerous scuba dive, Movile contains a poisonous atmosphere and no natural connection to the surface. Yet it hosts dozens of species of unique insects and other creatures that have evolved to feed on its rich microbial life, despite no sunlight and an atmosphere that would kill most terrestrial organisms (including any human foolish enough to breathe there without an air tank). Primarily a marine biologist and ecologist, Jamie and his talented undergraduates had nonetheless spent several years doing DNA research on the complex web of microbial life inhabiting the guts of cave crickets in Blanchard Springs in Arkansas. He and I had talked for years about finding a project on which we could collaborate.

When I described the online images from Secret Squirrel, he eagerly procured a small grant that would allow his students to process the DNA from a few samples, to see if the photos did indeed depict strange microbial life. He had planned to personally lead our collection effort, but when an illness sidelined him in December, he turned his collection kit and a long list of instructions over to me. I recruited my son Chris, a twenty-three-year-old engineering student and occasional caver, to come along as Sherpa (the job I had happily held decades ago in Lechuguilla, following Dr. Northup to the distant and incredible Oasis Pool). We set

Xanadu . . . Xanadid? What a day!

JIM FOX | Facebook post, March 10, 2017

Chapter 6

IN XANADU

Most TAG caves lie within a rugged limestone landscape too steep and rocky for agriculture or industry. This means that the roads to wild caves can be bad or nonexistent. One of the worst in Tennessee is the road to Xanadu. Depicted on old maps as a "jeep trail" or "logging road," it zigzags down nearly one thousand feet from a northern rim of the Cumberland Plateau into a cove near the Obey River. As I bounced down it on a damp spring morning, I saw a route littered with abandoned trucks and jeeps that had fallen victim to ruts and rocks. They would remain in place for days or weeks until the owners could arrange for a heavy-duty truck or tractor to extract them. Our small caravan of vehicles bearing Florida license plates had left the pavement for a succession of dirt roads leading to this horrendous jeep trail and Xanadu.

In the lead was a blue VW Beetle driven by Lee Pearson. He and Allen Mosler had begun caving years earlier at the University of Florida, where the main Gainesville campus encompassed three small natural caves, with many more only a short drive away. After taking a break from college, Lee had enrolled at Tennessee Technical University in Cookeville to pursue a degree in geology. He had become active in the local Upper Cumberland Grotto, whose members were involved in the ongoing exploration and survey of Xanadu. We met for the first time at a designated gas station along the only highway anywhere near our ultimate destination.

Lee had an infectious grin and the tall, thin build of a long distance runner. Beyond caving, I would learn that his hobbies were running, biking, restoring old VWs, watersports, and stage magic. Despite youthful good looks, at twenty-six his blond hair was becoming prematurely thin, headed the way of his bald father, a Methodist minister back in Florida. Lee lived in central Tennessee now and thought nothing of speeding down the narrow, twisting highway to the Xanadu turn-off, his wheels hugging the curves as though the Bug were a Porsche in the Alps. The Florida drivers struggled to keep up while the Florida passengers struggled to keep a drive-thru breakfast down.

Next in line was Allen's new 1981 Datsun pick-up. He had installed a camper top with a hinged plywood bed that allowed ample room for gear below and a foam camping mattress above. In the storage area he had added labeled, well-stocked compartments for everything that might be required for extended camping, canoeing, or caving trips. Despite having been purchased explicitly for caving, the interior and exterior of the truck were spotless. Two younger cavers in their late teens, one of them Allen's nephew, crowded the bench seat, their gear in the back of the truck.

Bringing up the rear, I drove a tiny yellow 1977 Honda CVCC, the early precursor of the Civic. Downhill, its nimble handling and five-speed manual transmission let me match the excessive speed of the lead vehicle. Uphill, the small engine—probably best suited to a motorcycle—struggled to keep up. The rear seat was collapsed to make room for caving gear and enough camping supplies to last two people for a week. The car belonged to my girlfriend, Kathy Steadham, who sat in the passenger seat fighting motion sickness. Like my two previous college girlfriends, I had met her at my sister's house. She had been my sister's new roommate the previous fall, shortly after I began caving.

In the ensuing six months we became increasingly close. We enjoyed several canoeing and camping weekends. After discovering that we both liked art museums, we drove to Georgia to see a traveling exhibit of Impressionist work. We both loved to travel, exploring small towns, restaurants, and antique shops along the way (she looked at furniture and Depression glass; I hunted carbide lamps). Her mother, who with Kathy's father ran a dive charter in the Florida Keys, had given her a pair of sturdy hiking boots for this trip, which I took to mean the parents approved.

A few months earlier, Kathy had joined Tim, Ed, Terri, and me on a grotto trip Allen led to Hollow Ridge Cave in Marianna—a muddy, mazelike crosshatch of limestone tubes near the Chipola River. (Allen would later purchase this cave and surrounding land in order to permanently preserve it from encroaching development.) Although Kathy didn't enjoy getting dirty or participating in any sort of planned exercise, she had gamely pushed through Hollow Ridge's crawlways and halfflooded fissures. She had later agreed to this caving excursion to Tennessee, provided we engaged in more traditional tourism along the way.

The road onto which we had turned off became increasingly rough. "Don't hurt my little car," Kathy admonished after a bump noisily tossed camping gear around the small cargo area behind us. As we neared the edge of the plateau, Allen pulled over at a wide sandy spot and got out of his truck. We pulled behind him and did the same.

"Around the next bend it gets really bad," he explained. "I think I can get my truck at least halfway down, but we should probably leave the Honda and the Bug up here. If everyone can throw their gear into the back of my truck, the extra people can sit on the tailgate. I'll go slow and get as close as I can get to the cave."

We did as he suggested, extracting our gear and locking the cars where they sat. The sandy spot was wide enough that any local traffic, as unlikely as that might be, could pass. Kathy, the two teenagers, and I crowded onto the Datsun tailgate while Lee climbed into the passenger seat. The truck was soon heading downhill at such a steep angle that we would have slid into the passenger compartment but for Allen's custom storage box. Its wooden frame provided a hard backrest to our seat on the tailgate. He drove slowly around obstacles and holes. Over the next mile the road devolved into deep, rocky ruts that seemed more of a mountain streambed than anything created for vehicles. After we passed the first abandoned jeep, Allen decided he had driven far enough. He found a bushy thicket where he could just back off the trail.

"We'll have to gear up here and hike the rest of the way," he said.

So we did. Kathy grumbled that her mother's boots were a little tight, but she thought she could make them work. We hiked deeper into the cove, overhead trees closing into a green tunnel. The air smelled of strange spices. The temperature dropped. Through occasional gaps in the foliage I saws wisps of mist rising from the opposite side of the cove and flashes of white from the dry cobbles of the Obey River below. As we reached the base of the gorge we passed another abandoned truck, one of its wheels hanging in air from the boulder that had stopped it. We seemed to have already left the surface of the Earth, to have descended into some fantasy netherworld.

Like nearly all streams around the plateau, the streambed we followed remained dry except in times of flood, when subterranean rivers below would overflow. We passed occasional calm pools and spots where water momentarily burbled along in sunlight before vanishing, but mostly we walked on a bed of dry cobbles and boulders. A half mile or so downstream I heard the sound of falling water, and we rounded a corner to see a thirty-foot waterfall cascading over ledges into a large pool that drained underground. We could see a dark mouth fifty feet wide and twenty feet high. This was Alph Caverns.

At the base of the bluff, near the river, was the much smaller Xanadu entrance. Together, these were two of three main entrances to the system. The third entrance, Zoroaster, lay more than one thousand feet farther along the bluff, and Lee explained that was our destination. We kept hiking, with Kathy grumbling about her boots. I barely noticed, caught up in the allure of big entrances. In a mock-redneck voice, Lee uttered a phrase I would hear him repeat many times over the next four decades: "This place is just eat-up with caves."

In an article for the *NSS News* that would coincidentally appear a few months after our trip, Charles Clark, one of Xanadu's early explorers, described the experience of three cavers who had first combed this largely inaccessible area in the mid-1970s: "Dozens of entrances opened in the picturesque bluffs along the river. When probing the wooded coves spilling into the gorge, waterfalls, bluffs and more entrances greeted them. It was a caver's fantasy come true. Names from ancient literature and mythology came to mind and each of the newly discovered nether-worlds was honored with one . . . Yggdrasil, Dragonsbreath, Zarathus-tra, Mountain Eye Cave, Zoroaster, Alph Caverns, Xanadu."

It certainly seemed a land of fantasy as we hiked beneath the cliffs and forest. A caver named Ray Lewis had first entered the small Xanadu entrance with two others on April 2, 1977. "We were sure it would end quickly, so we didn't take all our gear," he later wrote. After negotiating some low ceilings and breakdown, the three entered a sandy-floored tunnel where they were surprised to see two pairs of previous footprints leading in—but not out. They followed these past a side passage into a hole, using ledges to descend forty feet into a formation area with a "jungle" of columns and stalactites.

At a tight constriction at the back of the decorated chamber, they found a flat rock printed with the words, "This is as far as we got, Pat Stevens, 1927." Since they saw no bodies nearby, they presumed that the two explorers from a half-century earlier had found another way to the surface.

On their way back that day, Lewis and company checked the side pas-sage that they had passed while following the footprints in. After a short distance it popped into a "monster" trunk, fifty feet in diameter, which headed into the mountain. The borehole kept getting larger, and they soon encountered a steep impediment. With difficulty, they ascended the first few of what would become known as the fifteen sand hills of the Camel Raceway. "They just kept getting bigger and bigger and the passage kept going," Lewis wrote. "We were all in a daze. This was impossible, the biggest passage in the state! We came to the top of one mountain and looked off. We couldn't see the bottom or the other side."

Low on carbide, the three on that first trip had to return to the en-trance after climbing just five of the fifteen dunes. The following week-end, they returned and pushed the monster into a canyon that connected with Zoroaster's Cave, which they recognized. A full-scale survey began that July 4, led by Jeff Sims of the Smoky Mountain Grotto. Over the next decade more than a hundred cavers—many of them already TAG legends, some of them out-of-state visitors like Karen Witte—would map twenty-four miles of passage in Xanadu.

Their survey was not yet four years old as our party followed Lee Pearson to the Zoroaster's entrance near the river. This turned out to be not one but four entrances, each dotting the limestone bluff like gaps in a hillbilly smile. These outlets evidently dumped water from the cove above into the Obey during the rainy season. We planned a through-trip, entering at this wet lower entrance and ascending into dry, larger tunnels that would take us to Fort Sanders—a breakdown room encompassing three acres. From there we would find Cumberland Avenue, a one-hundred-foot-wide trunk discovered in August 1977 by Charles Clark, Jeff Sims, and Martha Clark. It had a smooth sandy floor down which you could race dune buggies, if only you could get them into the cave. We would then work our way toward the back side of the Camel Raceway and exit via a crossing of all fifteen sand hills.

Kathy asked, only half joking, if we'd all be happy just having done the hike. She took off the tight boots at the entrance, and Allen provided some moleskin to use in the spots where they rubbed her feet. That seemed to help, and she was soon keeping up as we eased our way through the entrance into the Zoroaster section. Over the next couple of hours, we stuck to the plan, more or less. As Florida cavers more accustomed to miserable crawlways than massive borehole, we kept stopping to check out small side passages—any of which would have been considered a stupendous find in the Sunshine State. Kathy would wait at the entrance of each such lead until we had momentarily gotten our fill of crawling. Then we would all hike down enormous tunnels only to poke into yet another miserable crack.

Eventually, we reached Fort Sanders, a junction hall that reminded the group's Climax veterans of the T Room there—only this space was much larger. We all sat for lunch atop a flat boulder longer than Allen's new truck, surrounded on all sides by darkness that stretched beyond the reach of our carbide lamps. As I removed my gloves to unpack tuna, crackers, and granola onto a bandana that served as tablecloth for Kathy and me, I studied the rocky surface.

It was a darker gray and much harder than the rock we knew in South Georgia. There, about thirty million years ago the Oligocene Suwannee limestone had been part of a coral reef within a larger Gulf of Mexico than we know today. It bristled with the shells and remains of sea creatures, some of which seemed as fresh as those for sale in any beachside souvenir shop. The Monteagle limestone surrounding us was perhaps ten times as old, laid down during the earliest unit of the Carboniferous period. It was a hundred million years before the dinosaurs, a time when shallow seas covered most of the North American continent. Thousands of TAG caves, including many of the largest, lie within the Monteagle formation; this was the rock that held Ruby Falls, where my childhood fascination with caves had begun. It felt smoother, denser, more serious than what I'd encountered in Florida and South Georgia. If you placed your palm on it—as I now did, resting my hand beside my bandana—you could imagine echoes of an ancient age stirring within its coolness.

Looking back from the vantage of the twenty-first century, the early 1980s now feel something like an ancient age. Ronald Reagan was president. It was a time of disco, the dawn of an era of big hair. Kathy's helmet could barely contain the massive black curls that that framed her long neck and highlighted her bright smile. We ate tuna with cheese and marveled at a view few humans had ever seen.

We didn't know it then, but great underground systems were being mapped for the first time all around us, not only in Tennessee but in bordering states and throughout the western hemisphere. Within fifty miles of our flat boulder, a dozen large caves waited silent and undiscovered, untouched by human presence for years and decades to come. Future parks and preserves lay everywhere. By chance I had begun caving at the perfect historical moment, when technology and human drive had combined in a way that would lead to discovery after discovery. It was like being young at a time when you could personally meet and perhaps join the first explorers of the Grand Canyon, Yosemite, or any of the great natural marvels of the surface world. A hidden and unknown continent awaited.

After a pleasant picnic in a field of blackness, our group packed up to head down Cumberland Avenue.

To be "on point" in a cave survey is to be the one who first crosses the virgin soil, the one who chooses the stations that will form the spine of the map to follow. In one section of the *NSS News* article on the discovery of Xanadu, Martha Clark described the experience of being on point in the survey of Cumberland Avenue, followed by her husband Charles Clark and by Jeff Sims, who would go on to discover miles of passage in Xanadu and many other nearby caves. The sandy floor of the seventy-foot-wide trunk bore no footprints. The smooth ceiling and walls were decorated with bright, unbroken streaks of calcite that sometimes reached across the pristine floor in brittle layers like a sugar glaze. As she pulled out her survey tape to take point, Clark planned her next steps:

> Realizing that I was the one to permanently mar this picturesque floor with the mark of Vibram, I walked forward carefully. I felt that the serenity of this passage should never have been disturbed.
>
> Setting a point 100 feet from Charles (on compass) I recalled the tale about Roy Davis and company racing down Virgin Avenue in Cumberland Caverns, throwing tackles on each other in their excitement of discovery. Here was our opportunity to literally *run* down virgin borehole screaming our delight. But it was not as I had imagined. Instead, I was overcome with humbleness. Regretfully disturbing the stillness, I called out each distance.

Beside her, Jeff "casually crossed the beautiful, unmarked passage to check beneath an overhang." She turned and saw that he and Charles had followed unaware of her carefully placed path, roaming everywhere as they scouted leads. Later, on the way back from the survey, the two men broke into a dead run, throwing tackles on one another, as Clark put it, "right down the center of my dream."

Following their path just three years later, I could understand that desire to run and whoop and holler in such a place. But we moved slowly. Lee knew the route to a couple of formation rooms hidden along the way, so we sidetracked to climb into these spectacular places. Kathy's feet were still bothering her and she needed to stop and rest more frequently, so side excursions to look at stalactites and flowstone afforded her that opportunity. And truly, all of us realized we were in a world-class cave—we wanted to take our time and soak up the experience. More than two hours passed before we reached the start of the Camel Raceway.

Since my early visits to Climax and Waterfall I had been climbing in caves, but when we hit the first sand hill I realized this was something more. Although each hill presented a steeply pitched slope, the soil—sandy in some places and semi-muddy in others—slid down with every step. You would gain a few feet of elevation, then lose half of it. We were all sweating and grunting as we reached the top of the first hill, only to see another ahead in the massive passageway. Standing at the pinnacle, I removed a glove in order to reach a few inches above my head and touch the flat ceiling. It felt cool and smooth, as though cut by ancient stonemasons. Once we stood in the valley of the cathedral-like chamber before us, this ceiling would be higher overhead than the ribbed vaults of Notre Dame above the tourists and penitents of Paris. I replaced the glove and plunged forward, sliding and slaloming my way down the other side like a dirty game of Chutes and Ladders.

"You said these were little sand dunes," Kathy accused me as we skidded toward the flat floor of the Raceway. "These are freaking mountains!"

"Yeah, it's great, isn't it?" I replied. This, I was later informed, was not a proper response.

We slowly moved forward, hill upon hill, Lee at the front of our group and Allen taking up the rear. I fell in behind Lee, listening to his tales of Tennessee caving as we conquered the slopes. Kathy and Allen began to recede behind us. Although we would disagree on this point for decades to come, I recall her saying she had to move slower and would catch up to us eventually. To this day she swears I "abandoned" her after the third or fourth sand hill. All I know is that I became intoxicated by borehole.

Watching Lee climb ahead of me, I realized that I could move more efficiently by carefully placing my feet where side pressure helped to keep them from slipping. Soon, like him, I was moving more quickly over the hills, sweating and panting, but making good progress. The headlamps of the rest of our group gradually became a distant cluster of stars in the rocky night.

One of the Xanadu's fifteen Sand Hills follows the trunk passage around a bend in this image.

I would eventually hear how Kathy's blisters and fatigue defeated her halfway through the Camel Raceway. She sat on the floor, unwilling to move forward, until Allen "saved" her by pulling a bag of M&Ms candy from his pack. She took strength from the chocolate, and with an occasional hand from Allen, slowly ascended the next sand hill, then the one after that.

I knew nothing of this as Lee and I finally left the monster trunk and entered a smooth, rounded tunnel that led toward the entrance. A dense fog from the warmer surface air rolled toward us as we approached daylight. I looked behind me and realized that Lee and I were alone, so I said I was going back to look for the others. I had to return to the last sand hill before I could see their lights slowly approaching, still a couple of hills beyond. Eventually, we all walked out together, where it was late afternoon.

The trip was far from over. Once on the surface, Kathy removed her boots, revealing the bloody blisters that had slowed her down. We still had a steep hike of a mile or so to reach Allen's truck. Using his first aid kit, Allen bandaged Kathy's feet as best as he could, but she still had to replace the boots and painfully make her way up the streambed and the jeep trail. The sun had dropped below the opposite ridge by the time we reached Allen's truck.

He pulled out garbage bags for us to store our muddy helmets and packs. One of the teens opened the passenger door to Allen's truck and casually tossed his muddy pack on the pristine dash. Allen angrily snatched it and sailed it down the road with the force of an NFL quarterback. But it was no use: After this day his truck would never be entirely clean again. We tossed the clean garbage bags full of gear atop Allen's foam mattress in the back of the truck. Once more, Kathy and I crowded next to the teens on the truck's tailgate as Allen began the slow drive up the bad road.

Going in, gravity had kept us rooted to our perch—now it tried to pry us off. We had to cling to the edges of the camper top to keep from rolling off the truck and down the road. With every bump, the bags of gear would bounce down toward us, trying to knock us off the tailgate. Our arms were cramping from the effort to hold on by the time we reached the other cars. At some point while we were underground, a thunderstorm had rolled through the area. We had passed many puddles on the way up, and the previously sandy spot where we had parked was now a wide, deep pond. Our cars sat on a dry bank at the wrong end of it.

Lee walked out into the water to see how deep it was. "Allen's truck can make it, but we'll have to get a running start to float our cars through," he said. "Watch how I do it, and you do the same thing."

As Kathy and I climbed into the Honda, she tossed the torture boots into the back, and sat in the passenger seat, resting her feet. Lee started his Bug and drove back toward the cave road, turning around in the spot where Allen had parked the truck. He floored the VW and splashed into the pool, sliding sideways as the light German car skimmed over the surface like a water bug. He drove up the far bank, pulled out of the way and parked, then came back to shout across the pool, "Whatever you do, don't slow down!"

It was my turn. Like Lee, I drove about fifty feet back toward the cave, then carefully turned at a wide spot, branches scratching the yellow finish as I moved forward and backward until the car was pointing up the road toward the pond. I floored it. We hit the water hard, throwing up spray like a ski boat on either side. We drifted two thirds of the way across, floated a second, and then sank to the bottom, where the wheels spun. We were stuck. My door rested above the water, but Kathy's side was slightly below it. A small amount of water seeped through the door seal into the floorboard. At least the engine still ran, somehow.

We rolled down our windows to decide what to do next. Allen had a tow cable, but he could not get past us to pull us out the in the direction we needed to go. We decided he would instead pull the Honda backward to dry ground, then we would try again to drive across the water.

"You nearly made it the first time," Lee said.

Luckily, Kathy's Honda had a sturdy trailer hitch. Allen backed his truck to the edge of the pond, hooked his cable to the hitch, and began to drive forward. The rear hatchback of the Honda CCVC formed an aerodynamic curve toward the bumper, and as Allen towed us backward, the tilt on Kathy's side became more pronounced. This curve dipped into the mud and dug in, and a two- or three-inch ribbon of mud began curling over the top of Kathy's little car.

She quickly rolled up her window as the mud came dropping toward her, and she burst into tears. "I'm sorry," I said, ineffectually reaching over the gear shift to hug her in the confined and rapidly submerging space. "We'll be okay." I honked the car's wheezing horn until one of the observers got Allen to stop pulling.

Lee came out to us in the water and scraped the thickest mud from my window—Kathy's side of the car hung down lower in the muddy water. After she cried for a while, I rolled down my window and climbed out of it, then Lee and I helped her climb out behind me. Allen once again tried to tow us backward from the mud hole. Without Kathy's and my weight, the car rolled backward onto solid ground, its engine still idling. Kathy watched red-eyed from the shore with the others as I once more went down the road, turned around, and gunned the little engine for all it was worth. This time, like Lee, I bounced and fish-tailed across the water and coasted onto the far shore. Allen followed, experiencing no trouble with his four-wheel-drive (although he would later discover that the cable he had used to pull us from the mud had somehow ruptured his gas line, and he would leak gasoline all the way back to Florida). Safely across the pond, we all returned to our vehicles for the bumpy drive out to paved roads.

We had planned on camping that night at a state park two hours away, but everyone was muddy and exhausted. Lee and his wife Sharon lived in married student housing at Tennessee Tech in a tiny one-bedroom apartment. He offered to let the five of us camp in his living room that night, an offer we readily accepted. For the next hour, we struggled to keep up with the taillights of the VW as Lee raced over the winding roads.

"I don't know why I ever married you after that," Kathy would say forever after.

Nearly forty years into our marriage, I still don't know why myself, but two years later we were married, and seven years after that our first child was born. All three of our boys are older now than we were on that first trip to Xanadu. Even though I thoroughly cleaned her little car the next morning, she probably would have dropped me on the spot if not for Allen's M&Ms and if not for Sharon Pearson, who first fed us all by opening every can of soup in her cabinet into a steaming pot. The next day she brought out a warm tub of Epsom salts in which Kathy soaked her feet as they talked, while Lee took me to another nearby cave, Allen and his nephews having headed south back toward Florida. Humans are social creatures, and friends born of shared adventure—or adversity—can be especially close. By the following night the four of us had entered what would become an enduring friendship, one that has never strayed far from caves.

SOCIAL INTERLUDE

Word spread that Marion O. Smith had been hospitalized with a skull fracture caused by a falling rock in a Tennessee pit. The following response is typical of over 250 Facebook posts by TAG cavers within twenty-four hours.

I started caving in 1972. Shortly afterwards, I began reading MOS's trip reports. There is no caver I admire more than Marion. Let's hope he has no head or neck injury that keeps him from exploring underground worlds.

BRIAN HOUHA | Facebook post, September 17, 2017

FROM: Taylor, Michael   April 4, 2018
TO chrisdtaylor; kathytaylor
SUBJECT: Small World

I just got off the phone with Joe Douglas, who is leading the Mammoth trip with Marion and Kristen Bobo next week. Turns out, not only have I caved with him before, but Chris, Ken and Alex have also—he was on the trip with Lee we took one winter to the small Cookeville cave that is in the back yard of Lea Ann's brother. Talk about coincidence.

Anyway, I have an assignment to write about this Mammoth Cave Civil War project for *National Parks* magazine. If Chris goes he will be another set of eyes to scan walls for signatures, so I am sending these articles for him to do a little homework on the scope of the project. Also, because of the number of trips and WNS protocols for most of them, I plan to put Chris in charge of cleaning/sterilizing gear after each cave. Quite possibly, Joe and/ or Kristen will also take us into an ancient Indian art cave while we are there. There may be ghosts.

MT

Chapter 7

GRAFFITI

The day after I joined a bat count in Tennessee, I drove into North Georgia to meet researchers at the Black Diamond Tunnel. Two months later, I stood two hundred feet below the Kentucky countryside looking at another scene affected by the Civil War. More than a mile from the historic natural entrance of Mammoth Cave, I stared at results of a human act that would probably get you arrested today within the boundaries of any national park: three lines of graffiti written in pencil on the white limestone wall. "A Rust 1861, W Garnett, V Hobartt 5th A G 1861," read the faint cursive of another era. The writers of this and hundreds of other messages in the canyon-like El Ghor passage are long dead, but their casual messages live on within the sheltered darkness of the cave.

The seventy-five-year-old-man beside me carefully copied the inscriptions into a small journal as photographer Kristen Bobo fired her flash at an oblique angle, teasing hidden details from the rough limestone. Later, she would run the images through specialized software to make the writing more legible. As Smith wrote, he placed question marks next to letters or symbols that were too indistinct to make out definitively with the naked eye. "Hobartt," for example, might have actually been "Hobarth." These names might—or might not—have been left by

Confederate officers during the war's opening months. With his dark, rough clothing and close-cropped white beard, Marion O. Smith might pass as the ghost of one of those long-dead soldiers but for his modern rubber boots and the caving helmet and lamp perched on his head.

A historian by training and a celebrated TAG caver by avocation, Smith had joined Joe Douglas, professor of history at Volunteer State Community College, and project photographer Kristen Bobo, also a well-known caver and conservationist, in a three-year study of historic Civil War signatures left within Mammoth Cave National Park. Their project focused on the interactions between soldiers in the Union and Confederate armies, the cave environment, and the larger karst landscape. So far the trio had proved that forty-one of the thousands of names they had found on walls and ceilings were left by soldiers during the war. Douglas estimates that over ten thousand total signatures are

Marion O. Smith records a historic signature in Mammoth cave.

scrawled upon the walls of Mammoth, not to mention ancient pictographs and other markings left by Native Americans.

Recording the names was difficult: Some signatures were layered atop one another in a confusing array; others were frustratingly incomplete, like "William," "Capt. Jones," or "1863." Names could be smoked onto ceilings in candle flame, scratched into walls with rocks or knives, or neatly handwritten in pencil or ink. Words might be printed or in cursive. The writing itself could provide clues as to when an undated signature was created. Douglas carried a guide to particular lettering styles and popular abbreviations of specific decades of the nineteenth and twentieth centuries.

After recording names on research trips, Smith would consult dozens of archival sources, from the register of the Mammoth Cave hotel to the official records of the Union and Confederate armies. Slowly, he pieced together the signatories' lives. "Much, much, much research needs to be done," he later cautioned me about the signature of A. Rust, which he suspected might actually belong to Albert Rust, an antebellum congressman. In 1861 Rust became a member of the Confederate Provisional Congress from Arkansas. By 1862 he was a Confederate brigadier general. If Smith could prove that he went to the greater Bowling Green, Kentucky, area in 1861 as a member of Congress, the signature might be his. But it could also be that of some wholly unrelated person named "A Rust."

The "t" might be an "h," Smith said, "but without archival verification, the writer remains unknown."

"There is a poignant aspect to the research," Douglas said of coming into such close contact with personal notes left by soldiers during wartime. Isaac McCann, for example, a soldier in the Thirty-Fourth Illinois Regiment, visited Mammoth Cave in March 1862, writing to his sister that the experience "stimulated one's imagination." In April he was mortally wounded in the Battle of Shiloh, dying in a St. Louis hospital later that month.

Some could not completely escape the horrors of war within the peace of Mammoth Cave. Enslaved tour guides would often take tour parties in a small boat across the cave's River Styx and fire a pistol (something they would never be allowed to carry on the surface), in order to demonstrate the echo.

Asa W. Slayton, of the Twenty-Fifth Michigan Infantry, described the experience in an article titled "Soldier Journal," published in the Grand Rapids *Weekly Eagle* on January 6, 1863:

> "The echo is good at this point," says Nick [Bransford, the African American guide] . . . and the sound is echoed and re-echoed from the water to the ceiling, and from wall to wall . . . down the river sounding like the sharp, heavy booming of a cannon, succeeded by volleys of musketry along the battle line to a great distance; and as we listen still, and hear the low, rumbling sound creeping along the darksome, distant way, it seems like the feeble moaning of the unfortunate victims of deadly strife.

Mammoth had no specific military value, but controlling the natural wonder became what Douglas called a "sign of prestige." As surrounding land was claimed by first one army and then the other, the cave itself remained generally open to tourism throughout the war—not only to soldiers, but to ordinary civilians and even Europeans willing to risk the travel. Many soldiers were aware of the site because of popular guidebooks published by Charles W. Wright in 1858 and 1860, along with articles praising its marvels in newspapers and magazines.

From about the 1820s, professional tour guides—many of them enslaved African Americans—led visitors through the complex maze of passages. Civilian and military visitors found moments of escape in the unchanging beauty and darkness. Soldiers quartered nearby would slip underground while off duty, leaving their names and the date behind, as was the nineteenth-century custom. Some shared a bit of art or a personal or political message.

"Confederate soldiers would write their name," Douglas says, "then Union soldiers would write theirs in the same passage, as though claiming the space." He describes a spot in the cave where someone wrote "hurrah for Jeff Davis," and someone else scratched it out. One wall bears a portrait of a Lincoln; other chambers contain stone "monuments,"

Historic signatures are smoked into the ceiling above a Mammoth Cave "monument."

piles of rock that tourists would make and name for Lincoln, Grant, or Sherman. Cave guides perpetuated these names long after the war ended. Even today, many hastily stacked monuments remain.

The three researchers had learned that some who wrote their names on the walls were killed or injured, while others lived long and productive lives. Recording never-before-cataloged signatures through field observation and photography, then verifying names through archival research, allowed small glimpses into the everyday lives of soldiers. By focusing on graffiti with complete, verifiable signatures left during the war years of 1861–1865, Douglas, Smith, and Bobo had begun to tease out a cultural story connecting dozens of fighters with but one thing in common: a trip to Mammoth Cave.

Marion Smith grew up in Fairburn, Georgia, where in the fifth grade he began reading historical accounts of the war and, when able, touring nearby battlefields. In 1953 he was fascinated by the Civil War "Cyclorama" at Atlanta's Grant Park zoo. In his early twenties, he started poking into the region's caves. As he was joining cavers in the first exploration and mapping of virgin discoveries, Smith became interested in historic Southern caves where saltpeter was mined from bat guano, mostly to provide gunpowder for the War of 1812. He first saw a Civil War-era signature in a cave in Alabama in 1972. Already familiar with many of reference works of the period, he soon located information on that soldier and began researching others.

Because saltpeter caves tend to be relatively dry, wooden vats and tools left behind by early miners can be remarkably well preserved. Smith recorded extensive lists of saltpeter caves in TAG, mining university libraries for clues to help him relocate previously lost sites. "It was a way to combine my twin obsessions," he later recalled. The quality of his historical research and the carefully arranged prose of his publications eventually contributed to his master's thesis on Georgia's delegates to the Second Confederate Congress, which helped him secure a job with the University of Tennessee as assistant editor and curator of the papers of President Andrew Johnson, a job from which he retired in 2000.

On September 14, 2002, I happened to visit Smith, whom the caving community has long regarded as the epitome of a TAG caver, at his comfortable log home on Bone Cave Road in Van Buren, Tennessee, on the occasion of his sixtieth birthday party. The next day he led me and others on a tour through the cave for which his road is named. Actually called Big Bone Cave, it was named after the remains of an extinct giant ground sloth found there in 1811. The cave's massive deposits of bat guano were mined for saltpeter during the War of 1812 and again during the Civil War. Smith led me over fantastic wooden catwalks created by the miners, practically running along loose boards laid in place nearly two hundred years earlier. The cave is gated and managed by Rock Island State Park. During an enjoyable hour or two there, we saw only a fraction of the mapped cave, known to be just under ten miles long, but we saw nearly all the portions that would have been familiar to nineteenth-century miners. In a wide room only about four feet high, we saw easily hundreds of signatures smoked onto the flat limestone ceiling. They stood out clearly, like ink on white parchment. Smith had catalogued all of them.

Marion O. Smith sits beneath an elevated wooden pipe used in saltpeter mining for the War of 1812.

Douglas had done historical research on caves in the early 1990s as graduate student, and in 2000 he began working with a Tennessee cave archeology group. He had met Smith on earlier caving trips, and the two began sharing information on historic signatures and artifacts. Together they studied Hubbard's, a bat cave with thousands of nineteenth century signatures.

"I didn't know what to do with them," Douglas recalls. Gradually he learned how different signature styles and writing methods could convey the approximate date they had been left, along with other clues that could narrow the writer to particular historical periods. He and Smith began presenting and publishing some of their research. They worked at first in Tennessee, but in 2009 they recorded signatures in a cave near Munfordville, Kentucky, not far from Mammoth. And then in 2015, they learned of signatures in a cave just outside the park's borders known among biologists for its large bat population. Smith began to look up some of the names they spotted there and confirmed they were Civil War soldiers.

"Nobody had published anything about it," Douglas says. "We found these magnificent Civil War soldier names, some very legible. That got us going regularly to Kentucky."

Smith knew of another small cave just inside the park's borders that had been reported to contain a single Civil War signature. But it was a sensitive location, normally closed to any research or visitation due to the presence of white-nose syndrome.

"If there's one signature, there's got to be others," Smith reasoned. "But the park will never let us in to look."

Douglas took this as a challenge. "Maybe in the summer, when the bats aren't there," he told Smith. "I think with the right proposal, maybe we can get in there."

"Oh yeah?" Smith skeptically replied. "We'll see."

Since Douglas was taking the time to write a fairly lengthy formal proposal for a historical research permit, he went ahead and added Mammoth Cave and "other caves in the park" to his request. The proposal eventually landed on the desk of Rick Toomey, director of the Mammoth Cave International Center for Science and Learning. It turned out that Toomey was a caver who had met Marion Smith before and knew of his reputation. With Toomey's recommendation, the park service granted Douglas and Smith a research permit for a three-year study. After each trip, Smith dug up archival material on individual soldiers, using more than just the official records of both armies. His first stop was often the detailed register from the Mammoth Cave Hotel, owned during the war by Edward K. Owsley, a Union sympathizer who nonetheless housed soldiers of each army, the Confederacy at the war's beginning and the Union for most of the duration. Douglas took extensive notes on the unpublished register in the archives of Western Kentucky University, then Jim Honaker later photographed the entire document for Smith's use.

In the late 1990s and early 2000s, I enjoyed a more or less annual gig at a summer camp for gifted teenagers called Project CAVES, an acronym for "Creative Adventures and Valuable Experiences through Spelunking." It was part of the Arkansas AEGIS program, which fosters various math and science camps throughout the state. Students had to apply to Project CAVES with an essay describing why they wanted to attend. Those selected received scholarships to spend a week in the Arkansas

Ozarks, where, in addition to normal camp activities like swimming and canoeing, they learned basic caving skills, surveying, and science, with evening lectures by a series of visiting experts, including me. I have always enjoyed talking to young people about caves, but my favorite part about speaking at the camp was that they let me bring my own children along for a couple of days of caving, camping, and general outdoor fun. At the 1999 camp, my oldest son Alex, then eight, learned an important lesson about caving: the trip ends whenever any member of the group wants to turn around.

I had given my evening lecture and was followed by an archeologist, who delivered a fascinating talk explaining how a few bits of bone and pottery could teach a great deal about the lives of Native Americans who had used area caves for thousands of years. With just a few clues, he was able to demonstrate how a particular male individual had occupied one cave for several years around 1200 AD, using it as a sort of manufacturing shop where he strung together leather cords with a device held in his teeth. The scientist had studied forensic evidence suggesting that the man likely died of a severe dental abscess, caused in part by a diet heavy in corn. The corn-rich diet indicated that the man may have been a member of a religious movement of the time that worshipped a corn deity.

My twins Ken and Chris were about five and a half years old then. Like their older brother, they were fascinated by the ancient artifacts that the speaker had brought along, some of which they were allowed to touch. After his talk, he let them handle a few tools actually used by the individual he had researched. He surprised both the boys and me by saying that he knew of another cave within a few miles of camp that still contained many undisturbed artifacts. If he could trust us to stay on the clearly marked trail and touch nothing, he said, he would give me directions to visit this little-known site. The boys and I readily agreed.

We set out the next morning on a thickly wooded trail. I carried a backpack with helmets and lamps, along with water, snacks, and a hand-drawn map to a particular room containing artifacts. It was a hot July day, so I was grateful when the trail came to a small river. All three boys could swim, and it was shallow enough for Alex and me to wade. As the water rose to their knees, however, the twins announced that it was deep and cold and they wanted to be carried across.

I piggybacked first Ken, then Chris, to the base of a white limestone bluff where the four of us began a fairly steep climb toward the cave entrance. This was the longest hike either twin had ever attempted. They weren't that happy about climbing in wet shoes, but we pressed onward because we knew that we were getting close.

It was easy to spot the entrance. The valley from which we emerged was rapidly heating up, and cool air flowing from the cave turned into visible tendrils of fog that rolled toward the bluff. Alex, who was walking point, turned to grin mischievously at his brothers.

"You know what that is, don't you?" he asked, pointing at the fingers of mist just above us. "That's Indian ghosts coming out of the cave to see who's out here."

To be perfectly honest, he gets that sort of humor from me.

On any given day I might have said the same thing. But it was exactly the wrong thing to say to a pair of five-year-olds already concerned about rivers and wet feet and possibly bears in the woods. They flatly refused to go inside, even as we reached the entrance and could see a small flagged path beckoning toward the darkness. Alex tried to argue in favor of leaving his brothers outside while we looked at the archeological treasures ourselves, but instead he got to learn the caving rule that the group turns the trip when any member of the team is finished.

For a couple of years after that, it was hard to get the twins to agree to any underground venture except an occasional tourist cavern. Alex, meanwhile, became fairly adept at caving. He learned vertical basics and rappelled into his first pit at thirteen or fourteen, as did Chris a year or two later. Ken began to gravitate more toward the virtual caves of role-playing games and online gaming. The first time I recall all three boys actually caving together with me was in Cookeville, Tennessee, several years after the ghost debacle.

It was a winter's day. I believe Alex had just turned sixteen and the twins were not quite thirteen. We had stopped in Cookeville to visit Lee and Sharon en route from a family vacation to Florida over Christmas break. Lee took the boys and me to several relatively easy caves that lay within the city limits. Joining us were two local caving friends of his, Kristen Bobo and Joe Douglas.

The most fun cave we saw that day lay in a wooded lot within a suburban neighborhood. We had to walk through fresh snow along the edge of someone's backyard to reach the entrance. Much later, I learned that it was the backyard of Steve Alexander, a federal wildlife manager and brother to Lea Ann Alexander, a librarian at my university and one of our family's closest friends in Arkansas. The caving world is full of such coincidences.

The cave was fun because it contained a jungle gym of crawls and climbs. At one fissure in particular the twins discovered that their legs had grown long enough to allow them to easily step across a gap perhaps eight feet deep. Bobo stood five feet four and weighed 102 pounds. While that size made her a champion at pushing though the tightest of crawls— Lee had introduced her to the boys as a "famous" TAG caver—her legs wouldn't reach across where the boys had stepped over, so she climbed down and up again to continue. When I showed them an article focusing on her and Marion Smith in *National Geographic* a few months later, Chris was quick to point this out.

All of this came back to me as Joe Douglas spoke over the phone about that day we had spent poking into Cookeville caves. I had "introduced" myself to him in hopes of joining one of his and Marion Smith's signature research trips, and he pointed out that Lee had introduced him to my sons and me a decade earlier. I was glad for the reminder, I said, because Chris also wanted to go with us to Mammoth. He had just finished a postgraduate internship and was taking some time off before starting graduate school in the fall; he had already accompanied me on several Tennessee caving trips over the previous year.

Joe said that was fine. He thought he could arrange for us to stay at the Cave Research Foundation field house at Mammoth Cave, which was managed by the geologist and noted cave surveyor Patricia Kambesis. I assured Joe that Pat was an old friend who had led me in surveys of virgin passages in both Lechuguilla and southern China, and that I would call her to set it up. The world of cavers is small.

. . . .

Historian Joe Douglas examines a saltpeter vat and wooden trough.

Mammoth is a cave of superlatives. The 1858 guidebook estimated its length at about one hundred miles—which would not be proven true until 1972, when cavers connected it to the Flint Ridge system in another valley, a tale thrillingly told in the 1976 book *The Longest Cave*, by Roger Brucker and Richard Watson. With 415 miles of passages known in 2019, and new discoveries every year, it remains by far the longest known cave on Earth.

Our signature hunt began that morning in a hallway of the park's Science and Resource Management Building. Rick Toomey, a few cavers, various park personnel and I crowded around a framed map of Mammoth Cave published in 1911.

"For signature trips, it's easier to look at an old map that shows only passages that would have been known in the nineteenth century," Douglas explained. A modern map would include literally hundreds of miles of new discovery stacked above and below, confusing our choice of routes.

He removed his glasses and leaned in close to the map.

"Rhoda's Arcade is right here." He traced one of two squiggly lines running near each other roughly ninety degrees to a large tunnel called

Silliman Avenue. "But Ike's Path is right here." He pointed to the other side passage.

"We went in there recently," said park ranger Larry Johnson.

"I know you went in there and got lost over here," Douglas said, sliding his finger an inch along the old map. "But there are names where?" he asked Johnson. "Right here?"

"Everywhere," Johnson said emphatically, waving broadly at that section of map. "Everywhere."

"We haven't looked at all here, and we haven't looked at Rhoda's Arcade." Douglas studied the map silently for a moment then pointed to an upper portion. "Now we could go all the way down to Fox Avenue. But I don't think we're going to find much there."

Immediately Smith and others clustered around Douglas began correcting him—he was pointing at Welcome Avenue, not Fox, which ran parallel to Welcome but well above it in a higher level of the complex system.

"You'll come out at Ganter if you do that passage," Johnson said. The ranger then noticed me standing in the crowded hallway and shook hands. We had met once before, he reminded me, at a caving convention in Tennessee. I nodded. I introduced him to Chris, and the two of us signed releases that would let us explore undeveloped parts of the longest cave on Earth without holding the park responsible should we never emerge.

Our group planned a traverse of between four and five miles over what soldiers would have known as the "long route" through the cave. Johnson would stay with us long enough to make sure we found and entered the Welcome Passage, which he said would involve three fourths of a mile of stoop-walking that he would just as soon avoid. He planned to leave us the at that point by an easier route out.

The spot where we stood would have been familiar to nineteenth-century visitors, but our group had a much easier time traversing it. We had arrived in El Ghor by way of an elevator and a short walk through the Snowball Room. For decades this large white chamber was famous for an underground cafeteria that fed tourists until it was closed a few years ago to avoid contaminating cave life. Reaching this spot in 1861 would have meant a round trip of fourteen or fifteen hours by lantern and candle.

Standing where they had stood, letting my eyes roam over a small section of wall, I spotted a signature no one else had noticed. Smith recorded it, Bobo photographed it, and we moved along. Chris and I soon became adept at recognizing more common Mammoth names. Most famous is the frequent signature of Stephen Bishop, an enslaved guide who began leading tours in 1838. For nearly three decades he explored on his own as well as with tourists. He was the first to traverse the "Bottomless Pit" and created an early cave map, eventually purchasing his freedom using his tour-guide earnings. (In 2003, park ranger Larry Johnson allowed Smith and Alan Cressler to rappel the Bottomless Pit, which they measured as actually an eighty-six-foot drop to six feet of water.)

A half hour after leaving El Ghor for another passage, Johnson stopped at a small opening in the right-hand wall. "I went back in there the other day, and there's a kind of dangerous little step-over I didn't want to do by myself," he said.

"Well we're here now, so we'll watch you do it," Douglas joked. He followed Johnson, adding, "I think this might be one of the ways into Rhoda's Arcade, but I think there's an easier way farther down the main passage. I'll go down and look."

As they checked the route, Smith noticed a signature. "I don't know if I have recorded Mr. Milroy," he said, pulling out his journal. He pointed out a series of X marks along one wall. "All my exes live in Texas," he mused. "Well, that's not true. Only some of my exes live in Texas." He, Chris, and I followed Douglas down the crawlway.

We checked out various routes, weaving our way separately through several interconnecting tunnels.

In one place, Bobo found two other guide names next to Stephen Bishop's. "We've long wondered what Alfred's last name was," she said, pointing. "I saw that and I was like, well, bingo!" She photographed the find in order to try to verify it later.

After reaching Rhoda's Arcade via two different routes, the group rejoined to catalog multiple new signatures there. Smith had left his walking stick at the entrance to a crawlway, and he grumbled that he would have to return for it. I said that we had in fact picked it up along the way, despite the fact that Douglas had suggested we "hide it back in the main passage."

"So if you actually took it here I should retract all my snide remarks?" Smith asked.

"At least half of them," Douglas quickly answered.

I admitted that it was Chris who had retrieved his stick.

"Well okay for him," Smith said. "The rest of you are still fair game."

Johnson led us to the start of the Welcome Passage before heading back toward an elevator to the surface, where Johnson joked he would be having a beer before we reached the other end. The Welcome Passage's tight walls and low ceiling required much stooping and some crawling in its three-quarter mile length. The tunnel rose vertically toward one of the most-traveled and graffiti-rich sections in the historic portion of the cave.

. . . .

In September 2017, six months before our trip, Marion was nearly killed in a Tennessee pit when another caver accidentally dislodged a fist-sized piece of flowstone. The rock fell forty feet before striking a glancing blow just below Smith's helmet, fracturing the lower left temporal bone of his skull. Bleeding from the ears, cold, and barely conscious, Smith climbed out under his own power. He was airlifted to a nearby hospital for treatment of concussion and other injuries.

It had been Smith's second caving injury since turning seventy—the first had occurred in 2014 when a loose boulder pinned him in a crawlway, also resulting in a helicopter ride to a hospital.

"I just yielded to the old temptation that I've yielded to for many decades and foolishly went in," Smith told a reporter covering the 2014 accident. "And as soon as I got in the thing, I literally said, 'I'll never get out of here.' I literally said that." He quickly added, "This incident, all it did was screw up my plans for the weekend."

Although he continued to enter hundreds of caves, since the more recent head injury he remained prone to periods of vertigo, especially when a passage required him to stoop or continually look up. As we got

As the group pauses for rest, Kristin Bobo and Joe Douglas examine Marion O. Smith's log of signatures obtained in Rhoda's Arcade.

farther into the upward-slanting Welcome Passage, we had to do a lot of stooping and looking up. Smith told the main body of our group to move ahead, knowing he would eventually catch up. They proceeded up the tortuous route and vanished beyond sight or hearing. While Chris walked along with Bobo and Douglas, I stayed with Smith, who moved slowly but deliberately, using his carved walking stick. His companion Sharon Jones had purchased the baby blue caving helmet he wore to replace the one destroyed by the rock.

Traveling with him at this slower pace, I was treated to several relatively obscure signatures that he spotted and paused to record. Most of these were from the late nineteenth century rather than the war years. We move steadily upward, occasionally pausing as he braced himself across the narrow passage, feet on one wall and back on the other in a sitting position. Poised comfortably between limestone walls, he regaled me with marvelous tales of the underground.

. . . .

The author examines a basket abandoned in a crawlway over three thousand years ago.

We reached the others at the Wooden Bowl Room, a junction area named for an artifact found by early explorers. From about 5,000 until 1,200 years ago, Native Americans mined gypsum from the cave walls. Possessing no lanterns or candles, they lit their way with torches made of river cane. Burned bits of cane lay everywhere on the floors. Black "stoke marks" from the torches lined the walls. I picked up a hollow, charred piece of cane less than an inch long and held it to my nose. It smelled of fire.

Near the Wooden Bowl Room, Bobo led me into a crawlway where we examined a beautiful but irreparably broken woven basket. It remained otherwise undisturbed, protected by its obscure location. The basket sat in a low-ceilinged chamber Bobo said was believed to have been a sort of restroom area for ancient miners. Archeologists estimate its age at more than three thousand years old, perhaps as old as four thousand years. Yet it looked as if it had been abandoned in the passage a few weeks ago.

Continuing toward the historic entrance, we found new signatures, several of which Smith later verified as made during the Civil War, even locating photographs matching these names. We spotted occasional art-work: a portrait of Abraham Lincoln dated July 1861; a woman in a dress, date unknown; birds and flowers. We saw a name and what is the oldest—but unconfirmed—date yet found in the cave: 1798. Proving that it was actually written in 1798, Douglas added, might be impossible. Such incidental finds eventually led the park to commission an ambitious new five-year study by Douglas and Smith, set to begin in 2020, chronicling *all* historical signatures within Mammoth Cave. As of December 2019, Smith at seventy-seven was still making frequent—if slow and grumbling—trips into the cave with Douglas and Bobo.

In a letter sent January 2, 2020, accompanying his comments and suggestions on a draft of this book, Smith requested that I "tone down" my portrayal of him as one of America's great cavers. "I believe that my main contribution to caving is through spelean history—the study of caves related to the Confederate Nitre and Mining Bureau and caves visited by Civil War Soldiers, including the ongoing Mammoth Cave studies," he wrote, exhibiting, in my opinion, the humility of a great explorer. In any case, as injury and age greatly slowed his ability to push virgin pits and caves, his ability to research historical data gathered underground remained intact.

After eight hours underground and five difficult miles, we encountered the glow of daylight coming from the Mammoth Cave's natural entrance. Smith slowly marched ahead, and I turned to look one last time at the darkness behind. I felt personally connected to those war-weary explorers who preceded us in this magical place. I sensed that they were caught up, as I had been, as all cavers are, in the thrill of the unknown.

For you vertical cavers, do you remember your very first cave related drop? Either in-cave or open air pit? About how deep and what state? Let's hear some stories!

CAVER SCOTT

ZEKE MCKEE: First pit was Bo Allen Pit in TN. 154' drop. About ¾ of the way out I decided it was a really dumb hobby and I'd never do it again. Needless to say that feeling only lasted 10 minutes or so and I was ready for more. 😂

STEVE T.: Davis Cagle's Chasm, 186 footer using borrowed gear from someone not on the trip. I was instructed how to use the gear (a rack and Mitchell system) onsite. Young and dumb.

TOM WHITEHURST: Similar experience here. Natural Well—190 ft.— Huntsville, AL, 1971. First pit and first time on rope, borrowed Goldline, two racks for four people, two Jumars total with climbing instruction provided at the bottom of the pit. Texas'd out with one Jumar and one poly ski rope Prusik. Still dizzy from the spinning. Young and dumb.

STEVE T.: Davis I'm sure stories like ours occur regularly even to this day. That makes me amazed that there are not more rescues, um, recoveries. NSS #21524 SCCI #9

CURT BUETTNER: Neversink . . . My first big drop. Was scared shitless. Lol . . . . . 168'.

MICHAEL TAYLOR: A really crappy 80-foot drop on the edge of the campground at 1980 TAG fall cave-in. I had practiced climbing in a tree with Prusiks, but Lee Pearson let me borrow a Mitchell system. About a million fire ants attacked us at the lip. I was hooked forever. In the morning I bought a set of three Gibbs, and sewed my first ropewalker harness at home later.
[Over 200 additional replies.]

Facebook post and comments, March 26, 2018

Chapter 8

THE BRIDGE

It was an Indiana Jones sort of moment, stolen from a hundred adventure films: that part where the heroes race over a collapsing stone bridge.

I was not yet thirty years old that summer in the late 1980s. Children were still in the future. Kathy and I had met up with Lee and Sharon Pearson in Cookeville, something we often did on vacation. By this time our wives seldom went caving, but Lee had somehow convinced them to join us in a short trip to a well-known, heavily visited wild cave about forty-five minutes from town.

"Nothing but easy walking passage," he promised. "Pretty formations."

"It's probably some hell hole with a belly crawl," Sharon said.

Lee insisted it would be fun, and, surprisingly, Sharon and Kathy agreed to go. We drove from Cookeville down a scenic county road along the edge of the Plateau. Through gaps in the trees and the haze of summer we could see rolling farmland and the twin ribbons of Interstate 40 before we turned south toward forest. We parked in a darkly shaded dirt lot just off the highway. The hike was short, with dramatic spires of weathered gray limestone rising through green brush beside us. The entrance appeared exactly as advertised: a tall portal to an easy walking passage.

We all donned helmets and lamps. The cool cave air was far more appealing than the rising heat and humidity outside. For perhaps two hours the four of us meandered through a limestone canyon about twenty feet wide, the sort of twisting, boulder-strewn pathway a cowboy would gallop down in a western, if it were outside. Occasionally we passed deep holes in the floor, but we easily skirted these by walking to one side. At a wide junction area Lee and I left our spouses sitting on a large rock, eating snacks. He explained that he and I would spend a few minutes scaling one wall of the canyon visible from the point where they sat.

"Just ten minutes or so," he promised. "There's a lead I've always wanted to check."

A couple of shadowy pockets in the wall beckoned, a good fifty feet off the floor. Even though we had chosen a well-known, well-traveled cave, the general inaccessibility of these high leads might signal previously unexplored side passages. Lee picked out a series of handholds and footholds and began ascending the wall. I followed. We finally reached the two openings, but both revealed dead ends. A lone bootprint told me we weren't even the first to check them out. So we edged along the wall, clinging by our fingertips to various indentations as we began slowly working our way back toward the floor.

Ahead, Lee pointed out a natural arch that joined the two sides of the canyon. From the main trunk below, this connection had appeared to be an uneven patch of ceiling rather than the bridge now visible from our higher perch. I flipped on the battery-consuming hi-beam of my headlamp. It seemed an easier route than the way we had come up. Lee said that the far side of the canyon was near a known formation alcove—one I thought we might have visited years earlier. I recalled that a much-traveled path, almost a natural staircase, led down toward the floor from the alcove, which glistened with yellow and white stalactites. It would land us in the main passage very close to the spot where we had left Kathy and Sharon.

We decided to avoid the exposed, somewhat dicey-looking downclimb by walking over to the other side.

Kathy and Sharon could see what we were up to from where they sat. Kathy recalls shouting toward us, "Don't try to go across that, you dumbasses!"

I don't recall hearing her.

Whenever constructions of nature sit for centuries undisturbed by weather or the hand of man, they may not be as immovable as they appear. A third of the way across the three-foot-wide arch, something shifted slightly beneath our feet. We froze.

Lee, leading as usual, turned toward me, a quizzical look on his face.

"That can't be good," I said.

Just then a chunk of limestone the size of a Pilates ball rolled off one side of the arch, followed by gravel sliding from a spot we had just passed. We ran as more chunks of bridge collapsed behind us to sounds of thunder. Powdered limestone rose through the air like smoke from an explosion. Lee reached the far side ahead of me. I was still a few steps behind, the path tilting beneath my feet like a gym treadmill moving toward a more difficult setting. Had there been an accompanying soundtrack, the music would have swelled ominously, horns blaring danger. I was two long strides away from solid ground and took a leap of faith.

Cavers will tell you that most injuries underground happen to ill-equipped spelunkers, that proper training and equipment make even extreme vertical caving a relatively safe activity. This is true, by and large: according to actuarial tables, you are less likely to die while caving than while participating in, for example, hang gliding, scuba diving, or boxing. Highly publicized cave accidents, like the boys trapped in Thailand who drew the world's attention for a week in 2018, generally involve novices overlooking basic safety precautions. And it's true that standard single-rope technique, first developed by cavers in the late 1960s to safely descend the deep pits of TAG, is so reliable that it has been adopted by rescue squads and SWAT teams the world over. Even the leading ropes for mountaineering and rescue operations—the brands PMI and Bluewater—were first manufactured in north Georgia specifically for caving. ("PMI" stands for "Pigeon Mountain Industries," named after the mountain housing Ellison's Cave, which contains the two deepest vertical cave pitches in the continental United States: Fantastic Pit, at 586 feet, and Incredible Pit, at 440 feet.)

But the reality is that caves are an ever-evolving and naturally unstable environment. Serious injury, even death, may be no more than a misstep away. *American Caving Accidents*, published periodically by the National Speleological Society and continually updated online, offers a sobering compendium of the many ways things can go wrong underground. It is thus required reading for beginning cavers.

Shortly after my 1980 Xanadu excursion, I joined the NSS and gleaned some basics from the series: Always check the weather before entering a cave known to flood. Secure your primary attachment to a rope with a locking carabiner. Beware waterfall climbs, which can lead to hypothermia and fuzzy thinking. Carry long pads to protect the rope from sharp ledges and projections. Inspect ropes and vertical gear frequently and replace them at signs of serious wear. When preparing to rappel off a slick or downward-tilting ledge, secure yourself to a nearby tree or rock prior to rigging the main line. Tie a figure eight at the end of every rope before tossing it off a ledge to avoid rappelling into space, should the line not reach bottom. Whenever possible, have someone else in your party look over your harness and rappel rack just before you begin to rappel. Once on the bottom of the pit, find an overhead ledge to protect you from incidental rockfall caused by any cavers who rappel in after you. And maybe fifty other things.

As I was learning vertical techniques while hanging in Frank Hutchison's backyard oak tree in Tallahassee, such dangers and how to avoid them seemed rather theoretical. But the first time I stepped off the ledge at Neversink—a must-see for nearly all new vertical cavers in TAG—the theory became suddenly real. Neversink is not the deepest pit in TAG: At only 162 feet, it doesn't even come close. Nor is it particularly difficult. The steep hike up the mountain expends more energy than does the climb from the pit. It is so relatively easy, as 162-foot-deep pits go, that it is often among the first five pits visited by vertical novices in the South. That is probably what makes it so memorable for TAG cavers: it is usually the first pit to take your breath away.

For Neversink is a vertical cathedral, a sculpted castle of stone and greenery and sparkling water that looks as though it were created by

Neversink Pit, which is now a flagship property of the Southeastern Cave Conservancy, Inc. (SCCi).

a fantasy artist for the cover of a sorcery adventure novel. On first approaching the sinkhole from the well-traveled mountain path, I could see a waterfall—a trickle most of the year, but occasionally a frothing cascade—straight ahead, on the far side of an opening two hundred feet in diameter. Like nearly every party that makes the trek up, we paused before rigging the drop to walk along a flat ledge about four feet wide that curves to the left of the most common rig point.

From this ledge, I could see all the way down. Although "all the way" is a shorter distance than in many other TAG pits, the series of concentric ledges and hollows that ring the shaft create a visual illusion of impossible depth. I steadied myself against a small tree and leaned out from the ledge to examine the log-strewn bottom, lit by a shaft of afternoon sun, feeling an almost magnetic pull, drawing me as though not into a strange world, but a strange universe. I walked with far greater care along the ledge as on my return to the rigging point than I had exercised while stepping out.

Rappelling into Neversink is an intensely visual experience. Because of this, it is one of the most photographed pits in TAG, perhaps one of the most photographed pits in the world. It adorns dozens of calendars and posters, has appeared in *National Geographic* and many other magazines. It was my second pit, with a group from Florida State. But from Neversink I hold an intense memory of that moment when I first pulled my foot from rock and trusted my weight to nylon rope and steel rappel rack. I fell two inches, no farther, as the webbing of my seat harness tightened beneath the rack. After that brief moment of panic, I was in control of my descent, gliding as if by magic beside moss-draped ledges. The visual explosion of depth beneath my feet demanded attention as few other caves—even much deeper pits—could manage. The shaft caught light in such a way that a daytime rappel felt more like mountaineering than caving.

In 1981, Frank Hutchison, for many years the vertical training guru of FSCC, spent a night on the flat left-hand ledge, a safety line around his sleeping bag, before a planned early morning film shoot. Forever after, he claimed to have dreamed the most magical dreams of his life that night. By profession an expert in medieval instruments and music, Frank woke the rest of our team the next morning with a haunting Gregorian chant that echoed through ring upon ring of stone as from the Earth itself.

Longtime Georgia caver Brent Aulenbach proposed to his future wife, diamond ring and all, hanging halfway up Neversink. He had attached the ring to his pack with string, so he wouldn't drop it down the pit. Nancy, herself a second-generation caver and co-star of the IMAX film *Journey into Amazing Caves*, accepted the proposal to the cheers of friends in on the plan, who stood watching from the ledge. Marion Smith was there. Alan Cressler took photographs. (And more than two decades later, their teenage daughter is an active TAG caver.) Marion was once married in the bottom of the pit with a party of about seventy in attendance. The marriage didn't last. "All I can say is that we had a beautiful day," he said many years later. "We had a shaft of light in the pit and we had a rainbow. You can't just get that anywhere."

Neversink is the sort of place to inspire uniquely human moments of creativity. And it is also a gateway drug to vertical caving. Hanging

View from the bottom of Neversink.

amid the lush greenery of the pit, slowly spinning as I slid down a singing rope toward the bottom, I fully understood what Karen Witte had meant when she had told us novices a year earlier, "That is the point," while tapping on a chalk drawing of herself in a gigantic Mexican pit.

Sometime between Xanadu and Neversink, I became addicted to longer, more adventurous, and potentially more dangerous trips. The following Thanksgiving, a group of us loaded into a university van and drove north for four days of intense vertical caving in northern Alabama. We went to Fern Cave, where in 1961 explorers from the Huntsville Grotto found 437-foot-deep Surprise Pit—a surprise because it appeared suddenly in the midst of what is otherwise an ordinary horizontal walking passage. We rappelled into the enormous chamber to the sound of a crashing waterfall before enjoying a Thanksgiving dinner of kippered herring, granola, and crackers, exploring just a bit of the cave's fifteen miles before exiting. We camped at Stephens Gap, a classic TAG pit where you could rappel 143 feet to the bottom and then, if you felt like it, hike out the horizontal entrance instead of climbing the rope back up.

On that trip we also explored 23 Dollar Pit, a complex system containing seven separate vertical drops, requiring a total of six hundred feet of rope to rig each successive shaft. The name came from the money that fell from the pocket of Bill Torode, one of the cave's first explorers (and also the discoverer of Surprise Pit), somewhere in one of the seven pits—presumably still there. The mountain in which 23 Dollar Pit lies had been logged, destroying the former path to the eighty-foot entrance pit, since anyone in the Florida State club had been there. We spent most of the day wandering around lost before we finally found the correct sinkhole near sunset. After successfully bottoming all seven pits, we derigged on the way out to emerge sometime after 2 a.m. We were tired and out of water, but damp from having climbed through several waterfalls.

While we had been underground, the outside temperature had dropped to below twenty degrees. It was grotto policy to carry a large trash bag in your helmet for use as an emergency poncho. We donned these and began stumbling around the mountain in the dark, a green-garbed garbage brigade. Paths that had been hard to find in daylight were impossible to follow with our fading helmet lamps. Lights from distant farms winked helpfully in the Paint Rock Valley below, but each time we tried to walk toward them, we'd hit an impassible cliff. We would back up and try another path, only to be stopped by another cliff. Twice, we accidentally found new pits, which we tried make notes on for some future return. Once as we sat on a log near such a pit, we noticed that several of us felt an overwhelming desire to sleep. We knew from *American Caving Accidents* that this was a sign of increasing hypothermia: sleep might bring death.

Ed Hill and I kept each other moving, as did other buddy teams we designated, singing songs and telling bad jokes as we tramped around until the sun rose. Dawn illuminated a dirt logging road not far below us. We crashed through the steep brush and brambles until we hit the road, then hiked a mile or so out to the van, utterly exhausted and shivering uncontrollably. After a restorative breakfast at a nearby diner and about a dozen cups of coffee, we started the long drive back to Tallahassee, trading shifts at the wheel every hour while all but the driver slept.

The feeling of competence that came from training and logical thinking, from not doing the thing that might otherwise lead people to call your death incredibly stupid, energized me. I began acquiring new knots and techniques: helical Prusiks, the bowline on the coil, how to rig a simple haul system using multiple carabiners. Encouraged by others, I joined trips in Climax, including one weekend where I spent over thirty-six hours hauling tanks through crawlways and providing support for the three teams of cave divers who were trying to connect underwater passages. At grotto meetings, I started trying to get myself onto expeditions more experienced cavers planned to distant lands.

As recounted in *Cave Passages*, a planned 1982 expedition to Guatemala that I hoped to join was canceled due to political unrest in the country. I quit law school and moved to Eastern Kentucky, where a cousin who was a young country doctor let me live in his large farmhouse while I attempted to become a writer. This was a perfect location for vertical caving. Kathy had graduated from college and taken a job in Orlando. We maintained a long-distance relationship as I attempted to find my footing after law school. While I visited her in Florida two or three times that year, nearly every weekend I made the two-hour drive from my cousin's house to Cookeville to cave with Lee. We dropped pit after pit. We mapped a little cave Lee had found within the city limits called Turkey Creek. One weekend we agreed to climb one thousand vertical feet between Friday and Sunday, which we did over the course of several pits. But this increased vertical drive also made me increasingly aware of potential dangers.

We did a two-person trip to Run to the Mill, a challenging cave found just a few years earlier. A series of short climbs and a wade through chest-deep water led to a 167-foot drop into enormous borehole that meandered toward the known location of Mill Cave. Hence the name: you could run for a mile down the sand-floored borehole in the general direction of the old mill, if so inclined. Lee and I did a quick jaunt to the end of the borehole one Sunday afternoon, which in hindsight was probably unwise for only two people in what was considered a "caver's cave."

We did not rig all of the short climbs en route to Tilted Well, the pit in the middle, and so we had to assist each other up and down in a couple of spots. A short fall and broken foot at one of those locations would have meant one of us would wait hours alone as the other left to call out a rescue. Among the many rules for safe caving I had learned in 1979 from the Florida State Cave Club was that three was the minimum group size for caving, so that in case of an accident, one caver could tend the injured party while the other left to seek help. But even then, I had soon noticed that some two-person trips were common: ridgewalking, checking out a potential dig site, making a quick visit to replace a cave register—these were often done in teams of two. Once I got to TAG, I noticed that yo-yo trips to various pits sometimes lacked a third member. With my weekend drives from Kentucky, Lee and I had fallen into the habit of breaking the rule of three. Occasionally we would join a local caver or two for an especially interesting cave, but only occasionally.

After the various free climbs in Run to the Mill, we crossed a chest-deep flooded passage that formed a natural trap for cold water forced through by previous storms. The bottom was a mucky sludge of rotting vegetation. Our feet dislodged massive bubbles of methane that rose like swimming jellyfish. They plopped to the surface with the intense smell of something flammable. I recall some sort of fart joke, but we neither exploded nor suffocated. No sudden storm surge drowned us. We pressed on to the pit without incident.

After a stunning rappel beside waterfalls that bounced off sculpted limestone, we enjoyed our hike to the end of the borehole. We walked beside a burbling stream, joking and telling stories as our voices echoed from the great rounded tunnel. Near the terminus, we followed bits of electric wire and fresh rubble into a side passage where Jim Smith and others had tried recently, without success, to blast their way into a possible continuance of the cave—another activity that could lead to tragedy without due diligence and experience.

As we returned to the base of Tilted Well a good while later, we noted an auditory oddity that I have since encountered in other caves: something about the waterfalls, the empty space, the air currents, and the human brain's constant desire for familiar patterns caused us to hear another group of people at the top of the pit, talking loudly. We tried to call out to them, but they ignored us and continued their conversation, which I could almost—but not quite—make out. Our rope hung undisturbed where we had left it, along with the heavy climbing gear we had shed for the borehole hike. We geared up and took turns ascending.

As we sat in the wet spray near the rig point, coiling the rope to carry it like a bandolier back through the water passage and up the many short climbs ahead, it sounded as if the noisy group now stood at the base of the pit, laughing and talking up a storm. I knew this sound was the distant susurration of falling water, naturally distorted by horns and curves of limestone, perhaps psychically amplified by our sensory deprivation while underground. It was no wonder, I realized, that so many cultures associate caves with ghosts, with portals to spirits and the underworld. And that's even when nobody dies in them.

· · · ·

One of the TAG classics we checked off our list that fall was Valhalla, an incredibly beautiful 227-foot, open-air drop with over a mile of cave at the bottom. Other than a difficult hike, it was a pleasant and unremarkable trip. I recall that Lee let me descend the sunlit shaft first. To avoid possible rockfall I stood under a large boulder that projected into the pit near its top. Two years after our visit, a team of three cavers descended Valhalla, and two of them waited beneath the protection of the same school-bus sized overhang as the third climbed out of the pit. Just before the climber exited, the massive rock released itself from the wall and fell nearly 100 feet, crushing both cavers below, sending up an enormous cloud of dust that obscured the bottom of the pit. The survivor immediately ran down the mountain to call for help, but there was no one left to rescue. None of them had violated any rule of safe caving. The cave was soon closed by its distant landowner.

On a visit with Lee and Sharon in February 1983, we happened to be watching the local TV news one morning in their small apartment when we saw Frank Bogle, a well-known Tennessee caver, on the screen talking to reporters.

As we learned later, Bogle had been on the fourth trip to a new-found cave with Joel Buckner, Joe Douglas, a young caver named Tom Pride, and six others. The entrance was a tight crawl, originally dug open in the bottom of a sinkhole by another young caver named Rodger Ling. A stream ran through the crawl, emerging into dry passage that led to a forty-three-foot pit, followed by a two-hundred-foot stream crawl to a series of wet climbs down to another, tighter, belly crawl in water to a wet twenty-four-foot pit. From the bottom of this a rope-assisted climb up a flowstone wall led to large borehole and going passage—a caver's dream.

That day the group had descended the twenty-four-foot pit then split into smaller teams to explore and map new passages down the borehole. The rope in the pit had been redirected over some chert projections to keep it out of the main force of the waterfall. It was bitterly cold on the surface, chilling the water in the crawls and pits—Bogle later estimated it at thirty-five to forty degrees Fahrenheit.

The cold flow caused each of the three groups separate problems as they left the cave at the end of the day. With the first group to climb the twenty-four-foot pit, the rope slipped ten feet when one of the chert nodules gave way, perhaps loosened by the excess water. The caver swung upside down during the fall, injuring his wrist and taking a hard blow to the helmet. Dazed, he was still able to continue exiting, the rope now hanging directly in the water. Everyone that followed became somewhat hypothermic from the frigid flow. Ling, in the second group, twisted his ankle while climbing the flowstone beyond the pit, but still with difficulty managed to leave the cave under his own power.

The final group included Pride, who had only recently begun caving and had no experience climbing in water. He became increasingly hypothermic while trying to work his wet ascenders in the pit ahead of Bogle, Douglas, and Buckner. Unable to go up or down, Pride was stuck in the frigid spray. Douglas got on rope and climbed to him, finding Pride dazed and incoherent. Douglas was barely able to work him off the rope and onto a nearby ledge, from which the two rappelled back down, retreating to drier alcove.

Pride was too hypothermic to move at all. Douglas left alone to call for rescue, while the other two used space blankets and carbide lamps to begin warming the hypothermic caver (and themselves, by that point). Hours later, a team re-rigged the pit in a way that moved the rope from the icy waterfall, allowing Pride to exit under his own power around 3 a.m., nine hours after his first try. The local sheriff's office had been notified of the event, which led to a medivac helicopter and several reporters waiting on the surface. The landowner was also there, and told reporters the cave was now closed forever.

"That's just a part of caving," an exhausted Bogle said into the bright glare of TV lights after exiting the entrance crawl. "Sometimes you get trapped."

Lee and I enjoyed this line immensely. We began repeating it to one another in each tight crawl we encountered.

Months later, I read about a fatality involving college students who had been granted permission to rappel into a scenic ravine at a public park. A younger, less experienced climber had been first to the ledge. He dropped the rope on the ground to scout for a spot to rig a "free" rappel off the cliff. The slope was slick and wet, and the young man slipped, falling to his death in full view of an observation deck across the ravine. According to news reports, his girlfriend was on the deck.

Lee and I talked about this tragedy—and how it might have been avoided—while hiking to a pit a few weeks later. I think it was me, but it might have been Lee who finished the conversation by twisting Bogle's line: "Well that's just a part of caving. Sometimes you die."

For decades to come, whenever Lee and I found ourselves in an even slightly dicey situation, one would often turn to the other and say, "Sometimes you die."

Good relations with landowners were essential to keeping pits open. Even so, many of the privately owned pits Lee and I visited in the early 1980s were later closed, often due to a highly publicized accident elsewhere. With all the bad publicity, we had to spend more time convincing landowners that we knew what we were doing in order to gain permission to risk life and limb on their property. More than that, as with country folk throughout the South, it was polite to spend time visiting with a landowner, getting to know one another, before you asked permission to cross their land, whether for caving, hunting, bird-watching, or anything else.

In our visit to Ferris Pit, a 251-foot shaft named (but not correctly spelled) after the Pharris family in whose cow pasture it sat, the owner told us that he had always believed the pit was bottomless until Bill Cuddington descended it in the late 1950s. This was because he threw stones into the opening and never heard them hit the bottom—which turned out to be a slope covered by thick mud in the spot directly beneath the entrance. Falling rocks would hit the ooze with only a soft plop, inaudible 250 feet away. Mr. Pharris said he had his sons hold him over the four-foot wide entrance by his arms and legs so he could watch Cuddington run around the floor with a flashlight. Finally he was convinced. If not for the strong grips and sure footing of his sons, the pit might never have become a Tennessee classic. Described in Barr's 1961 *Caves of Tennessee*, the pit is now closed.

For our visit to Stamps Pit, a 192-foot drop owned by an elderly farmer named John Stamps, we wound up talking for over an hour with the owner on the front porch of his simple cabin. Mr. Stamps had been born in Cookeville in 1903 and said he had lived on the property for

A caver rappels into Valhalla, a 227-foot pit. Several climbing fatalities have occurred at this popular TAG pit, now owned by the SCCi.

most of his life. He related the story of a local mailman named Jim Esser, who had made plans to be the first to descend the pit back in 1936. He enlisted several strong-bodied men to help haul him from the shaft, and arranged to buy a special rope in Nashville that was long enough to reach the bottom.

On the appointed day, his crew and many spectators gathered at Stamps' house to watch the attempt, but Esser never showed. He never mentioned the pit to anyone again. It was finally descended in 1971 by cavers from Tennessee Technical University using the new single rope technique developed by Cuddington. Mr. Stamps pulled out a logbook where he had collected signatures from the three who had first descended the pit: Ron Johnson, Stephen Ledgerwood, and Spencer Mason. A return trip that December had included Johnson, Bill Deane, David Stidham, Frank Campbell, and Marion Smith. By the time we signed the logbook in 1982, it held nearly four hundred signatures.

As he told us more stories, a striped kitten on his porch scampered about our packs and played with the end of the coil of rope I had set down. When Mr. Stamps finally gave us permission to hike through the field behind his house to the pit, the kitten followed. The field held knee-high grass, and we kept spotting our companion as he jumped up to see the direction we were headed. When we reached the broad entrance and set down our gear, the frisky animal immediately began playing near the edge.

"That kitten's going to go after the rope when we throw it in," I said. "Mr. Stamps will probably close the cave if we get his cat killed."

Lee agreed. He had carried some spare vertical gear in an army surplus duffel bag. He dumped this on the ground and stuffed the kitten into the spacious bag. It mewed piteously as we geared up for the drop.

"He might find his way out of the bag while we're in the pit," Lee said. "We better take him down."

He tied a cord onto the duffel and clipped the end of it into a carabiner on his seat harness, so the bag would dangle a few feet below him. He rappelled first. I could hear the muffled *mew, mew, mew*, all the way down.

As procedure dictated, once on the bottom and unclipped from the line, Lee hollered, "Off rope!"

I quickly racked in and followed. As I landed in the well-lit rocky bottom of the open-air shaft, Lee took pity and released the kitten from confinement. It immediately ran into an eight-inch tall passage along the base of the pit wall. We spent the next thirty minutes trying to coax it out. Eventually I found a nylon cord in my pack and dangled it enticingly at the entrance to the small opening. The kitten couldn't resist and attacked. I grabbed him, and Lee held the duffel open. Then it was *mew, mew, mew* all the way up the pit. Once we derigged at the top and stowed our gear, Lee let the cat out of the bag. As we hiked to Mr. Stamps' house, it once more jumped above the grass to spot us and keep up.

At the house, Lee knocked on the door. After few minutes Mr. Stamps came out and we explained that we had taken his cat down the shaft rather than risk it falling in.

"I don't know whose cat that is," the old man said. "It's been hanging around my porch for a couple days now, but I think it belongs to my neighbor. Ain't mine."

We thanked him for letting us go into the pit all the same and said our goodbyes. I never learned what became of the kitten. Not long after the trip, Mr. Stamps passed away, and his heirs closed access to the pit for fear of liability. Within a few years of those intensive months of vertical caving Lee and I enjoyed, many other TAG classics, including Neversink, Run to the Mill, and Valhalla, were closed to caving. It would take an intensive caver conservation effort a decade later to get them open again as cave preserves, purchased with private donations. In the meantime, a disturbing number of injury and fatality accounts continued to fill the pages of *American Caving Accidents.*

Not that I was thinking about making that particular publication as the bridge collapsed beneath my feet several years later. I leapt without thinking, landing solidly on the flat surface where Lee stood. We heard urgent shouting from Sharon and Kathy, some distance safely beyond the boulders. Gravel still rained down on the obscured floor.

"We're okay!" Lee answered. "We made it across."

As the dust cleared I could see that the natural arch still stood—just a little bit smaller than it had been a few minutes earlier. Our wives waited in the canyon, not directly below the boulder storm we had created, but close enough to have heard the crash and seen the dust cloud, to have wondered wonder whether we had killed our fool selves.

We had not. As this sank in, we grinned like madmen. We looked at the pretty stalactites and stalagmites in the alcove ahead before climbing down the gentle route to the main passage, where they waited to yell at us.

"You know, Mike," Lee said as we walked, "that's caving."

"Yeah, sometimes you die."

Years later, as the boys from a soccer team in Thailand were trapped underground and no one knew whether they could be saved, the eminent American caver Bill Steele wrote a *Washington Post* op-ed entitled "When Things Go Wrong in Caves." He described the balance cavers try to achieve between preparation and danger. "Caving means taking a calculated risk," he wrote. "I also drive. I've been hurt worse in traffic accidents than in caves. I still drive, and I still go in caves."

. . . .

I went home for Christmas during the nine months I lived in Kentucky. Just before New Year's Day 1983, I drove the six hundred miles from Daytona Beach to Cookeville in one long stretch in order to get in some caving time with Lee. I drove my father's old Pontiac Bonneville. The car had a powerful, dependable engine, but virtually nothing else on it worked, including the heater. Knowing I would encounter subfreezing weather on the way, I placed a kerosene camp heater on the passenger floorboard. With the windows cracked for ventilation, I sped north into the night, warm and toasty. Once I left Chattanooga for the winding highways beyond the Sequatchie Valley, I began to get woozy. On a tight curve well past midnight, a wheel went off the roadway and I nearly lost control. There was a steep cliff to the left, and I knew I had to be careful. Reasoning that my problem was fumes from the heater, I lowered the driver's window and one back-seat window—the only two electric windows that actually worked—all the way down. The twenty-degree air hit me in the face at sixty miles per hour, yet I still felt dazed. I don't how I made it safely to Lee and Sharon's campus apartment, but somehow I did. I quickly fell on their couch and into a deep sleep.

When Sharon couldn't wake me the next morning, she felt my head and discovered I was burning with fever. She eventually poked me awake enough to swallow aspirin and I went back to sleep. I slept for three days. Periodically, Sharon would force me awake to feed me a little broth and more aspirin, but I have no memory of this. When she and Lee would return from classes each afternoon, I would be in the same position on the couch as that morning.

"I kept thinking you were going to die," Sharon has said many times since. She asked Lee whether they should call an ambulance to take me to the hospital. He said if she couldn't wake me up to sip more broth, they should call the EMTs. I guess that never happened.

After three days I awoke on my own, weak, with no memory beyond the moment I rolled down the two car windows an hour or two from Cookeville. We never knew what disease had turned me into a driving zombie and near corpse on their couch. By the day after I woke up, I was feeling well enough to drop a pit, which we did. Life is risk. At least when Lee and I were caving, we knew the risks and were somewhat prepared for them.

Shortly after my time in Kentucky, I took another risk and proposed. In May 1983 Kathy and I were married. Not long after that, we both entered graduate school, her to study employee relations, me to study writing. My caving visits with Lee dropped off from weekend pit bombs to annual couples' gatherings like our meeting at the bridge.

Over Thanksgiving week 1984, I left Kathy in South Carolina to drive to a reunion of the Florida State Cave Club in Alabama. We camped in a field near Stephens Gap, where local residents had been dumping old furniture and appliances, with which we assembled an open-air "house" with a fully furnished living room, kitchen, and bedrooms. We took some silly photos and then hiked to Stephens Gap and dropped the pit. On Thanksgiving Day we rappelled into Surprise Pit in Fern Cave. Ed Hill and I shared a can of tuna for our Thanksgiving dinner, the waterfall crashing nearby. That was my last trip with the Florida State Cave Club.

As years rolled by, some of my visits with Lee were spent more in armchair caving than the actual thing. He and I would roll out topo maps, looking for Marion Smith's latest find or a rumored secret pit, and talk about going there. Sometimes we would spend a whole day tramping over a mountain with a compass, or—once it was invented—with a GPS unit, never finding the obscure entrance we sought. Other times we'd spend a few hours crawling in some Cookeville nerdhole, complaining to each other all the way that we needed to get in shape.

In addition to full-time jobs, each of us had three children, and raising them turned out to be a serious time commitment. Who knew? Yet we still found mutual time for caving, especially in Tennessee, well into our forties and fifties. Not only did we not kill our fool selves, but once in a while we discovered something new. In the 1990s, for example, Lee took me to Owen Spring Cave when the water was unusually low. This was considered a wetsuit-only swimming trip, but dry conditions made it where we could walk in waist- to chest-deep water.

We passed pure white catfish and many white crayfish as we sloshed upstream. We had no wetsuits, but easily reached the end by moving steadily to keep our warmth up. There the spring emerged from a pile of boulders. Lee managed to squeeze himself into the tiny channel from which the cold water flowed and crawled out of sight, well beyond the map of the known cave. I could just hear him when hollered from the distance that there was a loud waterfall somewhere nearby. He also hollered that he thought he was stuck.

We were both cold and wet and knew it was time to head out.

"You know I can't fit in there," I yelled back to him. "If I have to go for help, you'll be dead of hypothermia by the time I get back."

"Yeah, yeah," he replied. "Go ahead and sugar-coat it."

What followed was thirty minutes of much cussing, grunting, and the occasional sound of a sliding rock. "Man, I got to get in shape," he yelled at least once.

Eventually Lee's boots appeared down the crawlway where I could see them, meaning he had not found a space wide enough to turn around. He backed himself out of the crawl, steaming and panting in the moist air as he emerged.

"I probably shouldn't have done that," he said.

As we sloshed our cold way toward daylight, we talked about how someone might reach the waterfall he had heard and wondered whether anyone had studied the odd catfish. Later we learned that local cavers knew nothing of either waterfall or fish. That night, as we prepared for bed at a cabin belonging to friends of Lee who lived in the Sequatchie Valley, I said, "You know, I've read that hypothermia can cause some very elaborate hallucinations."

"So?" he said. "I don't think I had any hallucinations."

"What if we're both still at the back of Owen Spring, slowly dying of hypothermia while you try to get out of that crawl?"

"Mikey, don't say things like that!" was his answer.

I promised not to share my theory with our spouses when we caught up with them the next day. I did, although, suggest we would only be that much further into the hallucination. Our wives, whether real or the product of fervent minds clinging to life, would probably not have agreed with the notion, but I believed that each thrill of discovery was worth the attendant danger, to Lee and me as to the ancients.

I still drive, like Bill Steele, and I still go into caves.

We found a new pictograph site recently in the Cumberland Plateau—with Dan Calhoun. I am mostly posting the iDStretch enhanced versions. It is a shitty time of year for pictograph viewing in the South. They are very hard to see without enhancement. A couple of polychrome panels made it extra special.

ALAN CRESSLER | Facebook post, July 14, 2019

Chapter 9

THE SOURCE

The discovery of a cavern within a novel or film seems inevitably to lead to ancient treasure, monsters, or lost civilizations. Sometimes all of the above. The concept of the cave as repository of some "lost world" goes back well before the time of Jules Verne and his *Journey to the Center of the Earth*. Mysterious grottoes appear in the works of Homer, Plato, Virgil, Dante, and Blake, and in the religious texts and oral creation myths of many cultures. "The very cave you are afraid to enter turns out to be the source of what you are looking for," reads a possibly apocryphal quote attributed to Joseph Campbell, the master of myth and culture. "The damned thing in the cave that was so dreaded has become the center."

Real cavers, however, tend to have little tolerance for fanciful imagined scenes, asking practical questions, often to the irritation of anyone foolish enough to watch cave movies with them: Where does that mysterious light come from? How can a race of vampires, a herd of dinosaurs, and so many mole men survive long-term in a low-energy environment? How do you build the great palace, that bridge over the lava pit, and walls that shoot poison darts—still working a thousand years later—with no modern gear, not to mention no machinery for moving stone blocks? What can a giant spider eat when there are no team members left?

And yet most of the cavers I know enjoy bad subterranean films. The otherworldly nature of the cave provided suspense and horror for writers from the ancient Greeks thorough Mark Twain and Trevanian, but Hollywood's approach is something special. It might best be summed by the poster tagline from a 1959 film called *Beast from Haunted Cave*: "SCREAMING YOUNG GIRLS SUCKED INTO A LABYRINTH OF HORROR BY A BLOOD-STARVED GHOUL FROM HELL."

A comic strip in an occasional caver publication called *Speleo Digest* once described the typical Hollywood cavern as displaying a smooth arched ceiling and a flat, uniform floor suitable for truck traffic. Flying through the comfortable tunnel, suspended from a sometimes-visible wire, one generally sees a bat resembling "a hairy loaf of bread with cardboard wings." The bat is inexplicably drawn to tangle itself in the hair of any blonde woman within range. Both she and the bat shriek like wounded seagulls. And so on.

The zone where popular culture, myth, and reality actually intersect can be found in caves of true archeological interest. To see ancient artifacts, art, or human remains deep within a cave is to feel a connection with those who once stood, flickering torch in hand, where you stand now. Within the dark and intimate setting, their humanity sometimes reaches across centuries to touch the hairs on the back of your neck. Amid underground ruins in China, Mexico, and Jamaica, I have felt simultaneously the sense of deep reverence in a sacred space and an electric thrill very close to watching an Indiana Jones movie.

In a cave in north-central Tennessee in the 1990s that connection to ancient wonder first hit me in an immediate and visceral way. It began when I ran into Lou Simpson at a vendor's table at a caving convention, probably in 1995, although I've since forgotten exactly where or when we met. After contributing to *Speleo Digest* over the years, he was signing copies of a new, privately printed book called *Sex, Lies, and Survey Tape*, and we fell to talking. The book collected some his cave humor from the 1960s and '70s, including a wonderful description of Hollywoodesque elements of the Meramec Caverns tour, such as neon signs for Jesse James' hideout and a gigantic American flag projected over a wall of flowstone.

That evening Lou invited me to his camp, where we sat on folding chairs near a well-stocked beer cooler, swapping stories. He was a friendly older fellow, part of an active group of Ohio cavers that had been making discoveries in Kentucky and Tennessee for decades. When a Tennessee caver had once referred to the prolific group as "those idiots from Ohio," Lou adopted the name as a badge of honor. By the soft firelight he appeared a dead ringer for the bust of Socrates that sits in the Louvre: sloppy beard framing a broad face, forehead wrinkled in thought below ill-kempt hair, lips curled and slightly parted as if to release a wicked joke, a nugget of wisdom, or both.

We learned that we had read each other's work and both read the same caving authors. We talked some about Red Watson, a novelist, philosopher, and legendary pillar of the Cave Research Foundation, or CRF, the organization that grew from the study and mapping of Mammoth Cave in the 1950s to support permanent cave programs throughout the US. Red was co-author of *The Longest Cave*, the book that told the story of the connection that first made Mammoth the longest in the world. Red had helped create the CRF publishing arm, Cave Books, and had also helped establish the Antarctic Artists & Writers Program for the National Science Foundation. We both admired Red's wife, Patty Jo Watson, an eminent anthropologist and archeologist credited with helping to bring the scientific method into American archeological studies. It turned out that Lou had worked with her at an archeological site. Her detailed examination of dried human feces and other remains from a Kentucky cave had demonstrated the crucial role women played in establishing Native American agriculture, overturning theories that farming was strictly a male invention. Patty Jo had been the subject of a PBS documentary I had seen just a few weeks earlier, and our discussion of her brought us around to the almost mystical power we had felt when encountering truly ancient cave artifacts.

As we shared some these experiences, Lou slapped his thigh and proclaimed, "There's something you should see."

I glanced around, wondering where in a field full of cavers this thing might be. I grabbed the frail arms of my folding chair to stand.

"No, not here," he said. "In a cave. Near the state line between Tennessee and Kentucky. I'm going next month and you need to go, too. No arguments. I can't describe it—you just have to see for yourself. You can stay in the field house with our group."

Lou would say no more on the subject, but his mix of sincerity and mystery set the hook, and I agreed to join the trip. It fell on a Saturday, which I could just make without missing classes. Lou agreed that I could invite along my friend Lee Pearson, who was then working as director of the YMCA in Knoxville. He gave us directions to "Granny's" field house in Pall Mall, a nine-hour drive from my home in Arkansas. I left on a Friday afternoon and arrived near midnight to find about a dozen cavers sitting around a rustic bunkhouse, telling stories, playing guitars, and planning smaller groups for various projects the next day. Lee and I would join Lou and a few others in a place local farmers called Blowing Cave to survey a side passage about four feet tall.

"Blowing" is the Smith of cave names: Virtually every American state with caves of any sort contains more than a few by that moniker. The entrances to larger caves commonly expel cool air, which is especially noticeable in the summer months. A cool breeze hits a nineteenth- or early twentieth-century farmer in the face, and the cave has a name. This particular entrance opened near a river. It was one of a dozen Blowing Caves listed in Barr's 1961 *Caves of Tennessee*—dozens of others had been added to the Tennessee Cave Survey in the decades since. I knew that well-known caves sometimes revealed new passages, and I asked whether that might be the case here.

Lou assured me that it was. He was drafting the map, which now depicted over eight miles—compared with the 2,200 feet listed in the Barr book. The cave had another local name besides Blowing, which would appear on the map to distinguish it from the many other Smiths in Tennessee. Lou asked that I not publish that name, should I ever happen to write about the cave. We would be mapping virgin passage well into the cave, he promised, but that was not the reason he asked me to join the trip or the reason he thought I might want to write about it. He said, with something of a dramatic flair, that we would make a detour to an area discovered in 1976 and seen by very few people.

"You will have to be extremely careful when we get there," he cautioned. "Follow me exactly." Lee smiled knowingly at this—it seemed he was in on the mystery.

We traveled through a series of nice but unremarkable breakdown rooms and canyon passages, Lou leading us down several side leads to formation areas and other points of interest. Although we traveled with several other cavers, the three of us soon separated from the group, making plans to rejoin them in the day's appointed survey area in an hour or so. I didn't realize it then, but Lou was working to reduce the amount of foot traffic in the place he would take us—something he and others had diligently done in the two decades since their discovery of the chamber. Lee mentioned that he had noticed some of the Ohio cavers had seemed to be checking the two of us out, making sure we knew how to stay on trails and avoid bumping formations.

"They must think we're novices," he said, a little put out.

We left the group by means of a steep breakdown climb called the Towering Inferno. Although it had been named in 1976, not long after the Paul Newman/Steve McQueen thriller came out, Lou said the reason was that it was always hot due to the pit being overhead. At the top, we entered a side passage requiring some crawling and duck-walking. I asked about the black streaks I saw along the walls.

"Those are stoke marks," Lou said. "They were made by cane torches. You had to knock them against the wall now and then to keep them lit."

The crawlway opened into a large, well-decorated passage that Lou said was called the Tremendous Trunk. From here we climbed into another side lead, where I began to see more of the black marks. We came to what looked like a gate across the road, made of plastic flagging tape strung in fluorescent ribbons. A sign warned that a protected research area lay ahead. Parallel bands of tape on the floor beyond the "gate" marked a narrow path.

"Here we go," Lou said, stepping over the flagging barrier.

We passed a few small piles of ash, each of which had been carefully marked off with colored tape, like blood at a crime scene. These had been left not by vandals or sloppy cavers, Lou explained, but by Native Americans setting their torches down as they explored or rested.

I tried to imagine reaching this point without helmet or gear, using only a bundle of cane for light. Including side trips, we had been underground for over three hours, scrambling over boulders, crawling, and occasionally climbing to higher levels. Our route had passed intersections where Lou knew which way to turn only from years of work in the cave. I wasn't sure I could find my own way out from this point, and I tried to wrap my head around the idea of trying to do so by flickering torchlight.

Lou pointed to an ash pile that contained several bits of charred wood. Like the others, this blackened pile sat in a carefully laid circle of tape.

"Cane from here and a couple of other spots was carbon dated to over 4,500 years old," he said. "That puts it in what's called the Archaic Period. Now stay on this side of the tape and follow me."

Lou took a few careful steps forward and then sat in the clearly laid out path, shining his light beyond the tape beside us.

In soft mud no more than three feet away from our own fresh footprints were the clear impressions of heavily calloused bare feet. Bits of ash from torches lay scattered about, in some cases resting in footprints as though they had just fallen there. Lee lowered his head near the mud floor, so that his helmet lamp lit the prints from the side, bringing their details into crisp focus.

Looking at the pattern of footprints, torch, and formation bits beside, I could trace the movements of three people—a family, I guessed from the size variations—as they worked their way among the stalactites. In the nearest print I could see each toe clearly defined, with faint imprints of whorls and lines and what appeared to be the hint of a scar or two. Another print looked like that of a child, perhaps ten or eleven years old. I flashed back to my own wonder and amazement when my parents had taken me at the age of six to Ruby Falls. I tried to imagine what this child had thought of his or her strange surroundings.

Larger formations glistened just beyond the path, groupings of white and yellow stalactites that audibly dripped to a staccato beat. Lou said that in another passage not too far away from us were claw marks made by a jaguar that had somehow become trapped in the cave long before the humans came. The claw marks were estimated at up to thirty thousand years old, based on two jaguar skeletons found in the cave. They were found some distance apart, one at the end of Tremendous Trunk and the other in Horrendous Trunk. There was once apparently another entrance near the junction of the two trunks, because many paleontological artifacts were found there including a camel tooth and bones from horse, dire wolf, and passenger pigeon. Lou had found the camel tooth and was present when the Horrendous Trunk jaguar was found, mostly covered by a fallen rock slab.

Like the human prints beside us, the jaguar claw marks could easily be obliterated by a single careless caver. I realized that my own prints from that day, and prints Lee and I had made on other days in hundreds of other caves, might also last thousands of years if left undisturbed. For the briefest moment, I felt a connection to the vastness of geologic history, to a concept that I have more recently heard called "deep time." A human life fills but a blink of experience. This passage had barely changed, not just in the span of a few lives 4,500 years ago, but well beyond the lifespan of their culture and of a succession of other cultures that followed thousands of years later. Around us in Tennessee and the rest of the world lay undiscovered passages likely to remain undisturbed

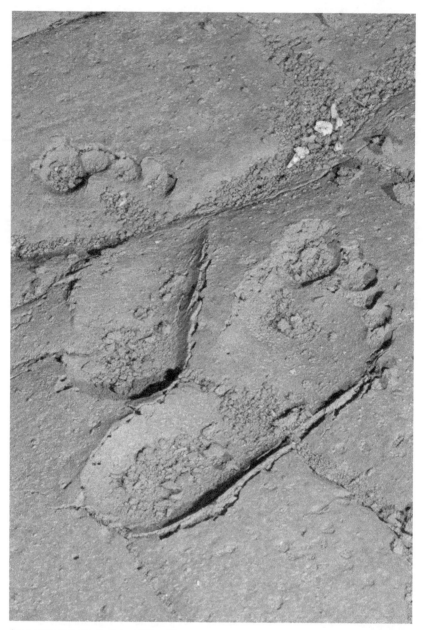
Ancient human footprints within a Tennessee cave.

throughout the existence of the human species, altered over millions of years only by the slow dance of continents and the sudden rush of groundwater.

We stared at the footprints for quite some time, to the sound of dripping stalactites.

"You were right," I said at last to Lou. "I had to see this in person."

Lee and I both thanked Lou as we left the research area and continued to our appointed survey target, where we helped map a few hundred feet of new cave that I can barely remember.

A decade after our weekend visit, two scientific papers with slightly different focuses, both coauthored by Patty Jo Watson, appeared in separate journals. Both focused on a place designated "Jaguar Cave" and footprints within a section called "Aborigine Avenue," as depicted by a portion of Lou's map (which, of course, had been made possible by dozens of cavers participating over many years of survey, including the extremely small portion I helped map). One of the papers focused on the discovery, mapping, and methods of protection of the prints (Willey et al. 2005), while the other, for which Patty Jo was principal author, gave a detailed account of the scientific analysis of the prints and what this revealed about the ancient explorers who left them (Watson et al. 2005). The papers reported that a few fainter prints had been stepped on and partially obliterated by cavers who found the passage in 1976, until they realized what they had found and carefully backed out. Unfortunately, less careful cavers had also walked over a few prints that had been untouched when I first visited with Lou. The conservation article reported that "sometime between 1996 and 2002, a modern caver ignored the sign at the entrance of Aborigine Avenue and the surveying tape circling the prehistoric footprints and walked across them, altering at least five of eleven prints near a pit edge." The paper added that sometime in the 1970s, a dog had accompanied a caving party into the area and that "its pawprints are now present among some of the prehistoric human footprints near the passage entrance." I must have passed those prints without noticing them as Lou and I approached the footprint area.

A gate had been installed in the cave in the year 2000, and damage
to the remaining prints had decreased since then. The abstract of the
conservation paper reads:

> More than 4500 years ago, a group of prehistoric cavers negotiated
> complicated cave passages and discovered a side passage approxi-
> mately two hours' journey from the cave's entrance. They explored
> the passage toward its end, came to the termination of the easily
> traveled portion, turned around and exited the same way they en-
> tered, leaving footprints and torch material in the cave mud. Their
> remarkable journey is the earliest evidence of human cave use in
> the eastern United States.
>
> A total of 274 relatively complete footprints remained in the
> passage's moist substrate when the passage was re-discovered ap-
> proximately 30 years ago. The malleable deposits were pliable then,
> and remain so today. This pliability made the prints' preserva-
> tion vulnerable to subsequent events, agents and processes. The
> purposes of this paper are to describe the prehistoric cavers' ac-
> complishments, document the alteration of the prints, and describe
> efforts to study and preserve them.

Both papers listed other sites where ancient footprints are found,
emphasizing that the footprints in this cave were the most prolific and
best preserved of any American site. They were also the oldest of any
prints found within "deep cave interiors of the eastern and southeastern United States." While one pile of ash had been dated at over 4,500
years old, as Lou had said, another appeared closer to 5,000 years old.
Moreover, minor changes to the prints called "microerosion," measured in the detailed photographs, suggested that two separate groups
may have entered the cave hundreds of years of apart from one another.
Unlike ancient Americans at other sites, such as Mammoth Cave, these
people appeared not to be mining for minerals but exploring just for
the sake of exploration. Further study of the site has continued, and
new efforts have been undertaken to protect the prints from goofball
cavers, which even the best of us may become when our minds are busy
being blown.

As the years went by after my experience in "Jaguar Cave," I began paying more attention to discoveries in the South containing Native American art or artifacts. While there were no new finds of significant footprints (at least none made public in such a way that I heard of them), the first two decades of the twenty-first century saw an explosion of discoveries of new cave sites containing prehistoric art, from Florida to the Carolinas—but especially in Tennessee. Many of these sites had been discovered by a prolific caver, photographer, and naturalist from Georgia named Alan Cressler. His photographic techniques had teased cave paintings and etchings that all others had missed. Working closely with Jan Simek, an eminent archeologist from the University of Tennessee and a leading expert in prehistoric art, Cressler had helped record and publish papers on seventy-six caves now known to contain ancient art. Most of these discoveries had occurred within caves in Tennessee.

I first met Alan in the mid-1980s on trips to TAG with the Northern New Jersey Grotto, and have seen his name in many caving and scientific contexts ever since. He had been a botanist in the late 1970s, studying unusual ferns in the area around Atlanta, where he lived. On one of his drives in search of ferns he stumbled upon the 1981 SERA Cave Carnival at Russell Cave National Monument, where he first encountered cavers. I was at that gathering but off with my Florida State friends most of the time.

"I didn't know any cavers, but they took me in and welcomed me," Alan later recalled. He camped near the cave's "canoe entrance" for the cool air wafting over the campsite and poked around a little inside the cave. That weekend he met a woman who happened to have an interest in ferns herself, and she put him in touch with cavers in the Huntsville grotto who were soon taking him to see unusual ferns growing near entrances. "Every time I would go look at ferns in Alabama, I found that most of the interesting ones were around cave entrances," he said. "I actually started carrying cave gear to look at ferns, and the next thing I know, I was caving."

Through his new friends in Alabama, Alan soon met Marion Smith and began accompanying him to caves and pits, where Smith quickly became his caving mentor. In one historic saltpeter cave the two visited,

Cressler spotted ancient petroglyphs on a wall more than a mile from the entrance. The thought of a small group of ancient explorers reaching that spot with simple torches intrigued him. Although he continued to join increasingly hard-core exploration trips with Smith, he also became fascinated with cave archeology. He befriended Charles Faulkner, a professor of archeology at the University of Tennessee, Knoxville, and was soon joining Faulkner's graduate students in caving fieldwork. A meticulous photographer in his botanical work, Cressler mastered cave photography and began creating an extensive photographic inventory of Tennessee cave art. By 2017, he had photographed ancient art at virtually all known locations where it had been discovered within TAG. With Jan Simek and others he had co-authored over a dozen papers on the subject.

That year, I began bugging Alan to take me to one of the seventy-six "unnamed caves"—but first I had some microbial samples to collect.

ROGGIE BRUCE: Why does that look like Lech?

BOB BIDDIX: It's very Lechuguillaesque. Is that a word?

MICHAEL TAYLOR: it should be!

ROBERT GREG: It's the best virgin cave we ever got into. Thanks for the awesome pictures, Bobby.

BOB BIDDIX | Facebook post, February 10, 2019

Chapter 10

ON TARBALL POND

Long before cell phones or GPS, cavers developed effective methods for people to meet for an expedition at an appointed time and place. Usually participants drove varying distances from different directions. Often some had never been to the cave before. These methods evolved to resemble the way one might meet a spy to pass secret documents. If in town, the meeting would be set in a public area with plenty of parking, usually near a diner where the first to arrive could comfortably wait for the last. In rural locations, the spot was likely to be a remote cabin or camping area within a short drive or hike to the cave. If the location appeared on maps, fine. If not, precise driving directions would be shared in advance of the trip.

Outside the US, cavers might set a gathering spot based on local transportation hubs. In 1990, I arranged weeks in advance to meet a New Jersey caving friend in Budapest on a particular date. Each of us would come to Hungary by train from different Eastern European countries, so we agreed to meet at or close to noon in front of a particular coffee shop in the Keleti train station. On the scheduled date, both of us experienced travel delays. Our two trains arrived in the city closer to midnight than noon, about thirty minutes apart. The coffee shop was gated for the night. My friend discovered me seated on a nearby bench, composing an intentionally cryptic note to leave on the shop window, telling him where I had booked a room. I crumpled the note as Tom sat on the bench. A short walk later, we were eating bar food, listening to local jazz, and discussing caving plans—a typical meeting in all respects.

Almost three decades later, Joel Buckner invited two cavers older than me to help lead a science trip into the Tennessee cave nicknamed Secret Squirrel. He had gone old school on our meeting arrangements, no cell phones needed. Approaching Murfreesboro via I-840 and I-24 under cloudy skies, I took a right and kept my eyes peeled for the Golden Arches. Joel and two friends, Bruce Robtoy and David Parr, liked to gather at a free city parking lot beside the restaurant for trips to this cave system. They could combine gear and people into one or, at most, two vehicles, safely leaving extra cars there for the day as they made the thirty-mile drive to a tighter parking area near the head of the half-mile trail to the entrance.

My son Chris and I had no trouble spotting the unshaven men in tattered clothing standing around the open hatch of a dusty RAV4. They chatted amiably, their breath hanging in the crisp December air. Except for their brightly colored bits of mud-stained ballistic nylon, they could have passed for Depression-era hobos in a rail yard. We said our hellos and walked to the restaurant to discuss the day's plans over coffee and McMuffins.

I had never met David, but I recognized him from videos on Joel's Facebook page. A musician best known for playing an electronic stringed instrument called a Chapman Stick, David often brings a small ukulele to cave camps. In one of Joel's videos, he plays a quiet instrumental version of the Beatles' "Across the Universe" while Joel sets a rock hammer at a blowing hole on a Tennessee mountainside. In another, he sings the Beatles tune "You Won't See Me" to a muddy group of cavers sitting at the edge of a sinkhole. A man with large hands and a beard that defines the firm jawline of a north woods lumberjack, David plays in these videos with a delicacy that belies his grizzled appearance. Underground, I would soon learn that he caves that way as well. Like Allen Mosler, he seemed able to belly-crawl through mud without getting dirty.

Bruce, whom I knew to be an active Nashville-area caver, was a thin, quiet man who, like the other two and myself, appeared to be in his late fifties or perhaps early sixties. As he joined us at the table, I apologized to the group for what was likely to be a very slow trip spent collecting ten to fifteen swabs for DNA analysis. I described the types of locations we were interested in sampling: unusually colored formations, especially the blood-red flow photographed on a boulder, and also the pool of floating "tarballs," one of which we hoped to place intact into a sample bottle. David and Bruce discussed the best route to the tarballs, which David described as a perched pond fed by overflow from the cave's active stream. Using a copy of the same simple line-plot map that Joel had given me earlier, David laid out a rough a plan that would circle us past some likely formation areas on the way there and back.

Loaded with carbs for the cold caving ahead, Chris and I returned to our rental car and followed the others in Joel's RAV4. We traveled a succession of ever-smaller highways to eventually turn left on a county road that led uphill. The ground rose in the continuous, undulating waves of the Eastern Highland Rim, an Ordovician geologic unit flanking the western edge of the Cumberland Plateau in a south-to-north line that roughly bisects the state of Tennessee. Unlike the Cumberland Plateau, which was capped by impermeable sandstone, the Highland Rim had an older, leakier roof of shale conglomerate. This created a dimpled landscape of countless low hills and valleys, unlike the scenic vistas and deep gulfs of the plateau.

We were surrounded by rugged country thick with oak forests and caves, land poorly suited, in general, to farms or towns. After miles of winding highway bordered by only a few widely separated houses, Joel pulled off the blacktop onto twin muddy ruts. We drove a short bumpy distance through a field to an overgrown parking spot where we could barely turn the vehicles. It was just wide enough that any other traffic, however unlikely, would be able to pass. After stretching and popping hatchbacks, we stripped in the chill moist air, changing into coveralls and boots, double-checking packs and the science kit. Within fifteen minutes we set off for the cave.

While still in sight of the road we passed a dripping limestone face beside a cave entrance that led 150 feet to a deep pool. Joel explained this was the natural underwater entrance to the cave's main stream. This portion of the cave had been known for decades—in fact it appeared in Tennessee cave descriptions dating from the early 1960s—but it ended at seemingly impassable water. In the mid-2000s, cave divers Forrest Wilson and Marbry Hardin managed to pass the sump and enter several hundred feet of walking passage, which they followed to a second sump they did not attempt. A record drought in 2007 exposed a low air space passage through the first sump that allowed Joel and Hal to pass, noses against the ceiling. Once on the other side they saw that the second sump had dried completely, with large borehole beckoning beyond where it had been.

"When we first entered it during the extreme drought, the passage was seven feet tall with a dive line hanging at eye level, with only ankle deep water," Hal recalled. "Marbry told me that the water was like chocolate milk during their dive, and they never were able to find a way through in zero visibility."

The discovery of miles of virgin cave soon followed beyond the temporarily exposed sump—along with an urgent need to find another entrance before the drought passed and the cave was blocked once more. ("The passage sumped the following autumn when the drought ended," Joel recalled recently. "It has been continuously sumped since.") On our trip we would use an artificial entrance in the hills ahead of us, dug open from a radio location that placed a particular crawlway in the "new" part of the cave very close to the surface. Following the cobbles of a dry streambed, we walked behind an old barn and a few ancient abandoned cars before taking a side path that rose into the hills of hickory and white oak. I had felt cold while dressing at the cars, but I was sweating in my nylon coveralls by the time Joel dropped his pack and announced we had arrived.

It took me a minute to spot the entrance: a small hole in the hillside that looked like a gap left behind when a tree had blown over in a storm. Incredibly, this inauspicious opening led to huge rooms, impressive formations, and still-going cave—a complex system that until this day had been seen only by a small group of original explorers. Joel and Bruce

The Biggly Borehole trunk passage in the so-called Secret Squirrel cave, a discovery first surveyed in January 2019.

discussed who would unlock the gate installed just inside the entrance. Like many cave gates I've seen over the years, it was known to have a tricky lock that required a dexterous reach to place the key into a hole not even visible from the outside. Bruce thought he could manage the left-handed keyhole and slipped his wrist into a nylon lanyard attached to the key. The lanyard was crucial for not dropping the key beyond the gate before we got it open. As Bruce struggled with the lock, his shoulder pressed into the dirt above the opening, we heard distant gunshots. They came from the shooting range several miles west of us, Joel suspected, but he added that at this time of year they could just as easily be local deer hunters.

Eventually Bruce unlocked the gate. One by one we entered the crawlway, with David, who knew this part of the cave best, in the lead. As was customary, the last person in line locked the gate behind the group. In the unlikely event that some local happened upon the entrance while we were there, no intruder could become trapped inside upon our eventual exit. I saw only Chris's boots for about sixty feet until we emerged into a stoop walk that soon led to comfortable walking passage. Before long we stood in a chamber that reminded me of the valleys between the sand hills of Xanadu. A flat ceiling covered borehole that dropped away precariously, then climbed up again to a similar level several hundred feet away. David scouted a few side entrances off this main trunk until he found the one that he wanted, which led to our first formation area.

The formation room was small, with barely enough height to stand at its center. Along one wall, a shelf held several small stalactites and stalagmites. Water drops trickled from these, depositing calcite over small terraces of stone that stepped down a slanted rock to the floor of the chamber no more than a meter below the shelf. What made this very common scene unusual was that one of the stalactites at the center of the grouping was bright canary yellow. It was as though Nature had run a helpful highlighter over the formation we should sample first. The glistening stone beneath its yellow point flowed into oranges and browns, mixing with colors from more typical creamy stalactites as the flowstone vanished down a crack in the floor. Chris and I unpacked the kit and traded our cave gloves for sterile latex ones we would wear while sampling.

As I had learned from Diana Northup in Lechuguilla, the trick to successful sampling for DNA analysis was to keep unwanted DNA off the sample. This meant using individually packaged swabs which had to be open to the air as little as possible. After a quick touch on the target substrate, the person doing the sampling would open a sterile test bottle and insert the swab, breaking off its wooden stick without touching the bottle. The head of the swab would then be quickly sealed in the bottle, with a label specific to that bottle recorded in a sampling journal. James Engman, who had prepared the pack, had told me he had enough project funding to analyze only about fifteen samples from the cave, but he had said I could take a couple of extras from each location to be stored on ice in case we wanted to later verify or reexamine samples from a particular spot.

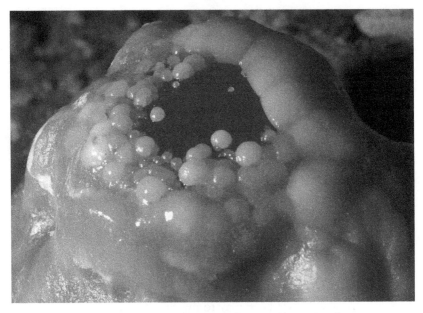

One of several Secret Squirrel formations exhibiting an odd orange color.

For this first stop, I labeled five containers Y1 through Y5, the Y standing for Yellow. Chris would pass me swabs, then open and hold the bottle for me to place each swab. The moment I broke the stick, leaving the tip inside, Chris would close the cap and place the bottle into a box that held a Styrofoam tray for easy storage and sample protection. One by one, we collected five swabs that I then detailed in the log, a yellow Rite in the Rain brand notebook commonly used for surveying in wet caves, according to location and nearby mineral features. The whole process took about half an hour. Then we removed our latex gloves and put them and the trash generated by the swabs into a Ziploc bag, stored everything, pulled on our cave gloves and set off for the next interesting feature. As we worked, Joel took photos to record the sampling location and shot a few videos of the process as well.

David led the way onward. I remarked how the cave reminded me first of Xanadu, with its impressive borehole, and then of Lechuguilla, with drier passages that seemed unusually rich in gypsum for an eastern cave. You could chart the predominant wind currents in the larger sections by which portions of the limestone walls had been converted to gypsum. Heading into the cave, the left-hand wall seemed to remain solid limestone, while portions of the right-hand wall had dissolved into a soft white gypsum crust. If you touched it, it crumbled like feta cheese. One could easily reduce a handful of wall to dust. I had encountered this sort of "soft" gypsum in Glacier Bay and other locations within Lechuguilla, where Northup and others had shown that microbes were continually dissolving parts of the cave, as I suspected was the case here.

Taking a short side trip, Joel led me up a steep slope to look at several gypsum formations that curled upward from the wall like bouquets of white lilies. One was called the "Buddha Hand" for good reason: the white formation resembled a larger-than-life human hand, reaching out from the limestone as if to bless the visitor. Our next sampling stop was a stand-alone formation an even brighter yellow than the first. The explorers had named it the Lemon Drop, so I called the bottle that held its swab LD. A short hike from there we sampled OT, a deep orange-colored stalagmite the size and shape of a small toadstool. We then climbed and crawled our way to the cave's central stream passage, which we hiked down for quite a ways, looking for a climb that would lead us to the isolated pool of tarballs.

The climbs were of an interesting and yet irritating sort common to TAG. Interesting, because they usually involved a chimney or free climb of ten to twelve feet, requiring an analysis of the rock face to solve the problem of where to put your hands and feet. They were irritating for the same reason: climbs not quite big enough to require rigging a rope, but hard enough to tire your thighs and upper body. Although Chris was the youngest and doubtless the strongest of our group, he was also the least experienced climber and cursed one or two spots mightily as I suggested hand- and foot-holds from below or above him. After three or four such places, I began to get what Lee Pearson had always called "the Jimmy legs," a twitchy involuntary dance of leg muscles bridging scary-looking gaps.

David, Joel, and Bruce had all traveled this part of the cave many times. They agreed that there were multiple routes to where we were heading, but disagreed as to which was easiest and most direct. At one point we climbed back down to the stream passage from a higher bypass and saw where an early explorer had left a chalk message on the wall for a comrade: "Dude, climb up here!" If only we had known ten minutes earlier, we would have done so.

As we splashed along, I noticed small flying insects darting over the water's surface. You could sometimes see insects lighting on a cave stream near an entrance, but we were much too far from daylight for these to be surface insects. They had to be cave adapted, which meant they had to have a food source in the water. This could be naturally carried in from above or might involve a food chain based on the native microbes. As we emerged onto one of the occasional sand bars we walked over beside the stream, I asked to step to the head of the line to examine the water before we stepped back into it.

Here and there I saw pellet-shaped rafts of a white mineral—probably calcite or aragonite—floating on the water's surface, near drips that fell from the ceiling. I had seen similar floating pellets emerge from a hot spring in Arkansas while working with a NASA team twenty years earlier. Under a scanning electron microscope, those rafts had contained the skeletal remnants of vast microbial colonies. Before disturbing the water, I carefully dipped one of our collection bottles next to one of these pellets, sucking it and a bit of water inside. This became sample CR, the initials standing for calcite raft. There seemed to be a correlation between the tiny insects and the spots where more rafts were visible—perhaps the rafts formed around the insects' decomposing bodies, which I had also seen in other cave pools. As I fussed with the sample bottle, Chris and Joel pointed out a bright orange salamander darting through the water, further evidence of a complex ecosystem.

I stored the sample and we slogged on, occasionally climbing out of the stream into a higher parallel tunnel. From this upper course, we reached a passage that looked like the primary stream, but was not, because that water chuckled and splashed as it flowed over rocks, while this water was clear and preternaturally calm. As we stood at an overlook before climbing down into the still pond, we could smell a strong petroleum odor. I had often smelled methane in caves, where surface debris washed in from a storm had begun to decompose, but this smelled more like someone had spilled a can of oil or gasoline. The smell had led the original discovers to dub it the Petroleum Passage several years earlier.

"Good thing we aren't using carbide," I joked, recalling old stories of how the flame of a carbide lamp had sometimes ignited gas pockets in mines and, once in a great while, in caves.

"Well, this is the place, but there don't seem to be any tarballs here today," Joel said. "I wonder if they're seasonal."

He was right: The surface was a flat mirror, with nothing tarlike in it. But I saw plenty of tarlike material on the white sandy bottom. The water varied between a few inches and knee deep. In several places pitch-black ovals, perhaps two feet on their long axis, lay scattered along the bottom. Most were ringed with bands of yellow and orange mineral crusts from which extended fuzzy filaments that appeared biological.

"Those bands look just like what you see at Yellowstone," I said excitedly. "And in Lower Kane Cave in Wyoming. We got microbes for sure!"

"How can you tell?" David asked.

Fifteen minutes later, I'm sure he wished that he hadn't, but he and the rest had experienced a short, enthusiastic lecture on hypogene speleogenesis, Lechuguilla's unique microbiology, and theories of the deep biosphere. Finally I shut up and turned to the task at hand.

We knew the clear water would become cloudy the moment we stepped into it, but we also knew we would have to enter it to sample, so we discussed the least obtrusive way to do so. Eventually I eased toward the first black patch, while Chris climbed almost to the water, stopping at a point where he did not have to get in to pass me the sample bottles. Everyone else stayed on the shelf above the pool. As Joel captured video from the side, I carefully swabbed one of the orange bands, reached over and grabbed a bottle from Chris, and promptly dropped my swab into the water.

"That's one for the blooper real," I said. "Buffoon science in action."

I put the ruined swab into the trash bag and tried again. This time I dug at the far edge of the tar patch and successfully bottled what became sample OB, for orange band. Unfortunately, gathering the sample stirred the water, hiding the yellow bands in mud before I could sample one of them. (On this particular day, the water level in the pond

One of the "tar" deposits and surrounding orange band, photographed at a time when the water level was low. Note insect at upper right.

appeared to be a good foot deeper than on the day Bob Biddix had photographed one of the "tar" patches a few months later.)

I eased forward, with Chris following me into the pool, and got another sample by digging my swab into the center of another black patch, labeling this one BB, for Black Bottom. I noted in the notebook, "Some dry deposits above the stream level suggest past seeps of small amounts of a dark substance, such as manganese or perhaps some form of petroleum." I saw an orange-colored stalactite hanging in a side rift above one of these deposits, and from it I collected sample OS.

Within thirty minutes of entering the pool, we had filled fifteen sample bottles. We had not seen any tarballs, nor had we reached the blood-red rock that had first piqued my interest in this cave. Dave thought he could "probably" find the rock, but said it would involve some "serious" travel from the point we had reached. I said that we had collected enough for a first effort and we began the long slog out. By the time we reached the exit, a gray winter twilight was settling in. I was third to climb up through the small gate and saw Joel and Bruce sitting on the hillside, watching something. Joel motioned for me to be quiet and join him, which I did. In a gulley below we saw a hunter who had killed a large doe. He dragged the heavy carcass over the cobbled streambed toward the road below, leaving a bloody trail in his wake.

"He was probably poaching on the gun range property," Joel said quietly. "So he's dragging it out to the main road."

As the other two exited the cave and joined us, we sat drinking water and snacking while marveling at the strength of the hunter, who dragged and carried his kill out of sight without a word. We packed up and followed the blood trail most of the way back to the cars, leaving it only when we were close enough to the road to hear its sparse traffic. As we reached our vehicles and began to change into street clothes, a light snow began to fall.

Months would pass before Dr. Engman's undergraduate lab students would process seven of the fifteen samples for analysis, and then weeks would pass before those first results came back. At my suggestion, the first seven samples his students worked on were four of the yellow series, the orange band, the black bottom, and one from an orange stalactite. I watched part of the three-hour process of isolating and refining the genetic material, each of the eighteen steps a direct descendant of techniques Norm Pace had established decades earlier. In July, I received an email from Jamie that included a couple of intriguing definitions he had pulled off the Internet:

A small number of hits, but hey! There is a chemolithoautotroph that has been associated with thermal vents, which is cool.

Euryarchaeota (Greek for "broad old quality") is a phylum of archaea. The Euryarchaeota are highly diverse and include methanogens, which produce methane and are often found in intestines; halobacteria, which survive extreme concentrations of salt; and some extremely thermophilic aerobes and anaerobes.

The Methanopyrales are an order of microbes within the class methanopyri.

It contains only one family, Methanopyraceae, one genus, *Methanopyrus*, and one species, *Methanopyrus kandleri*. This species is chemolithoautotrophic and its cells are bacillus in form. It grows comfortably at temperatures of 98°C and can survive at temperatures as high as 110°C, making it the most thermophilic known methanogen. They live in hydrothermal vents. They are similar to Methanobacteriales, but unlike other methanogenic archaea, their cell walls contain pseudomurein nitrosopumilaceae.

In all, the lab had identified over two hundred microbial species in the seven samples, several of them associated with life in the deep subsurface, including the species known only to exist in deep-sea thermal vents. Beyond the obvious problem—*What is a species that lives only in the deepest parts of the ocean, under high pressure and temperature, doing in the center of Tennessee?*—there were problems that had been introduced during the collection or lab work. One of the samples was clearly contaminated by human-associated microbes, and nearly all showed some slight evidence of human contamination. It was entirely possible that I had been careless in the collection process, especially toward the end of the trip when we were tired, although Jamie thought it most likely one or more of the students in the lab had introduced the contamination during the eighteen separate steps each sample went through as part of the complex protocol to extract and amplify the DNA for analysis by a distant professional lab.

"All it takes is one student coughing or scratching his nose while making a transfer," he explained. "If he's transferring parts of one sample after another, they all get contaminated."

In any event, the results were intriguing, but more sampling would be needed. At a caving convention a few months later, I managed to

Erica Sughrue admires hoodoos in Secret Squirrel.

corner the renowned microbiologist Hazel Barton and showed her a complete printout of our results. She confirmed that we had to deal with the contamination: "Just toss Y1 right out for skin contamination," she said. But Hazel also agreed that we were onto something unusual for Tennessee. "A couple of these hits are definitely worth further study," she said. "Let me know how it goes."

Meanwhile, the cave itself continued to go. Within a year of our collection trip, Bob Biddix took the first photographs of newly discovered selenite chandeliers in the cave that looked virtually identical to those found in Lechuguilla's Chandelier Ballroom—if a bit smaller. He photographed hoodoos, gypsum-rich totems seen in parts of Lechuguilla, and impressive large chambers. A more serious collection effort in Secret Squirrel needed to be planned.

Having some tea in my Edward James mug. Just like I remember him from so many decades ago in Xilitla.

PETER SPROUSE | Facebook post, October 29, 2019

Chapter 11

TAG ON STEROIDS

Beginning in the mid-1960s, cavers in TAG developed new tools and techniques to explore increasingly deep and complex caves. These improvements, aided by an unbridled enthusiasm for discovery and mapping, launched a golden age of exploration that reached far beyond the borders of TAG into the American West, Mexico, the Caribbean, and numerous locations around the world. Cavers pushing into ever-deeper pits in northern Alabama and Georgia soon realized that existing alpine techniques were insufficient to their needs.

Those methods had been imported from Europe, where climbing the Matterhorn was a very different undertaking than rappelling into undercut vertical shafts like Neversink or Valhalla. Rappels in mountain climbing—even in military commando raids—tend to be relatively short, well under one hundred feet. Dropping down a cliff face or skyscraper usually allows the rappeller to bounce his or her feet against the wall periodically, slowing the rate of descent. Solving the free rappel problem became key to pushing the deep pits of TAG.

As new developments were driven locally, geologic exploration in distant places revealed an opportunity. American cavers began to hear that the Sierra Madre Occidental of east-central Mexico, along with the state of Oaxaca five hundred miles farther south, both contained mountainous limestone geology resembling TAG, but with far thicker layers of porous rock. This made the potential for deep caves in Mexico an order of magnitude greater than anything in the United States. As in TAG, these regions were isolated and difficult to reach, usually covered in heavy vegetation broken by cliffs and sinkholes. They tended to be sparsely populated by insular locals who distrusted outsiders almost as much as they distrusted government officials. In short, the mountains of Mexico seemed like home to the first cavers on the scene.

For those early vertical cavers to leave their greater mark, it was necessary for TAG—as a region, as a group of dedicated explorers, even as a philosophy—to be born. The acronym itself was not coined until 1967, but the idea had begun several years earlier, in several places involving many people. The caver who pulled the separate threads together under a single banner was Richard Schreiber.

Born in Washington, DC, in 1943, Schreiber was first drawn underground, like many before and after him, as a child on family vacations, when he would pester his parents to stop the car at tour caves. He entered his first wild cave in February 1963 as a sophomore at Georgia Tech, invited by a fraternity brother who offered to drop him off at an entrance near Leeds, Alabama. Schreiber planned on camping alone at the entrance, but when he left the cave that night wet and muddy, with a couple of fading flashlights and no proper gear, he was unprepared for the twenty-degree weather outside. After a miserable night, he set off down the mountain near dawn, becoming lost among a chain of sinkholes that each struck him as rich with potential. Eventually he ran into a church group headed up to the cave he had just left. They invited him to join them. Schreiber agreed, turning to hike back up the mountain, where he was lent a helmet and carbide lamp by the group. Aided by their lights and knowledge, he saw many passages he had missed on his own.

Night was falling when he and the church group parted ways. Temperatures were still below freezing, so he decided to walk to town and seek a ride back to Atlanta. After hiking eight miles on a lonely country road, he reached the edge of town muddy, disheveled, and somewhat incoherent. The first person he encountered was the sheriff, who nearly arrested him. After taking Schreiber to the sheriff's office and hearing his story, the lawman gave him a cup of hot chocolate and directed him onto a bus back to Atlanta. Schreiber boarded the bus in the dark, still cold, wet, and muddy. As with others before him, rather than being finished with caving forever from this experience, Schreiber was hooked.

Before long he had joined the NSS and gathered a core of young cavers at Georgia Tech. When they couldn't manage the drive to where the caves were, they practice rappelling off Stone Mountain and other surface features closer to Atlanta. But every weekend that they could, they found their way into mountains and valleys where they mapped new caves and found new passages in familiar ones.

"Anything you could stick a dog in was a cave as far I was concerned in those days," Schreiber recalled in an interview for the guidebook to the 1989 NSS convention, held that year in Sewanee, Tennessee. "I'm surprised I didn't get snakebit by some of the holes I poked around in." He and his friends dove into the rapidly developing field of vertical caving. One of those friends was John Cole, an engineer at NASA's Marshall Space Flight Center in Huntsville, Alabama, who had a knack for creating mechanical devices.

On July 3, 1961, Virginia caver Bill Cuddington had been the first to descend 437-foot Surprise Pit in Alabama's Fern Cave shortly after it was discovered. He used a complicated wooden rappel spool held in place by a metal frame. No cavers at the time had possessed ropes of such great length, so Cuddington tied a manila rope to a nylon one in order to reach the bottom. He spun as though on a carnival ride while ropes slid rapidly around the spool, cutting deep grooves into the wood before he became the first human to touch the base of the pit. By 1965, as new pits in the two-hundred-foot-plus range continued to be discovered throughout the region, it was clear to Cole, Schreiber, and others that better gear was needed. Cuddington, meanwhile, also shared reports from the Association for Mexican Cave Studies (AMCS) of three-thousand-foot-thick limestone beds in Mexico for which the current methods were wholly inadequate.

"Everybody was positive they were going to find a really deep pit down there," Cole recalled in a 1981 interview. "We hoped to be a part of all this by contributing the expertise to make a safe descent."

The standard Prusik style developed by Cuddington and others worked fine for climbing—using such knots to climb out of a one-thousand-foot pit would simply require more time and stamina than using them to climb out of a two-hundred-foot pit. Descent was a different story. To rappel longer pits, cavers had been using either Cuddington's complicated rappel spool or a method that involved creating a chain of carabiners and "brake bars"—metal bars placed across the middle of a carabiner. The bars would be attached on one side of the carabiner, with a groove on the other, so that they could swing closed when needed. Rope would be threaded over the "closed" bars through a pair of carabiners, creating enough friction for a safe descent. But both spools and brake bars became difficult to control in pits deeper than two hundred feet. In such pits the weight of rope hanging below a caver gradually decreased during the rappel, speeding the rate of descent—sometimes to a potentially dangerous degree.

Cole theorized that the brake-bar method would provide better friction and control if several of the bars were threaded together on a single U-shaped steel frame instead of multiple carabiners. This would allow cavers to flip each bar into place or pull it aside as they wished, with rope snaking through holding the engaged bars in place. Someone could begin a long rappel with the rope strung through fewer bars, adding additional bars as speed increased. After working through dozens of sketched concepts and fabricating several prototypes with materials at hand, Cole and his friends purchased lengths of cold-rolled steel from a hardware store. With this steel and a few simple tools they fashioned the first rappel rack on a backyard forge made of a barbecue grill hooked to a vacuum cleaner.

They tested the device's strength in a garage. Satisfied it would hold at least 750 pounds without failing, in quick succession they tried it out in rock quarry, a 91-foot pit, and a 227-foot pit. They were amazed at how easily they could control speed of descent simply by pressing the bars together or spreading them apart. Coming to a complete stop halfway through a descent had been nearly impossible, but now it was simple. They could easily add and remove bars while descending, solving the problem of the changing rope weight beneath them. Bill Cuddington soon asked Cole to build him one of the new devices, as did Richard Schreiber and others.

The racks came just in time: someone had found the big Mexican pit.

. . . .

In December 1966, residents of the village of Aquismón in the state of San Luis Potosi guided three Maryland cavers, members of AMCS, to a massive nearby pit. Native Huastecans had known of the shaft for thousands of years, calling it Xol Oclif. They considered it a hazard to be avoided. Spanish explorers named it Sótano de las Golondrinas, or Cave of the Swallows, after its many thousands of nesting birds (which were actually white-collared swifts, not swallows). The Spanish also considered the giant hole in the mountain to be of little use, although occasional hunting parties would trek through the jungle to shoot at the rising columns of birds there for sport.

Upon arrival, the three cavers were confronted with a far deeper pit than they had gear to descend. As they peered at the distant bottom, they guessed the depth to be about three hundred to four hundred feet. But by moving around the perimeter to a lip where they could toss large rocks, they realized that the rocks were falling much farther than that distance. Estimating the drop at seven hundred feet or more, they resolved to return in the spring with vertical experts and longer ropes.

Before this trip could be organized, on February 19, 1967, twenty-two cavers from Tennessee, Alabama, and Georgia gathered at the Gouffre, a 241-foot pit in central Tennessee. Two ropes were rigged, and several on the group spotted going passage at the bottom. Their survey effort followed a meeting in Oak Ridge, Tennessee, of SERA, the Southeast Regional Association of the NSS. Richard Schreiber had entered graduate school at the University of Tennessee, in Knoxville, where he became chair of the local Smoky Mountain Grotto. He often caved with members of several regional grottos who had attended the meeting. Later that year, he convinced many of these friends to join him in a large push of the Gouffre's unexplored leads.

"We were all college age," Diane Cousineau recalls in a video on the birth of TAG produced for the 1998 NSS convention. "We had the same types of interest, the same very middle-class backgrounds. We were all equally poor. We either didn't have cars or had ones that ran marginally."

"At first we called ourselves The Family," Jim Wilbanks says in the same video. "We didn't really have a name for what we were. All we knew was that every Friday night we were all piled up together . . . whether it was in some grove of trees or in a parking lot, and we were caving together until Sunday evening. And it was every weekend. . . . We found a kinship, which any caver knows about today."

In the same video Marion Smith puts it more succinctly: "The truth is we were a bunch of nerds who thought we were hot shit."

Wilbanks points out that it was the mid-1960s, the age of the "generation gap," a time when young people "were looking toward ourselves for leadership, rather than our parents." Younger college students like Wilbanks, in their teens, looked to slightly older graduate students like Schreiber, Smith, or Rick Foote, who were in their twenties, as "father figures." On his first trip with Schreiber, Wilbanks rappelled into Engle Double Pit in Alabama. Prior to that, his longest rappel had been about fifty feet. "Here he was, putting me down into a 236-foot entrance shaft, then a 30-foot intermediate drop, and a 150-foot wet drop to the bottom, and I was way out of my element."

Somewhere on the long Sunday-night drive back from the Gouffre, Schreiber said to Wilbanks, "We need to come up with a name for this group."

"Diane calls it The Family," Wilbanks replied.

Schreiber didn't like being cast in a paternalistic role and said it should be something else. The two tried out and discarded several names as the Tennessee countryside rolled by in darkness. "What about the three states?" Schreiber suggested, referring to Alabama, Georgia, and Tennessee.

"TAG!" Wilbanks said. That evening he wrote a letter to share the name with Diane Cousineau, and it spread rapidly.

After finding virgin passage in the Gouffre on their first try, the TAG group began planning regular exploration projects in the region and were soon finding pits and caves everywhere. They liked to go big. On a single day fourteen people—most equipped with a new John Cole rack—descended Surprise Pit, setting a record for the most to descend the pit in a single party before they headed farther into the depths of Fern Cave in search of virgin discovery. On a later trip, a prolific caver called Foxy Ferguson was surprised with a birthday party at the bottom of Surprise, where champagne and cake waited on a clean tablecloth.

"That was the beginning of TAG and the idea of caving without a fixed organization, but caving with a purpose," Schreiber recalled in 1989. The active group acquired use of an old house near Garth, Alabama—within hiking distance of Engle Double Pit—that became known as the "TAG House" from 1966 through 1971. An old sharecropper's shack, its floors were piled with mattresses to sleep several dozen cavers on some weekends, with coolers of beer on the porch and rock and roll playing on Schreiber's portable record player.

In April 1967, two months after the first TAG trip to the Gouffre, Cole and Cuddington joined eight members of the AMCS in the first descent of Sótano de las Golondrinas. First they outfitted and trained other cavers from Maryland and Texas in the use of rappel racks (although some still used the double-carabiner-and-break-bar-method for the big drop). They landed in a mossy chamber with a much larger diameter than the entrance, the walls gradually widening away from the rope throughout the long descent. At the rig point they used, the actual depth measured a whopping 1,094 feet. At the highest possible rig point it increased to 1,235 feet, or slightly higher than a rappel from the observation deck of the Empire State Building.

By either measure, Golondrinas became the world's deepest known free-fall pit. Word of the find spread, launching an explosion of vertical caving in Mexico by many groups. (By 2019, however, the pit's rank among the world's deepest had slipped to twentieth. Such is the nature of discovery during a golden age.) Simultaneously to the Mexican expeditions, the TAG group continued finding and descending new pits in the United States. That June, Richard Schreiber led the third group to descend Golondrinas—a party containing mostly TAG cavers. They also explored many other pits and caves in the region. He brought yet another group to the pit in December, all the while continuing work in TAG, where his greatest discovery was yet to come.

. . . .

Cavers ascending from the base of Sótano de Las Golondrinas.

A few years after my first TAG trips, I had gained enough experience—more from writing about caves than from any notable prowess underground, where my skills were decidedly average—to bluster my way onto some big expeditions. When Kathy and I finished our masters' degrees at the University of South Carolina, we moved to Park Ridge, New Jersey, where she went to work in the corporate offices of Sony and I went to "work" as a freelance writer specializing in caves and adventure travel. The pay was usually lousy, but the trips were always amazing.

The 1980s saw increased American cave discovery not only within TAG, but throughout karst regions in the American West, the Caribbean, Canada, and Central and South America. Meanwhile, European and American teams found vast new cave systems in Asia, Europe, and the Pacific. There was plenty to write about. From 1986 to 1988, various outdoor magazines sent me caving in the Black Hills of South Dakota, the Big Horn Mountains of Wyoming, the cockpit karst of western Jamaica, and the fog-shrouded karst spires of southern China. Rough work, but someone had to do it. Between magazine gigs in 1988, I snuck in recreational visits to Xanadu and Ellison's, worked support for cave dives in Virginia and upstate New York, and attended three caving conventions. In January 1989, I led the first caving expedition to the rugged John Crow Mountains of eastern Jamaica, a jagged hell of jungle and sharp limestone pinnacles, with unexplored pits everywhere—none of which, alas, led to a significant system. Upon my return, I lined up what would be my second trip to Lechuguilla, a wondrous new find in New Mexico's Carlsbad Caverns National Park. That expedition was set for May, but I had also received an invitation to join my first-ever caving trip to Mexico in March, if I could just find a way to pay for it. This was to be the exploration and mapping of a cave including a large, as-yet-undescended pit—no mere tourist trip to yo-yo Golondrinas, as several of my caver friends had done. I was determined to make it.

At the time I was writing regularly for a magazine called *America*, aimed at college students with a focus on low-cost adventure travel. While I couldn't talk my editor there into paying for a Mexican cave expedition, she said that if I could find actual college students doing more "normal" adventure travel anywhere in Mexico, she'd be happy to assign a feature on that.

"You could always go caving afterward," she added.

On a whim, I called the student activities office at the University of Texas to ask whether they had any planned recreational trips heading to Mexico over the coming spring break. Just one, the student worker manning the phone said, an adventure travel and diving trip being run by an Austin cave diver. She gave me his name, Jim Bowden, and a phone number. It soon turned out we had several friends in common. He was happy to have me along as writer, since he was regularly leading adventure travel groups at that point and could use the free publicity.

A few weeks later I rode south from Austin in Bowden's old school bus with sixteen University of Texas students and a freelance photographer. Bowden, I learned, was an experienced cave diver and instructor with long experience in Mexico. He had discovered many cenotes, or water-filled sinkholes, in eastern Mexico, some of which had led to significant cave dives. While he routinely led very dangerous cave dives, he and a partner had contracted with the university to take students on a far more relaxed spring break adventure. With this group I explored ancient ruins, rappelled into crystal springs, swam in spectacular mountain cascades, and consumed much local food and beer. A few dive students completed a SCUBA certification dive in a cool cenote as the rest of us snorkeled, observing wildlife in and out of the water.

We dove off limestone cliffs into Manté, a turquoise lake where the year before American cave diver Sheck Exley had set a world SCUBA depth record, descending 780 feet underwater to the base of the spring that fed the lake. While we were camped at Manté, the famous diver himself stopped by the site. He was spending a few days testing equipment for an upcoming attempt at a new depth record at a cave in South Africa. I had met Exley in 1981 on a Florida State Cave Club dive project in Climax Cave in South Georgia. We talked a bit about friends in common there. Five years later I would be present when Sheck died and Jim Bowden nearly died, as the two attempted a new SCUBA depth record at Zacatón, an even deeper pit in this same part of Mexico (imagine Golondrinas filled with water). But on this sunny summer day, he was happy to share dive stories and tips with eager college students from Texas.

The tour group spent its last day at an estate called Las Pozas, or the Wells, built in the 1940s by Edward James, a British surrealist poet.

American cavers called the place "the Birdhouse" and had been using it as an inexpensive, beautiful, and stunningly strange campground since the mid-1960s, when groups from TAG and Texas first began making regular trips to Mexico. James had been a patron of both Salvador Dali and René Magritte, and art historians consider him a driving intellectual force behind the surrealist movement. Dali famously called him "crazier than all the surrealists together." Unlike Dali, James believed that nature itself contained all the strange juxtapositions associated with surrealism. In 1947, he purchased eighty acres on a mountain a few miles above the village of Xilitla, and began the project that would prove his theories and occupy him until his death in 1984.

We wandered through that project: blue concrete platforms high above the trees, spiral staircases leading to a forest of columns topped by massive flowers, pathways lined by ten-foot sculpted hands, and fountains that seemed to flow uphill. Eerie grottoes hid beneath a riot of natural vegetation and exotic birds. On a pinnacle stood the odd home in which James had lived at the site, turrets and gables poking from jungle fog like the opening of *Citizen Kane*.

Somewhere in the green forest nearby, I knew, was a difficult-to-reach pit called Hoya de la Luz, considered by some TAG cavers to be the most beautiful pit in North America. Resembling some elfin keep from a fantasy film, its multiple waterfalls crashed into a forested bottom 591 feet below the lip of white limestone walls encircling it. But our group was not equipped for such a climb, let alone an allegedly miserable hike to get there, so we made do with the sunset, warm cervezas, and cold burritos. We camped amid surrealist sculptures, and I woke to a cacophony of parrots just outside my tent. At the end of it all, we piled into the bus and Bowden dropped me at a roadside motel near Ciudad Valles as he headed north toward the border with his load of sunburned students.

That afternoon I was met by three friends, New Jersey cavers who had helped pick our meeting location on a tourist map weeks earlier. They had built an extra day into their somewhat flexible travel plans, so we planned to spend it swimming amid some spectacular nearby waterfalls that I had visited with the students. First we went to a local discount store and bought several large mirrors, one of them bordered by an elaborate frame. My friend Bob Cohen, nicknamed The Guru by Jersey cavers, thought these would make for interesting photographs at the waterfalls. He was right—I think Edward James would have approved of what we produced that day, odd reflections and illusions involving crashing water and human faces. So as not to waste the mirrors we had purchased, we dried them off and hung them on empty walls in our motel rooms, where they may have confused observant housekeepers.

That night we enjoyed a traditional dinner with a local family and took in a Mexican disco. The next morning we coaxed a rented Volkswagen up a mountain highway to the Valle de los Fantasmas, named for its ghostly rock formations. From there a series of increasingly rough gravel roads led us to a campsite where we were to join a multinational caving team in the first exploration of a large vertical cave system.

When Maureen Handler, a biomedical engineering major from Massachusetts, transferred to Virginia Tech in 1981, she knew nothing about caving. One day a classmate mentioned that she and her roommate were headed to a cave club meeting. She invited Handler to go along, but Handler declined. A skier and hiker, she had already joined the university's ski club. She was focused on getting good grades and decided that crawling in mud didn't appeal to her.

Her friend returned to class the next Monday, excited. "Oh, you've got to go to the cave club meeting," she said. "You've got to go. It's all guys and they love to party."

"Guys who party?" Handler asked. She had just turned twenty, moving out on her own to Virginia. She didn't know many people. "Okay, I'll check 'em out."

Many times in the decades that followed, when delivering talks about caving to civic and school groups she would say, "Who would've thought that two simple sentences like that would change the entire direction of my life?"

She joined the group in October 1981 and began caving with them in TAG the following March. By June she was dropping Fantastic Pit in North Georgia's Ellison's Cave, the deepest pit in the United States. Handler also dropped out of college—to travel with Texas cavers to even bigger caves in Mexico—before returning to school in 1984 to

Mike Newsome, right, captures photographer Bob Cohen in a mirror as the author enjoys a waterfall near Xilitla, Mexico, in March 1989.

Maureen Handler in Borbollón in 1989.

pursue a new major in civil engineering. She became involved in mapping local caves in southern Virginia and West Virginia. She continued traveling frequently to TAG, eventually moving to Chattanooga after earning her degree. For six years in a row she also joined annual expeditions to Mexico. The biggest by far began at the end of a Christmas trip in 1988 that included Gerald Moni—the long-time best friend and caving partner of Marion Smith and the primary data-keeper of the Tennessee Cave Survey for four decades.

They met some local Mexican cavers who stopped by as the Americans geared up on the side of a road. One joined them to rappel and climb a roadside pit, and the locals invited the Americans to spend the night at their houses in San Luis Potosí. The TAG group accepted the offer and partied into the night with the Mexicans, swapping cave stories in two languages while drinking homemade mescal. They were heading back to the States the next day, and one of the locals asked Handler whether her group would like to see an unexplored thousand-foot pit.

"Um, yeah," she answered.

He explained in Spanish that the deal was that his group needed to help explore the cave and its massive pit. "We don't have the gear to get down there," he said. "If we call the Mexico City cavers to help us explore it, they'll just take over the project."

"I'm sure," Handler agreed. It was the same with big-time cavers everywhere: those who had the gear tended to dictate the survey. The two shook hands and agreed to plan a joint expedition if the site was everything he claimed it would be. The next morning they drove up into the hills for a look. *Resumidero* translates as "drain," and it was clear that the cave drained the tiny village of Borbollón. Bits of trash, old tires, shoes, and occasional large logs had been periodically flushed into the entrance area by floods during the rainy season, bits of flotsam left behind as the water rushed toward some hidden recess.

"So he takes us into a kind of nondescript cave," Handler recalled thirty years later. "We got to this balcony and we started dropping rocks down and timing them. Each time it was seven seconds. And each time the reverberations echoed from a big room. There was a big, impressive flowstone formation flowing down into the pit."

Handler returned to Chattanooga and began making calls. At the time she was dating Bruce Smith (no relation to Marion), co-author of the book *On Rope*. When his comprehensive guide had been published by the NSS the year before, it had been hailed as the bible for single rope technique in North America—a position it would fill for decades to come. Smith would co-lead the expedition in March, and the two would invite some of the strongest vertical cavers they knew. By the time Handler and Smith arrived in San Luis Potosí—on the day I was swimming in waterfalls with my New Jersey friends—word had spread. Over fifty people showed up for the first expedition meeting at a local hotel.

"Oh my God, what are we going do with this crowd?" Handler asked herself. About half of the group were Mexican and the rest American, with two Canadians in the mix. And she had given permission to three more from New Jersey to meet directly at the cave in a couple of days. I was to assist Handler in taking the first-ever photos of the big drop and the chamber at its base, while my friends Bob Cohen, Mike Newsome, and Chris Stine would rotate onto the mapping crews spreading throughout the cave.

It was to be a true North American exploration of an unknown deep system, one that no one on the team would never forget.

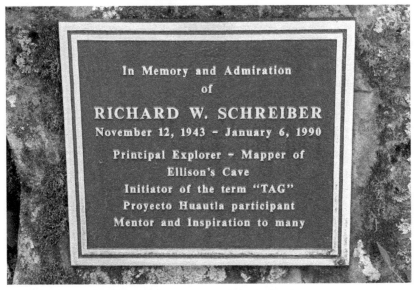

In Memory and Admiration
of
RICHARD W. SCHREIBER
November 12, 1943 – January 6, 1990

Principal Explorer – Mapper of
Ellison's Cave
Initiator of the term "TAG"
Proyecto Huautla participant
Mentor and Inspiration to many

A bronze plaque placed at one of the entrances to Ellison's cave.

He is 18 years old. He goes caving for the first time. He explores, learns about cave conservation and protection. He buys his own gear. He learns how to rappel and ascend ropes. . . . He is now 22 years old. He gets involved in organized caving. Starts a grotto and gets other cavers involved. He is 30 years old and finds a great cave, it becomes a major discovery. He experiences finding virgin passage and is hooked. He is now 35. Has gotten married and has a young family. His job and career take a lot of time. He is 43 now and dreams of going caving, but there is never any time. Maybe he can go caving once or twice a year. He is now 50 and envies the young cavers at the grotto meetings that he faithfully attends. The ascenders and gear all looks strange. The lights are now all LED. He is 58 now and the kids are grown. He makes a trip and tries to climb. His strength and stamina is going. He is now 67 years old and fully retired. He usually daydreams of caving. Still active though, he hikes the mountains and stumbles across an undiscovered entrance. As he looks in the opening . . . he is 18 years old once again.

BILL BENTLEY | Facebook post, September 14, 2017

Chapter 12

THE CAVER TREE

In July 1967, less than a month after his first trip to Golondrinas, Richard Schreiber began a survey of Pettyjohn's Cave, which local cavers also called Bronco, Atwood, or Ellison's, on Pigeon Mountain near Lafayette, Georgia. As it turned out, Ellison's was an entirely different cave, which Schreiber learned from a local farmer who gave him directions. At the time Schreiber was also helping TAG caver Foxy Ferguson with the survey of Byers Cave. Together they began what would become the Georgia Cave Survey. Simultaneously Schreiber worked with TAG cavers surveying Engel Double Pit.

These various projects, combined with graduate school, meant that he had time for Pettyjohn's only occasionally, although he knew that geologically Pigeon Mountain offered a potential for deep caves. In March 1968, Schreiber and TAG caver Rick Foote followed the farmer's directions to an entrance north of Pettyjohn's, the "real" Ellison's Cave. They quickly traversed a half mile of passage. He wrote to Marion Smith, who was serving an army stint in South Korea, that the cave "could be Ga's deepest and the deepest in the East," although it would be about seven months before he returned to it. Schreiber also wrote that

he and Rick Foote had agreed to keep the cave a secret "until either"—
which was underlined— "one or both of us have a chance to return."

During that year Schreiber began dating a fellow graduate at the
University of Tennessee named Della McGuffin, and of course he took
her caving. It turned out she had a knack for it. While caving was
generally a male-dominated pursuit in the 1960s, there were many
notable women caving in TAG, such as Foxy Ferguson, Gemma Morri-
son, and Diane Cousineau. Gender was no predictor of endurance and
disposition on long underground trips. Larger men might be able to
easily bridge a canyon passage in one step, but smaller women could fit
through tight crawlways that filtered out nearly all men. Della proved a
strong climber on rope and efficient at reading survey instruments. Rick
Foote had returned to Ellison's in the summer, when Schreiber was in
San Luis Obispo, California, visiting his parents. Foote and three others
(including his wife's ten-year-old brother) did what amounted to a tourist trip. They saw no new passage.

Schreiber wrote to Marion Smith that the cave "might make an easy
survey, since there weren't any side passages." On October first, he told
a friend that the next weekend he, Della, and her roommate Sue Cross,
were going "to map all of Ellison's cave on Saturday, finish it up on
Sunday, and then visit Rusty's"—an easy cave with a short pit and many
beautiful formations. On the appointed Saturday, the three entered and
began mapping at a junction point, heading down a wet crawl Schreiber
had never traversed. Cross began "having a fit" because she hadn't expected to get wet, but Schreiber and McGuffin urged her onward.

"Della didn't mind," Schreiber recalled. "I was having a ball because
we were bombing through virgin passage with running water and air—
the same sort of thing leading to Surprise Pit, which we had both seen
previously. What could be more exciting?" (Later, Marion Smith would
note that someone had previously entered this portion of the cave and
used a carbide lamps to draw a skull and crossbones on the wall, adding
the year "1927.")

They pressed on until they reached a pit that appeared to be over
one hundred feet deep. They had no rope, and Cross was not trained for
vertical work in any event, so they left the cave and returned to camp
for dinner. The next day, October 6, 1968, Schreiber and McGuffin

carried a three hundred foot rope with them, along with vertical gear. Cross had had enough of caving in her single trip. The two reached the bottom of the 125-foot drop, which would soon be named "Warm-Up Pit," and followed a winding stream crawl. McGuffin squeezed through a small keyhole in the rock where there seemed to be no other way to go.

As Schreiber attempted to follow, she said, "Hey, there's a drop."

Her "hey" echoed into the darkness of a clearly vast space. He forced himself through the tight keyhole (later bypassed by an easier route). He stood at McGuffin's side and saw a black void. Schreiber grabbed a rock from the streambed and dropped it over the side. The returning boom took so long that they knew they had found a pit many hundreds of feet deep. It would take a few weeks to organize a full TAG team.

A few days before the scheduled return to descend the great pit, Jim Wilbanks went to Schreiber's apartment. "Richard, I'm dying," he said. "You have got to tell me what is coming off this weekend."

Schreiber grinned conspiratorially. "Follow me," he said. The two went into his bedroom. Schreiber closed the door and pointed to a bumper sticker stuck on the inside, which was printed with the single word, "Fantastic."

"Okay," Wilbanks said. "Now what does this mean?"

"I found an eight-second pit."

Wilbanks says he still feels the goosebumps from that moment.

Without knowing exactly what it was for, John Cole supplied an eight-hundred-foot length of Sampson rope, which Schreiber and McGuffin hoped would be long enough. Fantastic Pit, as they named it, turned out to be 586 feet deep from the highest possible rig point—then and still the deepest free-fall pit in the continental United States (three deeper pits in Hawaii and Alaska would be found much later). On November 1, 1968, the first descents of Fantastic Pit were made, with cavers rappelling 510 feet and climbing back out on Prusik knots. Richard Schreiber was first down, followed by Della McGuffin, Jim Wilbanks, Mike Lemonds, David Stidham, and Rob Culbertson.

The caving trip took over nineteen hours.

The next day, a large group of ten TAG cavers, including John Cole, whose invention of the rack, not to mention the supply of a long rope, helped make the descent possible, yo-yoed the pit. Bill Cuddington and two others got tired of waiting for their turn to rappel and put their descent off for a later trip. Meanwhile, Schreiber, McGuffin, and Lemonds mapped over a thousand additional feet back to the entrance of the upper cave. That day was much wetter, and those in in the pit basically climbed in a waterfall. Bill Torode, who had discovered Surprise Pit, soon descended Fantastic and was later able to dig open a new entrance that made reaching the pit much easier than the long journey via the natural entrance. The TAG group launched in earnest the survey of Ellison's Cave, spending up to six days at a stretch in underground camps, pushing miles of complex vertical passages. In the following eight years its mapped length grew to nearly twelve miles, with a total vertical depth of over one thousand feet, far exceeding Schreiber's first estimates of its potential length and depth.

One of the cavers who eagerly joined Schreiber in the lengthy survey project that followed was Marion O. Smith, fresh out of the army. Smith had been in Korea when Fantastic was found, but he was back in Georgia in time to join Schreiber in the discovery of Ellison's second great shaft, Incredible Pit, 440 feet deep, on April 19, 1969. They returned with rope for the first decent on May 3. After Schreiber, Smith, and McGuffin reached the bottom, they were followed by a group of five visiting Indiana cavers that included Bill Steele, who would go on to earn acclaim for his deep cave discoveries in Mexico. Smith accompanied Schreiber on dozens of mapping trips further extending the length of the cave. On one trip that summer he rappelled Fantastic Pit, traveled through the lower cave beneath the mountain to reach the base of Incredible Pit, then pushed onward to several large chambers beyond.

Not long after my first Tennessee caving experience in 1980, I began to hear from Lee Pearson the occasional expression, "a Marion Smith passage." The phrase applied to any wet, miserable crawl that after hours of effort might (or might not) lead to a vertigo-inducing pit. The man attached to the name, I learned, was something of a TAG legend.

A caver begins the 440-foot descent of Incredible Pit in Ellison's Cave in 2017.

Whenever I'd go to caving conventions or join expeditions to remote places and wind up sitting around campfires or waiting for climbers at the edge of a pit, I would hear seasoned cavers say Marion this and Marion that. Any surname was superfluous, as when basketball fans speak of Kobe.

Marion was, he insists, merely part of a great group of TAG cavers then pushing the limits of vertical exploration, among them Jim Smith, E. T. Davis, and Tommy "Teddy Bear" Thurman. "At that time Jim Smith had more 500-meter-deep turnaround trips than anyone!" he wrote, suggesting that in comparison he was a "wuss." Perhaps it because Jim Smith had focused his attention on Mexico by the time I was regularly caving in TAG, and some of the others had simply slowed down, that I heard Marion Smith's name so often. Perhaps it was because he was small enough to wriggle into the nastiest crawlways and pits imaginable, leading to more colorful expletives and humorous trip reports. For whatever reason, his name seemed the most frequently mentioned in those days.

In emails, cavers might shorten a Marion reference to his initials: MOS. Some who knew him well called him "Goat." I was never sure whether this was because of Smith's scraggly white beard, his skinny build, his uncanny climbing skill, or his general obstinacy. Maybe it was Greatest of All Time. Marion was such a celebrity in the small universe of caving that for years I could never quite screw up the courage to approach him at caver gatherings like the TAG Fall Cave-In or the summer SERA Cave Carnival. His stern visage at such events discouraged casual conversation.

I had, at least, managed to speak several times with Gerald Moni, the head of the Tennessee Cave Survey and one of Smith's closest friends. The two had met in 1969 and were jointly responsible for dozens, if not hundreds, of new caves added to the survey over subsequent decades. But I did not actually meet the famous Goat in person until March 1989, when I found him up a tree in Mexico.

Our rented VW bounced into the Borbollón camp, where we found only three cavers from Mexico City there to greet us. The big drop had been rappelled the day before, they said—we were too late for the first descent. Its depth had been measured at 713 feet from the lip of the entrance passage to the sloping floor of an immense chamber that funneled downward toward a series of deeper pits and junction halls. Some of the team were in the cave staging ropes and gear for the next day's push, one of the cavers explained. Others were still en route from San Luis Potosi or exploring other pits near camp.

He added that several Americans who had descended the main pit that morning and returned to camp were now in a tree. He pointed toward a nearby hill, where a lone ancient tree of a species I did not recognize stood silhouetted at the summit, its massive canopy casting shade from the subtropical sun.

We climbed the hill. Sure enough, scattered overhead sat a who's who of TAG caving. Reclining among the branches were Marion O. Smith and Gerald Moni, who was smoking a fat cigar as was his habit. Near him sat Alan Cressler and John Stembel, strong cavers from the Atlanta area whom I had met previously in TAG and West Virginia. Stembel was widely known in the caving community as "Rocco"—it would be a couple of years before I learned that he was actually named John. Another American team member was a young Texan, Joe Ivy, whom I knew from his reputation as a gifted climber and designer of caving gear, some of which I had purchased. Ivy had also gained a national reputation at an early age as an expert in teaching cave rescue techniques and safety. Eleven years later he would perish tragically, if ironically, in an accident while climbing a large dome in a Texas cave.

I followed my New Jersey colleagues into the tree—there were plenty of empty branches—to say hello. Chris Stine had shown the foresight to trudge up the hill carrying a heavy beer cooler, so as we climbed we were able to pass cold bottles from the ground to whomever wanted one. A breeze rustled the shaded leaves. I settled onto a branch, beer in hand, and realized that something other than comfort had led to this arboreal gathering.

On the grassy hillside just beyond the tree I saw two cavers I had met a few months earlier at Lechuguilla Cave in New Mexico. One was Neeld Messler, a young man in his early twenties with blond hair and an un-caver-like tan. His cherubic face and ample muscles had led two of the women then leading mapping efforts at Lechuguilla to nickname him "Speleobabe," a name that had stuck. The other caver was his equally young, fit, and tanned girlfriend, Bethany Jablonsky. Beyond them rose a spectacular view of forested mountains and limestone cliffs. The two lay sunbathing on a plastic camp tarp, wearing nothing whatsoever.

"Michael Ray Taylor," Marion Smith said, drawing my attention away from the view. "I read your article in *Sports Illustrated*."

He was referring to a story published the previous year on Wyoming's Great Expectations, at that time the deepest known cave in the United States. One of the two principal explorers I profiled in the piece was Jim Smith—no relation to Marion, but also a very well-known caver in TAG and Mexico, and, I had heard, one of Marion's closest friends. I was curious to learn what Marion thought of the article. Frustratingly, he said nothing else on the subject and began conversing instead with Gerald about some lead in TAG.

Marion's voice was a melodious mixture of backwoods inflections and deliberate delivery such as central casting might assign to a Confederate field commander. Over time, I would realize that it had been unconsciously copied by a generation of younger explorers in exactly the same way as a generation of test pilots once mimicked Chuck Yeager. Much later, I would also recognize that even his mention of my article was in fact a compliment.

Back in camp, we met Maureen Handler and Bruce Smith returning with some of the crew. One of the Mexican cavers asked her which way the cave now appeared to be heading.

She shrugged and said, "China?"

Maureen explained that all the passages seemed to be heading down, down, down, with new pits yet to be dropped. Fortunately we had plenty of rope and plenty of eager cavers. Over the next two days, some surveys lasted as long as twenty-five hours. Separate small teams followed the downward course of the cave, setting bolts and rigging ropes. In camp there was always fresh local cuisine, with plastic two-liter bottles of homemade mescal stacked like firewood. During the night whenever the main campfire waned, someone would spit a mouthful of the stuff on the coals and they would reignite with a *whoosh*.

The second day, I joined Maureen and three others in a ten-hour photo trip. She placed us on the rope and around the big room, firing flashes to her shouted commands. Sitting on rope about four hundred feet above the floor and three hundred feet below the lip, flashgun attached to my arm by a wrist strap, I would drop a hot spent bulb into one pack, then remove a fresh bulb from a separate bag to pop into the gun. Then Maureen would again yell, "Fire!"

For a brief moment the blackness below me would become a cathedral-like space bordered by columns of sparkling flowstone. Then I would climb to a higher place on the rope and repeat the process. Later in the day, as the photo crew took final pictures of the big chamber at its base, a tired exploration crew met us there to say they had bottomed the cave. It appeared to end in a terminal syphon—a pool that flooded the remaining passage, which might continue to descend underwater. The small lake was full of strange red larva and blue fungus, with wispy bacterial mats floating on its surface. No one wanted to go in.

Although the end had apparently been found, mapping side leads and pits continued for the next couple of days. The night after the photo trip became a party, with several guitars strumming mariachi songs and the frequent *whoosh* of mescal hitting the fire. Mike Newsome, Bob Cohen, and I were in no condition to head down the big pit the next morning with the crew that was going to map a secondary passage found the day before, then begin de-rigging and hauling ropes from that part of the cave. Instead we joined Bruce Smith, Maureen, and several of the Mexican team members for a recreational hike to a nearby pit that had been discovered and mapped a few years earlier.

Sótano la Cacalotera, which one of the Mexicans translated as "Well of Shit of the Earth," was 245 feet deep and reminded me in many ways of Neversink, Valhalla, and other classic TAG pits. Basically a straight shaft about one hundred feet wide at its mouth, it belled out slightly wider toward a fern-covered sandy floor. Any cavers on rope thus hung an increasingly farther distance from any wall as they descended.

Part of the reason for this yo-yo trip was for Bruce and Maureen to train some of the San Luis Potosi cavers with gear they had brought down from Chattanooga and planned to donate to the group. Bruce thus rigged two ropes into the pit about ten feet apart from one another to allow twice the number of people to practice rappelling and climbing at any given time, and also to allow side-by-side instruction if needed.

As the afternoon wore on, Maureen wanted a photo of Bruce on rope, so he began posing halfway up. I had an idea and yelled up to him to wait there. The second rope was free, so I began to climb, stopping when I reached a point just a foot or two below Bruce's level.

The author on rope in expedition leader Maureen Handler's time-lapse photograph of Borbollón's 718-foot pit.

"Okay, Bruce. You have brought vertical caving to the masses," I said. "How about if we dramatize the on-rope moment of creation? I'm thinking Sistine Chapel."

Bruce smiled, getting the message, and began swinging toward me. I began swinging toward him. We each stretched a finger toward the other. It took a few tries, but eventually our swings became properly coordinated when I braced against the wall just as Bruce reached out. Maureen managed to snap a photo of our fingers just touching in a God-and-Adam splendor, both of us hanging about one hundred feet off the floor of the impressive pit.

The following morning, the fast vertical team of Marion Smith, Alan Cressler, and Terry Raines began mapping the bottom section of Borbollón before removing ropes and hauling them slowly toward the main drop. As John "Rocco" Stembel related in the official expedition report, published in January 1991 in issue number 18 of the newsletter for the Association for Mexican Cave Studies:

At the supposed sump, Marion was burning up and decided he needed to cool off. Dog paddling around, Marion noticed a very

Climbing guru Bruce Smith, left, swings over to touch the author's hand over one hundred feet above the floor of Cacalotera.

small airspace and could hear water splash down some sort of void on the other side. The largest area was wide enough for a nose and maybe three centimeters high. So the sump was not a sump, but a nasty, low airspace. There was no noticeable wind, but very little wind could ever be felt in Borbollón.

In short, the cave continued, albeit in a Marion Smith passage that would have to wait for another expedition by Mexican cavers. Late that afternoon, Maureen, Rocco, and Neeld met the team on their way to the entrance. True to his reputation as a strong caving pack ox, young Speleobabe was soon carrying seven wet, heavy ropes that others had de-rigged, working them slowly toward the main chamber and the bottom of the long drop.

Word spread to those above that help was needed to haul the remaining ropes and gear from the cave. I joined a team of thirty in spreading ourselves from the entrance to the lip of the 718-foot drop. We made a human chain that would ferry ropes and gear to the surface. To quote again from Rocco's expedition report, in which he refers to himself as John (even though I somehow still didn't cotton to the fact John and Rocco were the same guy until years after the report was published):

> Marion, Alan and John uncoiled all the ropes and snaked them end to end. Maureen and Alan climbed the pit, then Marion and John waited as the eight hundred meters of rope was hauled out. An old Modelo beer can affixed to the tail of the rope signaled the end. After six hours of hauling, everyone was out of the cave at sunrise Friday morning.

In the end, Resumidero de Borbollón was mapped to a depth of 2,226 feet with a total horizontal survey of about 4,500 feet. At 713 feet, the main drop became for a few years the second-deepest in-cave pit known in the Western Hemisphere. Despite the bits of refuse from the village that had washed through it, it was by far one of the prettiest pits I would ever see, as well as one the deepest I would ever climb. While the space beyond the lake was supposedly pushed into some new passage by Mexican cavers, to my knowledge no map of the new section has been published, and the pool's odd biology has not been scientifically sampled. Some return trips have reported sufficiently bad air near the bottom of the main pit that one later Mexican group carried oxygen for the climb out and did not descend any of the lower pits. The bad air was believed related to pollution washing through the cave from the village, but such a relationship has not been proven.

I should add that the day after the rope haul, just for sport Neeld and I took a short drive to yo-yo a 660-foot drop called Sótano de Puerto de los Lobos. There was a deep pool at the base, so we each rappelled solo, switching over to ascent a foot above the water to climb out alone. I rigged, so therefore I went first. I was young, in reasonable shape, and maybe a little stupid, taking what amounted to a solo trip into such a deep pit. I enjoyed the view as I descended, spinning slightly, finally pushing my brake bars together in full stop. I leaned backward in my seat harness to reach down and touch the dark water just below. I hung awkwardly for several minutes while attaching my ascenders to the rope, removing my rappel rack, and then hanging the heavy metal bar from a clip on my side. Then I climbed the equivalent of a skyscraper back into daylight without incident. Neeld did exactly the same after me. I am sure he climbed faster.

It may be worth noting that *ACMS Activities Newsletter* number 18, edited by famed TAG geologist and surveyor Patricia Kambesis, contained several other expedition reports in addition to that of Resumidero de Borbollón. Some described deep, complex systems with many pits, one or two of which are still being explored thirty years later. Nearly all of the trip leaders who wrote these accounts—including most of the Texans—had honed their vertical skills in hills and hollers of TAG, where many of them continue to cave today. Schreiber had been an important early explorer in Huautla, a cave system that continues to be explored and may yet become the world's deepest, and descendants of John Cole's racks continue to sing in deep pits as rope flies over the bars.

I was never able to meet Richard Schreiber, who died after a sudden illness in January 1990, although I did catch glimpses of him once or twice at caving conventions. After he died, his friend Marion O. Smith wrote a moving tribute to his life of discovery for the *NSS News*. "As the experienced one, he always initiated interesting, adventuresome trips, and became my caving mentor," Smith wrote, "showing me both the serious and ridiculous sides of caving."

At Borbollón, I barely got to meet Schreiber's legendary protégé—first in the caver tree, then a couple of times while passing in the cave, and briefly, I later realized, when his battered truck had pulled into Las Pozas with other cavers while I was there. Somewhere over the dozen years between climbing that tree and writing a lengthy article about him for *Sports Illustrated*, I came to see Marion O. Smith as more than an accomplished cave explorer: he was one of the most remarkable humans I would ever encounter and a living embodiment of caving culture.

Perhaps his greatest discovery was a deep system that in some ways resembled Borbollón, in that it contained massive pits and chambers, in this case running on for miles beneath Tennessee's Cumberland Plateau. This cave too was profoundly threatened by pollution from a small mountain town, which made Rumbling Falls not only Marion's greatest find but for a while also made him one of caving's more controversial figures.

And it eventually prompted me, just as I began to write this book, to spend some time digging alone in a little cave below the plateau, where one fall day I would pull out a blue antique bottle buried within the mud of a blowing lead.

Images courtesy of the National Speleological Society.

On November 1, 1968, a group of young cavers gathered to descend a virgin pit. Richard Schreiber and Della McGuffin were the first two people to descend (see attached photos from that moment). Fantastic Pit in Ellison's Cave Georgia became the deepest free-fall pit in the US. It has since been eclipsed by pits in Alaska and Hawaii; however, it is still the deepest in the continental US at 586 ft. deep and free. These college-age explorers are now fifty years older, so few are still active cavers. Many are no longer with us.

Imagine: The rappel rack was a new invention, everyone climbed with three Prusik knot systems, carbide lamps mounted on construction hats were standard. Blue jeans and denim jackets were common cave attire. If it was wet, a wool sweater was added. Everyone's NSS number was four digits. Ropewalker systems did not exist, poly clothing did not exist, cave suits were unheard of. Some have called this the golden age of caving in TAG. The cave was discovered by simply asking a farmer in his field did he know of any caves nearby. Everything below the Warm-Up Pit was virgin. The cave was mapped as it was explored, and it was an amazing time indeed. So much virgin cave to see.

Since that day fifty years ago many people have explored this amazing cave. Visitation has remained steady over all these years at about 300 to 350 people per year. They come from all over the US and the world.

Three people have died there, several have been injured and required rescue. It will happen again. The lure of the big deep cave calls out to many who lack the skills to survive if anything goes wrong. For many of these folks everything goes right, and they unknowingly escape death or injury. Some are not so lucky.

ALLEN PADGETT | Post in the TAG Caver Facebook group, November 1, 2018

Chapter 13

GOAT'S PARADISE

A native of the tiny farming community of Fairburn, Georgia, Marion O. Smith first toured Ruby Falls in 1958 as a high school student. Over the next two years he toured larger commercial caves including Mammoth, Carlsbad, and Luray Caverns, but it wasn't until 1965 that he became interested in exploring wild caves with a group of friends at West Georgia College. They started with Tumbling Rock in Alabama and Case Cave in Georgia, where they camped for twenty-six hours. Like many college students who know cave locations but nothing of the NSS, he and his friends did almost everything wrong, "but lived," as Marion would say in later years.

Gradually he and his friends formed their own caving club, the now-defunct West Georgia Grotto. Rusty Mills, a more experienced caver from the Dogwood City Grotto in Atlanta, showed up for their second and third meetings in January and February 1966. Richard Schreiber and several other active cavers attended the fourth meeting March 9, showing tantalizing slides of new exploration in Fern Cave, including Surprise Pit. On March 16, Smith recalls, "Mills put me down my first pit, Cemetery"—a scenic 153-foot drop near Trenton, Georgia. Smith found the experience terrifying and probably not for him.

The entrance to Gary's Chamber, Rumbling Falls Cave, on Saturday, July 27, 2002, with caver Tim Curtis standing at center. The author sits high on the right-hand wall.

Still, on April 9, 1966 (as Marion recalled in an interview for the 1989 convention Guidebook), he ran into Schreiber and Foxy Ferguson at Moses' Tomb and was soon joining them in survey trips, becoming a key explorer of Ellison's by 1969 after serving eighteen months in the US Army. From 1958 forward, he had kept a daily diary, and as his interest turned to caving, Marion's diary evolved to meticulous journals of every cave entered, awarding special status to those containing pits. By August 21, 1982, he had entered and recorded 1,673 different caves, including 1,003 and pits. Like his mentor Richard Schreiber and his friend Gerald Moni, Marion had been honored with a coveted Lew Bicking Award by the NSS. But of these early explorers, Marion also claimed a personality that prompted one TAG caving group to bestow an entirely different honor: the Horse's Ass Award, a cookie shaped like a hand imparting the finger. While Schreiber would also earn this award, Marion became the only one to receive the cookie twice, an honor bestowed at Marion's sixtieth birthday party in September 2002.

"Marion can be difficult to be around for extended periods," one friend confided to me. "He has no tolerance for fools." Even my caving pal Lee Pearson, as easy-going an individual as I am ever likely to meet, once had his fill of Marion's frequent critiques when the two did some dicey climbing together in a passage Lee had found in a Cookeville cave.

As of the 2002 party where he received his second Horse's Ass Award—a party I attended at his log home near Bone Cave, Tennessee—the Goat had explored 5,182 wild caves and rappelled into 2,762 pits (he only counted those over thirty feet deep). Sixteen years, three near misses, and two nearly fatal cave accidents later, shortly before celebrating his seventy-sixth birthday in the fall of 2018, he entered his eight thousandth cave—a feat unlikely to be matched. He has descended over 3,500 pits and despite age and injury was still descending and climbing new pits with some regularity at the age of seventy-seven as this book went to press.

His journals sometimes record everything else about those trips: who was on them, what the weather was like, where they ate and what it cost, whether the food and service were good or poor, what the loud couple at the next table discussed, and many other details. Yet as I came to know him, I realized that Marion's journals were in a sense superfluous, because he is the only person I ever met with a truly eidetic memory: give him almost any date from childhood to last Tuesday, and he will fill in the minutiae of where he was, what he did, and who was there. ("I'm date conscious, I always have been," he said in his 1989 interview. "I got that from my Daddy, I think.") Cavers have long observed that it is difficult to catch him in an error. "I misremember often," he claims, "but I'm generally in the ballpark." As I type these words, I dread the many errors of my own memory that he will undoubtedly spot and correct within these pages.

A dozen years after our meeting in Mexico, Marion agreed to let me tell the story of his greatest underground accomplishment—and biggest secret—in the pages of *Sports Illustrated*. Although the publication was not particularly known for covering outdoor adventure, let alone any pursuit as obscure as caving, several times its editors allowed me to do so because in each case the cave I described was a significant new discovery. And in each case the caver at the center of the story was a truly heroic, larger-than-life figure. These articles tended to be controversial within the caving world, not only because I was sharing secrets with the general public, but because at the center of each story was inevitably some conflict that had caused disagreement among cavers long before I chose to write about it.

None of these controversies were larger than the Tennessee case of Marion O. Smith and Rumbling Falls.

I've been reading and writing about caves online for almost as long as there has been an online. In the spring of 1993, I was invited to write an essay on the more claustrophobic aspects of caving for *Destination Discovery*, a print magazine produced by The Discovery Channel (which would drop "The" from its name in 1995). I chose as my topic a nasty passage in West Virginia called the Devil's Pinch, where Lee Pearson had grabbed my arm to forcefully extricate me from what seemed a limestone cheese grater, in which I played the uncomfortable role of the cheese.

After writing a couple more pieces for the magazine, in early 1994 the cable channel decided to transition the news-and-feature publication from print to a new sort of animal housed entirely on the World Wide Web, invented by Tim Berners-Lee only a few years earlier. When Discovery.com went live it included my nonlinear digital feature on an ill-fated dive of a one-thousand-foot-deep Mexican spring called Zacatón by Jim Bowden and Sheck Exley, in which Exley died and Bowden suffered a severe case of the bends. Over the next decade I wound up covering frequent science (and occasional cave-related) stories for the website. In the process I became aware of the rise of online news, and began to follow what we now call social media.

As the millennium approached it seemed everyone was online, especially the more tech-savvy cavers. Online you could learn the latest advancements in vertical gear, lighting, and mapping technology. And there were chat rooms where cavers argued about everything—including whether cavers should discuss anything as secretive as caving in such a public place as the Internet. I reconnected with my Florida State caving buddy Ed Hill, who in 1999 was a marketer in Atlanta. I recall long exchanges in which we argued whether or not Y2K would bring major

The Rumble Room, beneath Stupendous Pit, as photographed by Chris Anderson for a press conference announcing the cave to the public in 2000.

disruption. About that time various Tennessee cavers began referring online to an environmental battle being waged over a planned sewage plant in Spencer, Tennessee. It was clear from the posts that the plant, if built, would seriously endanger an amazing cave.

The thing was that no particularly amazing cave existed near that small town on the edge of the Cumberland Plateau. At least, none that I knew about. That changed in November 2001, when my morning news feed showed a stadium-sized chamber with colorful rock layers ringing its rounded ceiling. A tiny rope in the photograph showed a tiny caver rappelling into the room from a great height. According to the CNN article that accompanied it, the photograph and the existence of the enormous cave system where it had been taken had been made public at a press conference the day before. The purpose of the press conference was to prevent sewage effluent from being pumped into a seven-mile-long subterranean river that wound through the cave, which bordered Tennessee's Fall Creek Falls state park.

Marion Smith, I learned, was one of the discoverers of the Rumble Room—a chamber larger than the Louisiana Superdome—and the principal explorer of Rumbling Falls, the cave connected to it. But as he and a tight-knit circle of associates pursued that discovery in secret, the cave itself became threatened by the construction of a $6.5 million sewage plant upstream. The exploration and the protracted environmental battle that followed bred controversy not only within the narrow confines of the caving community, but also far beyond its borders.

I started making phone calls.

"Get a move on, fatso," Marion said. "Don't just lie there a lollygagging."

He reclined on a boulder, looking as casual as when he had draped himself over a branch in Mexico thirteen years earlier. His scraggly off-white beard remained mud-free, as did the wisps of reddish-white hair curling from beneath his battered helmet. Most of the eight other cavers on the trip wore pricey nylon coveralls, but Marion, as usual, was dressed in brown thrift-shop trousers and a mud-colored long-sleeved shirt.

I lay panting on my side between tight rock walls, my left arm stretched to shove my muddy pack forward. Over the past hour, I had rappelled down a sixty-eight-foot pit; climbed two waterfalls; crawled several hundred feet along a shallow streambed lined with shin-bruising cobbles; shinnied up, down, and across stone fissures; and squeezed through a hole the size of an office wastebasket in order to reach the rope that I knew lay just beyond this little narrow gap.

Rolling the pack forward like a muddy ball, I got a move on.

Think of the Cumberland Plateau as a vast layer cake, with cave-rich beds of limestone stacked atop one another and capped by a thin icing of hard sandstone. Along the edges of the plateau, great wedges have been carved away by erosion, creating steep-walled valleys the locals call gulfs. These share the name of the creek that drains them: Dry Fork Gulf, Cane Creek Gulf, Camps Gulf, and so on. Fall Creek Falls, the highest waterfall east of the Mississippi and the central attraction of Fall Creek Falls State Park, flows into such a gulf.

In times of heavy rain, the creeks become dangerous whitewater torrents. But most of the year, they remain bone dry. Their water vanishes

underground, through porous gravel beds or, occasionally, through swal-
lets that suck streams in like bathwater down a drain. Cavers know
that hidden river systems must carry this water to the various distant
springs where it resurfaces, but most of these rivers have eluded human
exploration. A notable exception was Camps Gulf Cave, where explorers
worked their way into a series of huge chambers that followed the course
of a wide subterranean stream. Lee Pearson took me there in 1982, when
the system was incompletely explored. Our names were among the first
twenty in a logbook placed in a great natural rotunda there.

Although it remains relatively easy to find virgin caves and pits along
the edges of the plateau, these are usually small and unremarkable, ending long before reaching the base level. That has never stopped TAG
cavers from trying to find more. In early 1997, John "Fred" Hutchison of
White House, Tennessee, went ridgewalking at Fall Creek Falls State Park.

In warmer months, the wooded gulfs and coves form an impene-
trable hell of poison ivy, briars, and ticks. Just finding a cave you've
visited before is hard in the summer; finding a new one is even tougher.
But in the dead of winter, with the vegetation gone, black holes stand
out from a distance. On cold, dry days when fog condenses from warm
cave air blowing from an entrance, the rocky ground steams like sewer
grates on a Manhattan Street.

One hole that Hutchison found that winter went a few feet horizon-
tally before dropping into a pit. A few weeks later, he returned with
another caver and descended the sixty-eight-foot shaft, exploring five
hundred feet up a small stream to a short, noisy waterfall. At the top of
this his friend Walter K. Crawford found the base of a second fourteen-
foot falls that appeared too wet and difficult to climb. Hutchison noted
the thunderous, bone-jarring rumble of the falls that had stopped exploration. On March 1, 1997, he dutifully filed the name "Rumbling Falls"
and its location with the Tennessee Cave Survey.

There is an ethic among cavers holding that those who discover
new passages should adequately map them, and there is also an etiquette holding that one shouldn't go mapping in a newfound cave
without the discoverer's permission. Marion had done a short solo trip
into Rumbling Falls two months after it was listed in the TCS. He approached Hutchison at a cavers' meeting a year later and asked whether

he intended to climb the second waterfall in Rumbling Falls. John Fred said no.

"I didn't know how very important that conversation was," Marion recalled two decades later. "I should have recorded it in my diary. I didn't. John and I have different memories of the conversation now. But I maintain I had no obligation to say anything to anyone if I returned to the cave."

On July 5, 1998, he, Gerald Moni, and Debby Johnson went to the cave. Marion climbed the second pit and scooped "about fourteen hundred feet" of passage, which at the time he believed was all the cave contained. He thought it would be an easy mapping project of three to four trips. Marion enlisted John Swartz—a noted mapmaker who was to become the chief draftsman of the survey—Gary Chambers, who was then forty-four, and Bill Walter, sixty. Debby Johnson was the baby of the crew at only thirty-eight, but she too was no stranger to mapping pits or wet crawlways. John, the cartographer, insisted that this would be a "map-as-you-go" project—no one would be allowed to run ahead of any discovery until it had been thoroughly measured and recorded. This would turn out to be a key decision. They began mapping on September 19.

A second mapping trip on October 18 yielded a crawlway that everyone had missed until then, resulting in 755 feet of passage. Marion expected the third effort on October 24 to be the last. The cave was getting increasingly small and difficult to push. A wastebasket-sized hole led into a series of narrow canyons with shoulder-hugging walls. This was typical of caves where explorers follow a stream uphill—as you get closer to the surface, the stream often branches into impassable tributaries. In this case, the stream had emerged more or less whole from a slot too small to enter. Beyond this point, a tight maze trended back downhill, but everything seemed to be getting smaller.

The team began mapping through a narrow fissure, climbing up and down through the widest places, following a faint breeze, often the sign of larger passage ahead. Because it was a Sunday afternoon and no one lived near the cave, they stopped there, but the breeze offered enough encouragement that another trip was planned for the following weekend. That day, when Marion reached the point where I would one day lie lollygagging, he stepped around a corner and saw the last thing any of them expected: a ledge and a vast expanse of blackness. He yelled what he saw to those behind him.

"No fucking way!" Swartz answered.

Marion tossed a loose rock off the lip. It tumbled silently for what seemed a very long time before exploding with a thunder that rumbled across the floor of an enormous chamber.

"How are you making that noise?" Swartz asked, convinced it was some sort of trick. Then he caught up and saw for himself.

"Okay, I'm coming already," I said, sliding forward as I told myself, for the millionth time, *Man, I gotta get in shape*. I grunted and shoved and slithered out of the tight spot to where I could sit up. I felt a knot rising on one elbow.

Just beyond Marion, Chris Anderson, an amateur cave photographer from Kentucky, had clipped himself into a rope rigged to bolts set in the ceiling. The blackness at his back seemed to swallow all light.

"On rappel!" he shouted to those already at the bottom. He stepped backward and vanished.

Anderson, a highway patrolman by day, devoted thousands of dollars and hundreds of hours to photo-documenting the large chambers of Rumbling Falls. He took the photo CNN had carried the previous fall. On this day in 2002 he and a team of seven assistants would record the first-ever images of Gary's Chamber (the name is a play on Gary Chambers, who discovered it), a gigantic room nearly two miles downriver.

It was a crowded day for the cave. Stephen Alvarez—a Tennessee photographer famous in the caving community for his *National Geographic* images taken around the globe—was there, scouting locations for a later photo shoot. Marion and caver Steve Collins, meanwhile, were leading Anderson's team to Gary's Chamber. Then they planned to survey a side passage that remained incompletely explored.

If, that is, Marion could get the writer he was tour-guiding to get a move-on.

"Off rope!" a distant voice echoed.

A caver descends into the black void of Stupendous Pit.

I rappelled next.

At first, the only view was colored bands of rock on the nearest wall and the tiny twinkling lights of cavers twenty stories below. They appeared to spin slowly as the rope twisted under my weight. I saw essentially the same view at Borbollón, even though the distant cavers there were five hundred feet farther away. Because two of the most famous pits in TAG are named Fantastic and Incredible, Marion decided to name this drop Stupendous Pit. From where I sat, the name fit.

The far wall and most of the room were lost in darkness. I had heard that the Rumble Room was unusually black, not only because of its size, but because of suspended dust. Looking around me, I saw that was not exactly the case. What surrounded me appeared to be millions of tiny, discrete water droplets floating in air. They undulated in waves reflected by the light of my helmet lamp, like phosphorescent beads within the body of some monstrous jellyfish.

I wondered what sort of microbial ecosystems might be hovering about me. Although blind fish, cave crayfish, and other endangered species had been found living in the river below, I knew that no microbiologist had yet entered this cave (and to my knowledge that remains the case today). While the Rumbling Falls exploration appeared to be winding down, its scientific study had barely begun.

Not for the first time, I marveled that the state of Tennessee came within a hair's breadth of dumping millions of gallons of treated effluent into this hidden wonderland.

Spencer, founded in 1840, sits atop the Cumberland Plateau just outside Fall Creek Falls State Park. The town of 1,600 is home to a small college, long defunct, that now serves as a library; the Van Buren county courthouse; a Mayberry-sized jail (in 2002, when I was there; fifteen years later it was destroyed by fire, replaced with a new jail and sheriff's office in 2018); a gas station-slash-pizza parlor-slash-convenience store; three diners; and a passably good horse show. Just out from the center of town, Spencer claimed a great deal of undeveloped real estate, much of it offering stunning mountain views suitable for vacation retreats, but for one thing holding developers back: the sewage problem.

Like many small towns, Spencer had no municipal sewage system, requiring residents to install septic tanks. The sandstone cap that protects the limestone beds of the plateau is very slow to accept drainage, especially at times of heavy rain. Translation: the contents of septic tanks sometimes bubbled up out of the ground like crude oil. A 1996 study showed that 46 percent of Spencer's 538 septic systems were releasing sewage into the yards of houses, schools, and business.

The tank behind the sheriff's office and jail routinely overflowed to cover the floor of one cell. "It backs up here and you can't stand the smell," Sheriff Donnie Evans said. "You just have to put up with it."

When the jail sludge would finally dissipate, it tended to flow downhill into a residential backyard—the one behind the frame house where the mayor's parents lived at the time. Mayor Terry Crain, a high school teacher and basketball coach, at that time also worked as a real estate agent with a company listing those undeveloped sensational views. (He later cut his real estate ties). The mayor, like other local politicians, was no stranger to phone calls demanding that something be done.

Some of the undeveloped property belonged to a resident in a position to do something: Shelby Rhinehart, a Spencer native and the senior member of the Tennessee House of Representatives. First elected in 1958, by 1989 he had become chair of the house commerce committee and one of the state's most powerful lawmakers. A former Spencer mayor, he was well aware of the problems faced by current residents. Over several years in the mid-1990s, Rhinehart procured federal grants and long-term federal loans to pay for a sewage plant.

The original plans called for discharge of the treated effluent into the Caney Fork River, eight miles away. But when bids came in, easements and pipeline costs would have pushed the residential sewage bill to over $100 per month. So the town settled on a smaller drainage close at hand: Dry Fork Creek, a wooded stream the state had designated "Tier II," or highest quality.

Although no one knew it at the time, Dry Fork Creek was the principal source of the river flowing through Rumbling Falls Cave. Nashville cavers, aware of other caves in the area and the potential for new discoveries, began fighting the plans through a variety of means, to little avail.

Town managers insisted that the treated outflow from the plant, which would serve fewer than seven hundred households, would not degrade the stream. State officials offered only minimal public notice and held no public hearings on the plan. But before it could become official, the town had to obtain a permit to discharge effluent into Dry Fork from the state's Water Quality Control Board. Rhinehart assumed it was a forgone conclusion the permit would be granted.

Rope zipping through my rack, I touched down on a rocky hillside. Boulders the size of cars and trucks lay scattered below me, vanishing in the darkness toward what I knew must be the Rumble River. The floor of the room encompassed over four acres, making it the second largest cave chamber known in the United States. But at any one moment an individual caver could illuminate only a few feet of it. One reason cavers volunteered to hump gear for photographers was that the elaborate exposures would enable them to finally see the places they had been.

The team gathered atop a flattish boulder in the center of the room to wait for the rest to drop in. We drank water, snacked a little, and stowed our vertical gear, which we wouldn't use beyond this point. Although I had never met Anderson or any of the members of his photo team, as usual in TAG we had several friends in common.

I was reminded of one of the truths of caving: the greatest pleasure is not the cave, but the group. Whenever you travel with other people— even strangers—into places that noncavers can barely imagine let alone pass safely through, you share a bond far deeper and immediate than that of, say, Sunday golfers. An almost magical camaraderie spreads through a team as it moves away from the surface world and into a truly alien realm. You become instant veterans of a deeply involving physical experience, one that will remain unknown and unknowable to anyone who wasn't there.

I suspect this is part of the reason that Marion kept the survey of Rumbling Falls secret for twenty months after the Rumble Room was found.

"It's a group thing," he insisted. "It was always a group thing. All the decisions were made by the group." The primary mapping team by that point included Marion, Swartz, Chambers, and the addition of Knoxville caver Jack Thomison. Marion insisted they all had "equal say" in the project.

It is human nature to feel proprietary about one's discoveries. There's a phrase in TAG: "scooping booty." It means pushing into virgin finds within a cave already discovered and under survey by someone else. TAG caver Jim Smith became briefly notorious in the 1980s for scooping booty in Great Expectations. Marion chose not to tell Smith about the Rumbling survey, and as a result Jim wouldn't speak to him for nine years.

"I decided I didn't want anyone with an ego as big as mine involved in this project," Marion said in 2002, although he added that the primary mapping team had discussed "several times" inviting Jim to join the project, but "they always deferred to a later occasion." Altogether nine people knew of the survey, including Gerald Moni who descended Stupendous Pit in November 1998 but did not participate in mapping trips.

We followed Marion and his ego downriver, plodding along the muddy bank before cutting to an upper-level bypass on the right.

"We'll have to crawl some this way," he said. "But if we went the other way, you'd have to wade through chest deep water in places. Besides, I left a rope up here that I need to fetch."

I moved just behind Marion. Revitalized from resting in the big room, I was mostly able to keep up. Rumbling Falls is not a terribly difficult cave, as cavers judge difficulty—it just keeps going and going. "The first mile isn't that remarkable," Steve Alvarez had said at the top of the big pit. "But by the time you hit the third and fourth mile, it's pretty amazing."

Gary Chambers puts it more succinctly: "It's the death of a thousand cuts."

Although the passage size remained large, at least in the main river and for quite some distance in the bypass Marion led us down, every step required attention and vigilance. Movement in a cave is constant problem solving. It's like driving a four-wheel-drive truck down a bad mountain road: *If I steer to the right, I can straddle that big trench, but then I need to cut to the left to avoid that crumbling ledge, and I better put the left tire on that big rock to keep it off my oil pan.*

The difference is that in a cave your feet, knees, and hands take the place of knobby tires, and you move in three dimensions: *It'll be easier if I go around this rock to the right, but then I'll have an overhung climb, so I better go over the top now. If I dig my boots in sideways on this mud bank, I can scramble to that ledge for a few feet of fairly easy walking. And if I walk with my head tilted to the left, I won't be coldcocked by that rock dangling from the ceiling.*

My choices were easier at that moment: I crawled where Marion crawled, climbed where he climbed. In 2002 there were young TAG cavers stronger and faster underground than Marion, but he possessed an unmatched endurance and determination. Despite a bad back, fading eyesight, and other infirmities of age, he seemed impervious to pain, unable to sit still with going passage ahead of him.

Eventually we left the crawlway and returned to the river in a spacious junction hall, Marion sprinting ahead. The next half-mile became a muddy slog. Sometimes I walked in the cool shallows of the muddy stream, other times I scrambled over slick rocks poking from deeper water.

Luckily, the water level that day was relatively low. On one occasion during the survey, Marion, Chambers, and Swartz had attempted to head downriver at high water in one-man rafts. Chambers launched his raft and was quickly swept fifty feet downstream. He managed to paddle to shore and grab a rock, and shouted at the others not to follow.

"John didn't believe me," Chambers recalled. "He jumped in and shot farther downstream than I had. He looked like a little cartoon character, paddling for all he was worth. He barely made it to shore, and as he did a rock punctured his raft and sank it."

From that point forward, Marion had cancelled any survey trip when the river was up.

As we moved along the rocky path above the river, we hit an obstacle I dubbed the Butter Horse. It was the only way forward: a piece of limestone about the size, shape, and height of a horse, deep holes to either side. It was covered in at least four inches of slick mud. The fast and the brave could cross its spine in three or four strides. I chose instead to straddle the rock horsy style, moving forward in little hops on my hands. At the far end, I slid down a muddy shoot, taking care to keep a boot forward to break the slide, as using my shin or hand could have proved enormously painful.

Shortly beyond the Butter Horse, I caught up to Marion waiting for me on a high ledge with a commanding view of the river. Beside him a survey station was burned onto the wall: B94.

"Look at this," he said. He gestured toward the winding river and the darkness beyond, reminding me of a painting I once saw of Lewis and Clark. "We reached this survey station and the end of a long trip, so that was the last one we set that day. Map as you go means map as you go, so we turned around here. I've never in my life turned around with that much virgin cave ahead of me. Gary wanted to go ahead, but I restrained him, saying, 'We'll be back next weekend.'"

I looked at the view and marveled at their forbearance.

While Marion and his crew were surveying by the book, they weren't exactly sharing. As the Nashville Grotto of the NSS prepared to fight the state to keep effluent out of the small, known resurgent caves down Dry Fork Creek, they remained in the dark about the discoveries in Rumbling Falls. At one point, John "Fred" Hutchison, who had found the cave, asked a member of the survey team how mapping was going.

"Marion's mapping miles and miles of crawlway," was the answer—true as far as it went. Nothing was said about the many more miles of gigantic walking passage being mapped.

With every survey effort, some of them lasting as long as twenty-five hours, Smith and his crew mapped their way into new chambers. There was Gary's Chamber, approximately 350 by 150 feet, with a 150-foot high ceiling; John's Room, 300 by 100 feet; and Birthday's Bonanza—found during the week between Swartz's birthday and Marion's in September 1999—an 800-foot-long breakdown chamber with walls over 150 feet apart. Not to mention that they found many hidden formations, including a profusion of white helictites within a passage that his friends named Goat's Paradise.

The Rumble River flowing through Gary's Chamber. The author held the flash array lighting the lower right.

"A lot of people will tell you Marion Smith is greedy," Smith told a reporter who later questioned him about the secrecy. "Well, we were greedy. It was a gift from the caving gods late in my career."

But as news of the sewage plant and the Nashville Grotto's fight against it spread, the survey team realized they would have to go public. The only question was when. Gary Chambers argued privately in favor of doing so at a public hearing, but none was scheduled. A few back-channel efforts by the group led to nothing. Jack Thomison convinced them it was time to act, so on March 23, 2000, Marion met privately with officials in the Tennessee Department of Environment and Conservation to describe the cave and their concerns for its future.

To no avail. Despite strong internal dissent from within TDEC, construction was soon underway. In September 2000, a coalition of environmental groups filed suit in federal court, seeking an injunction to stop the town from using federal funds for the plant until an alternative discharge method could be found. That lawsuit ultimately failed, but continued efforts by the coalition and supporters from within TDEC and EPA led to the public commentary that had been denied the first time. During one meeting where commentary was allowed, Rhinehart attacked the environmental coalition as "a bunch of city people from Nashville" who knew nothing about the area or the needs of its citizens.

Since no environmental study of the cave had yet been done or ordered by the state, area cavers and environmentalists decided to counter the town's efforts by funding one on their own. Julian Lewis, an Indiana biologist, discovered nearly a dozen species of aquatic cave life found in fewer than ten locations in the world, and two small organisms found nowhere else.

The discharge of effluent into Rumbling Falls "would poison it just as surely as if you put arsenic in it," Lewis said. "It would have a devastating impact."

The night before a public hearing in November 2000, when it seemed the sewage battle was all but lost, Marion agreed to go public with the Rumble Room and the true dimensions of the cave's passages. His former girlfriend Debby, then president of the Nashville Grotto, called key cavers who had been working with environmental coalition to fight the sewage discharge to invite them to a private meeting that night.

"It was all very hush-hush," recalled one of the cavers who received the call. "She said the meeting was important, but she wouldn't say what it was about."

At the meeting, Marion displayed eighteen photos of the cave, its gigantic dimensions plain to see. The group had been calling Rumbling Falls by a code name, "Ursula Newman Cave," and Marion placed the name on a list of the longest caves in Tennessee.

"At first we were stunned speechless," the caver said. "Then we felt betrayed. This was the cave the Nashville Grotto had been hunting for over twenty years, and Marion had kept it all to himself."

Chris Anderson used $800 worth of antique flashbulbs, hauled in by a crew of ten strong cavers, to take a panoramic photo of the Rumble Room that was used at the press conference. "For the first time ever, everyone could see the immensity of the room," he recalled in a later interview. "Five seconds, a fleeting time for sure, and then the bulbs faded out, the camera shut down, and the applause broke out."

The Nashville cavers and Marion's crew presented a united front at the public hearing where the photograph was revealed, but shortly after the meeting, Debby Johnson was asked to step down as grotto president for her complicity in the Rumbling Falls deception.

"They're basically jealous," Swartz said unapologetically. "They wish they had found this cave, and they didn't." While Swartz admitted that the Nashville crowd included "some good, strong cavers," he added, "If they had found Rumbling, we wouldn't have a 15.7 mile cave today. We'd be lucky to have five or six miles mapped. They would have scooped a lot of passage, and would never have pushed the leads as thoroughly as we did."

None of the publicity, however, seemed to influence the Water Quality Control Board, which again reversed itself and granted a "final" discharge permit for Dry Fork Creek in December. After failure in federal court, the only legal recourse left open to environmental groups was to seek an injunction against the plant in local chancery court, while persuading the legislature's conservation and environment committee to look into the irregularities in the permitting process. Both efforts were considered unlikely propositions by local legal observers.

Shelby Rhinehart told the conservation committee that the sewage plant was "none of its business." "I just cannot fathom why people that's probably never been in that area very much would all of a sudden make this a project," he said in a committee hearing. "You're jumping on the wrong horse."

Sidney Jones, the TDEC engineer who had advised against the permit nearly two years earlier, resigned over the issue, writing to his supervisor, "The opinions of field staff like you and I, who deal directly with the consequences of any problems created by the discharge, apparently counted for very little."

A hearing was set for February in Davidson County Chancery Court. Less than ten days before the sewage plant was to come online, Chancellor Ellen Hobbs Lyle ruled that the state's permitting process was "substantially flawed by incorrect procedure, and incorrect application and construction of the law." Lyle declared Spencer's permit invalid; the cave was safe.

The battle was won, but so far as many cavers of the Nashville Grotto were concerned, Marion Smith's name was mud.

Marion Smith exiting Rumbling Falls on the early morning of July 28, 2002.

Which was the substance I slipped in when at last I rounded a corner and spotted Marion and the team gathered on a broad gravel bank. Beyond them, an arch of proportions suggesting a Broadway proscenium framed a blackness that could only be Gary's Chamber. The tired photo Sherpas had dumped their loads and settled in for a meal before a planned two-hour shoot. I did the same. Marion, of course, was antsy to survey, so he and Steve Collins vanished into the gloom, their lamps rising like distant rockets as they scrambled up a one-hundred-foot slope toward an unmapped lead above Gary's Chamber.

After lunch, I passed through the arch to hike up a rock-strewn underground hillside, dodging skittering breakdown blocks loosed by the cavers ahead of me. They sounded like breaking china as they tumbled toward the dark river. I ducked under a protective overhang to watch the explosive flashes of Chris Anderson's lighting system paint the gigantic room with light. For two or three seconds, the vision was seared into my retinas: a huge, gracefully curving space, lined with rust-colored bands of limestone, dwarfing the few human explorers strung along its flank. Then the flashes faded, and I was once more alone with the small cone of light projected from my helmet.

Many hours later, I sat alone in the Rumble Room. The last member of the photo team, Tim Curtis, was on rope, nearing the top of the two-hundred-foot climb. Tim and I had walked together in the river for over an hour after we left Gary's Chamber, but we had chosen different routes and became separated.

"I ended up alone in the river," he said later. "I missed the high and dry bypass so I found myself in a rough predicament, headed into deeper water, alone as far as I could see, hugging the wall."

The floor became giant slabs of angled rock covered in mud. He couldn't stand on it without being pulled into the river. He didn't want to swim because it would douse his carbide lamp. "I just had to work my way through it," Curtis said. "It was quite scary."

We finally met up again in the Rumble Room. Meanwhile, the first pair up Stupendous Pit had found a dangerously worn spot in one of the two ropes rigged on the way in, so it was hauled up. I had quite a wait as one by one Anderson's team ascended the remaining line, but I needed the break. *Man, I gotta get in shape.* Marion and Steve were still somewhere down the Rumble River, mapping virgin passage, shining their lights where no light had been.

I was to be the last one up. I turned off my lamp to savor the silence and dark that is the cave's natural state. I could barely make out the climbing caver: a single star floating in an empty sky. It would be midnight by the time I exited, a fifteen-hour trip. Marion wouldn't be out until long after three.

I could feel bruises and scratches forming a map of the cave on my body. I knew it would be many weeks before I would feel the call to go underground again, to see the places that only a few skilled and determined—and sometimes lucky and greedy—cavers can reveal in a world so thoroughly explored. But I would return in a few months to follow Marion into a historic saltpeter cave and into many other caves over the ensuing years. Less than two weeks before his sixtieth birthday party, Rep. Shelby Rhinehart would suffer a fatal stroke near the end of the legislative session.

I knew, without having to ask, that Marion would be back underground within days, would have made a dozen trips long before my bruises began to fade and I contemplated another drive to TAG.

It's what he does.

Kristen Bobo laughs at the buffoonery of Gerald Moni and Marion Smith, Scotts Gulf Area, White County, Tennessee.

CHUCK SUTHERLAND | Flickr post, August 2008

Went spelunking with my two favorite old geezers, Marion Smith and Gerald Moni. Not much changes. Marion grunts, complains, and cusses. Gerald endlessly pontificates about the world according to Gerald. It was nice being underground with both of them.

ALAN CRESSLER | Facebook post, December 23, 2017

Chapter 14

SAVING SECRETS

Among the many pits and caves Lee Pearson showed me during the year I lived at my cousin's house in Kentucky, several were kept secret due to delicate landowner relations, delicate formations, or some combination of both, but only one was actually named Secret Cave. It was located at the edge of a growing real estate subdivision. The entrance pit dropped twenty-two feet to a ledge, followed immediately by a second thirty-four-foot pit. We did them both on a single eighty-foot rope. Regardless of rigging, such a drop could present a grave danger to children within the subdivision should they happen to discover it. But the main reason the cave was kept secret was where you landed at the bottom: an enormous room profusely decorated with stalactites, stalagmites, rimstone, and flowstone that resembled rivers of chocolate and caramel ice cream. The active formations, glistening with a sheen of water that constantly added tiny mineral deposits to their mass, dripped and flowed in a dozen hues. They circled the large chamber in greater profusion than can be found in many tour caves. If their delicate existence became widely known, the site would likely be overrun with visitors. Moreover, additional pits led from the main room, and the injury or death of a careless spelunker so close to a residential street would probably close

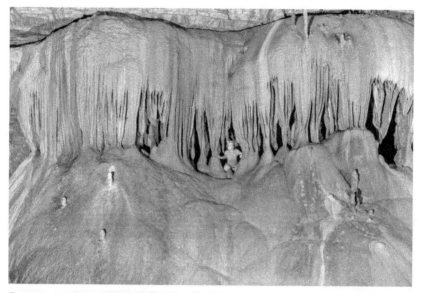

Formations in Secret Cave, Cookeville, Tennessee.

the cave to everyone. I followed Lee's instructions, staying on the path cavers had laid and promising not to mention Secret Cave to others once I was away from Cookeville.

Six years later, a geologist and caver named Albert Ogden (who also happened to be the founder and lead singer of the all-caver rock band Terminal Syphons) moved to Cookeville to become a geology professor at Tennessee Technological University. Not long after he arrived, members of the Upper Cumberland Grotto took him to see Secret Cave. When he climbed out he boldly exclaimed, as he put it in 2019, "If this land ever comes up for sale, I'm going to buy it to protect the cave." A year later, he did exactly that, developing a management plan for the cave. He produced a video showcasing the cave's beauty and need for safekeeping. Three decades later, in the fall of 2018, he oversaw the transfer of ownership to the National Speleological Society, making it the society's eighteenth NSS cave preserve.

On August 17, 1980, Tom Miller and Pete Shifflett entered a small, un-explored cave near a dry streambed in a remote canyon of Wyoming's

Bighorn Mountains. Just inside the entrance of what they named Dumb Luck cave, the two encountered the stream absent from the surface: a surging force of thirty-nine-degree-Fahrenheit whitewater constrained within a wide crawlway. The passage was seldom more than two feet high—and often much lower than one foot. They pushed their way upstream through the icy water, snagging clothing on razor-sharp rocks and losing bits of gear, ripped free by the current. Several times, the two had to back up in places only inches high in order to try other routes. But they pressed on, in hopes of connecting with a larger known cave whose entrance lay five miles away and 1,400 feet higher in elevation.

After hours spent exploring 1,500 feet of the most miserable—and potentially deadliest—belly crawl imaginable, Miller and Shifflett emerged to walking passage. They began a series of exposed climbs up waterfalls and through plunge pools, until eventually they reached familiar tunnels and beyond them the upper entrance, over seven miles up the canyon from the spot where they had entered. Theirs would ultimately be remembered as one of the single greatest US caving trips of the twentieth century. By connecting Dumb Luck with Great Expectations Cave, the two established a new US cave depth record (one that would be surpassed a few years later by Lechuguilla Cave). Dumb Luck was later renamed Great Exit, and the traverse from upper to lower entrance became known as the most difficult caving through-trip in North America, perhaps the most difficult anywhere.

On August 17, 2005, a quarter century after his discovery trip through the "Grim Crawl of Death," Pete Shifflett returned to Great Expectations. In celebration of his fiftieth birthday, Shifflett led what he called "an old fart through-trip" of five of the cavers who had played pivotal roles in the original exploration and mapping of Great X, the nickname by which cavers everywhere know the challenging cave. These six (some of whom began their caving careers in TAG), along with six younger cavers, safely traversed between the two entrances with amazing speed for such a large group, reaching the Great Exit a mere sixteen hours after entering the Crisco Crack at the upper end.

"There are moments in the Grim Crawl of Death when the seat is torn out of your wetsuit and rocks are scraping your bare bottom that you begin to question the intelligence of doing this," recalled Bob

Montgomery, who at fifty-one was only second oldest on the 2005 through-trip, "but then you realize that this is world class alpine caving, a true once-in-a-lifetime experience."

It was Shifflett's eighth—and, he claimed, final—Great X through-trip. "I'm probably no longer strong enough to do serious work in the cave," he admitted. "I have a distinct feeling that I've beaten the odds more often than I deserve."

The cavers, like much of their gear, had changed appearance somewhat in twenty-five years, although the cave remained the same. With its isolated mountain location, snowed-in most of the year, Great X sees very little human visitation. Its passages appear just as they did in 1980 when the first carbide lamps penetrated their darkness (although the fossil-lined walls may shine differently in the glare of modern LED headlamps). Yet in human terms, the cave had invisibly undergone great change in the quarter century since Shifflett and Miller first established the entrance connection: it now belonged to the explorers who traversed it. Specifically, Great Expectation's upper entrance and forty surrounding acres (including several other known caves) were purchased by the NSS in 2003 as its twelfth underground preserve. By Shifflett's trip in the fall of 2005, contributors within the society had nearly repaid the purchase price of $192,936.16.

Like Secret Cave, Great X is just one of dozens of celebrated American caves that once lay in private hands. In a growing national trend, researchers, conservationists, and recreational explorers have banded together to preserve their most precious resources, raising money to purchase and protect caves and karst lands. The NSS and a host of other nonprofit organizations, including the American Cave Conservation Association, the Southeastern Cave Conservancy, the Texas Cave Management Association, and the Nature Conservancy have become legal owners of hundreds of caves. Additional cave-bearing properties are leased or managed under long-term arrangements with cooperative landowners. With large-scale purchases and acquisitions, these private organizations have begun to take a seat at the table with state parks and other public preserves in developing comprehensive regional plans for cave conservation and management.

As underground wilderness becomes increasingly threatened by expanding development and shrinking forests, as cave life suffers from groundwater pollution and increased human traffic, group purchases offer hope for preservation. And to explorers like me, they offer a promise of future access to caves once closed by private owners fearful of accidents or lawsuits.

A popular pit with cavers for decades, Neversink was always located on private property. When the land changed hands in 1991, the new owners, fearful of lawsuits, immediately closed the pit. By this time many "classic" TAG pits and caves had been similarly closed, including Valhalla, South Pittsburg Pit, and Run to the Mill. Georgia cavers Jeff and Alexis Harris called a meeting of about twenty TAG cavers to discuss not only buying Neversink, but creating a conservancy modeled after the Nature Conservancy to purchase and manage many cave preserves. The founding notion of the Southeastern Cave Conservancy, Inc. (SCCi), is that these caves would be "preserved" not only for the sake of conservation and education, but for continued—if well regulated—recreational access by cavers.

Just as the fledgling organization was developing its plans, Georgia caver Chuck Henson offered to donate property containing an entrance to Howard's Waterfall, a popular cave, to a caving organization. None of the Atlanta area caving clubs felt ready to take on direct ownership, but the new group realized that by incorporating in order to manage Henson's donation, they could possibly gain control of Neversink and other popular TAG caves. They began negotiating with a real estate agent to buy the property, but in 1993 the cave was sold to another private owner who bypassed the agent.

"Neversink was a learning experience," recalled John Hickman, a former director of SCCi. "It was sold twice while we were trying to buy it."

In 1995 the organization finally acquired Neversink for $51,000. Most of the money used to purchase the property was donated by individual cavers in exchange for an "I Bought a Piece of the Pit" T-shirt. I would see them at almost every caver gathering over the next decade. After Neversink, other pits and caves soon followed. By 2019, the organization managed over 170 caves on thirty-one preserves within six states, including the fabled Surprise Pit entrance of Fern Cave. The stakes in acquiring these caves were urgent: beyond the much-needed protection of cave life and formations, SCCi offered the best hope for keeping TAG classics open to human exploration.

On September 7, 1867, while en route to Mammoth Cave, Kentucky, naturalist John Muir stopped in the vicinity at lesser-known Horse Cave, so named because "horse" was a local synonym for "big." In his book *A Thousand-Mile Walk to the Gulf*, Muir wrote of the place: "It seems a noble gateway to . . . springs and fountains and the dark treasuries of the mineral kingdom. This cave lies in a village of the same name which it supplies with an abundance of cold water. Cold air issues from its fern-clad lips. In hot weather crowds of people sit about in the shade of the trees that guard it. This magnificent fan is capable of cooling everybody in town at once."

Within fifty years of Muir's visit, Horse Cave proved capable of disgusting everybody in town at once. In the 1920s and '30s, raw

A caver descends into Neversink, now managed by the Southeastern Cave Conservancy, Inc.

sewage—thick with spoiled whey from a local creamery—was piped directly into the underground stream. The "magnificent fan" spread the stench for miles, making the town virtually uninhabitable every summer for six decades. Heavy metals from a chromium factory further polluted the abundance of cold water. Various commercial tours failed, including one that changed the name to Hidden River, which is the preferred name today. In 1943, the cavern was closed to the public as a health hazard—at a time when cavers had spotted tantalizing unexplored passages leading from the known trails.

After nearly fifty years of closure, a project begun in 1986 made Hidden River Cave, née Horse, once again safe for human visitation. The American Cave Conservation Association (ACCA), a small nonprofit founded in Richmond, Virginia, relocated to Hidden River Cave that year with the goal of restoring the cave and establishing a karst museum and educational center at the site. On September 8, 1991, David Foster, longtime president of the ACCA, led the first Cave Research Foundation survey trip into the cave he had spent five years cleaning up, both figuratively and literally.

"This cave may be longer than Mammoth," an excited Foster said after that first trip. Once beyond the restored scenic entrance, Foster's team followed a fifty-foot-diameter trunk lined with massive mud banks. For two thousand feet they skirted the remains of an old wooden tourist trail.

"It was a gloomy, dark place," recalled caver James Wells. "Chunks of rotting wood poked up from the mud. They crumbled at the slightest touch. The walls seemed to suck up light. But the cave was amazingly clean. We crossed a place the old-timers used to call the Cottage Cheese Swim, because of all the floating whey. I didn't see a trace of white in the water. The air smelled fine."

The "cottage cheese" had vanished thanks to two new waste treatment plants, a $15 million project that diverted sewage and whey from the cave. Volunteer crews removed decades of refuse that had blocked the entrance area. The town of Horse Cave (it kept the name) supported Foster's efforts by joining in the construction of a $2 million museum devoted to caves and cave conservation. The American Cave and Karst Center opened in July 1992. The restoration of the cave—once one of the most polluted sites in America—became a model for cave and karst managers on public lands, as well as a model for cavers interested in purchasing and protecting caves currently in private hands.

Throughout the 1990s and early 2000s, Foster and others mapped over seven miles of new passage in Hidden River Cave. Using software that aligns the map of Hidden River Cave with satellite photographic data, a study by the Cave Research Foundation was able to locate contemporary sources of groundwater pollution entering the cave stream. While the river of whey and horrible stench are distant memories, the fight to preserve karst waters is ongoing and continues to improve with technology. Meanwhile, casual visitors can tour the karst museum and cave, while the more adventurous can try its commercial zip line or rappelling experience.

The sheer drive to explore and experience the underground draws many to caving, but personal interest often gives way to furthering science and conservation, in both individuals and in groups that own major cave systems. Although the SCCi had been founded primarily to insure recreational access to popular caves such as Neversink and Howard's Waterfall, the organization soon became involved in conservation and scientific management. Working with the Nature Conservancy in Tennessee and other states, the SCCi began identifying properties that contained rare species and important archeological material. Soon the SCCi owned many caves that were significant for reasons beyond thrilling rappels.

In 2002, with help from the Tennessee Nature Conservancy and Bat Conservation International, the organization purchased property containing the cave commonly known as Jaguar at an estate auction. This cave combines all of the good reasons for preservation and management by a cave-specific organization: it contains miles of passage, with portions decorated by pristine and beautiful formations; it is home to a large colony of endangered bats; it contains claw marks and remains of ice age mammals; and it contains the oldest known human footprints in the dark zone of a cave, left 4,500 years ago by Native American explorers. When I had entered with Lou Simpson in the 1990s, we referred to it as "Blowing" or "Jaguar" just to keep potential vandals

A caver admires a flowstone formation in Howard's Waterfall, now a protected cave.

from learning its location. Now that its location is secure, SCCi uses the actual name in describing the cave's many wonders in preserve literature and on its website. In keeping with the conventions of Tennessee's Cave Archeology Research Team, as established by Jan Simek, Alan Cressler, and others, I prefer to stick with Jaguar in print—but by any name, this archeological treasure is now protected.

On a recreational trip to Great Expectations in 2002, cavers discovered the entrance area was for sale: A real estate agent was showing the property to a prospective buyer who hoped to develop it as a vacation retreat. Cavers had long enjoyed positive relations with the owner, a third-generation cattle rancher. (He once helped me haul my camping gear out of the canyon with his ATV after I visited the Grim Crawl of Death in 1987.)

"I'd rather see cavers get it than that it be developed," the owner told a group of Wyoming cavers who approached him about the sale.

Bob Montgomery contacted the NSS, which was by then owner of a dozen other cave and nature preserves in the east and southeast, about purchasing the organization's first western cave. "The problem was that we had to move quickly," Montgomery recalled. "There was already a prospective buyer. The NSS Board of Governors was meeting just two weeks after we found out the property was available, and we convinced the board to bypass its usual decision making process because of the urgency." After unanimous approval from the board, Montgomery began the complicated process of negotiating a deal.

No good survey of the property existed, so it was difficult to establish the precise location of the entrance. Moreover, the rancher was interested in acquiring a parcel of land within his ranch that was owned by a third party; rather than selling Great X directly to the NSS, he offered to trade the Great X property in exchange for this parcel, which the NSS would purchase. The entrance property would include a two-hundred-foot buffer zone and two other caves, all requiring surveys that didn't exist at the time of the negotiation.

"This was December," Montgomery recalled, "and the property was snowed in. So we built a clause in the contract that allowed us to move the deed location of the forty acres according to later survey results. As it turned out, we had to shave acreage from the southwest corner and trade it for acreage on the southeast corner."

But once all the surveys were complete, the cave belonged to the NSS, and a management plan was created. "The NSS owning Great X preserves the ability of trained cavers to access a world-class cave," Montgomery said. "But more than that, it insures the continued study and preservation of the cave. There is now more scientific research taking place in Great X than ever before."

"I'm really hoping that some of the younger cavers I've taken through during the past three years will want to go back and make a project of surveying various leads deep in the cave," Pete Shifflett told me after his 2005 through-trip. He said that he believed the cave hides unrevealed secrets, adding, "Maybe. Maybe. It only takes one lead."

In 2006, my old friend and early caving mentor Allen Mosler donated a Florida cave and five acres to the SCCi. Well known to Tallahassee cavers, the small cave near the Chipola River had been the site of several of my earliest grotto trips. Allen had purchased the land many years earlier when the cave had been threatened by surrounding housing developments. The cave has over three thousand feet of passage, nearly all of it involving a great deal of mud and water. Shortly after its donation to SCCi, Alan Cressler found it to contain archeological significance as well.

Protecting caves involves much more than ownership. Jim Wilbanks, part of the group that cofounded SCCi, has deep roots in TAG: he was among the first cavers to stay in Richard Schreiber's TAG house in the mid-1960s and was the third person to descend Fantastic Pit after its discovery in 1968. For over half a century, Wilbanks has been the sort of person to cheerfully volunteer for clean-up crews, convention planning staff, and other not necessarily fun jobs that need doing within the caving community. A generation of TAG novices, myself included, first met Wilbanks by staying at his house, which was generally open to traveling cavers. I recall camping in his yard with a group from Florida State and then later with a group from New Jersey. When the SCCi first formed in 1991, he was soon attending grotto meetings in the region to help promote the idea of a cave conservancy.

At one of these presentations, Maureen Handler signed up as SCCi member number sixty-eight. In the years since, she and Wilbanks have worked together on a variety of conservation projects. After finishing college, Handler used her engineering degree to form a Chattanooga-based business, Southern Environmental Technologies, specializing in environmental monitoring, restoration, and mitigation (company motto: "Cleaning up our world, one acre at a time"). This turned out to be a specialty crucial to cave protection. At a 2001 meeting of the Southeast Regional Association of the NSS (SERA), Wilbanks formed a committee called the SERA Karst Task Force (SKTF), designed to provide resources to other groups—whether cavers, land managers, or conservation organizations—wanting to do cleanups in karst areas.

Well-known caves were often covered in graffiti, while roadside sinkholes often became convenient trash dumps. The first SKTF cleanup was a graffiti removal project in 2002 at popular Lost Creek Cave in Tennessee. Before volunteers could attack decades of spray-painted graffiti on the walls, Dr. Jan Simek first checked for possible Native American artwork and Marion Smith and Joe Douglas checked for possible historic signatures that the modern graffiti might have covered. Satisfied that the

Trash hauled from the Russell Cave National Monument watershed by the SERA Karst Task Force.

damage was relatively recent, volunteer crews used low impact methods to clean the surfaces. A few months after the Lost Creek cleanup, a large group at Stephens Gap filled a thirty-yard dumpster with construction trash in just two hours.

Shortly after this effort, Wilbanks approached Handler about applying her professional expertise to help with even larger projects; she readily agreed. Their first "major" cleanup was Rocky River Cave in Warren County, Tennessee, where Handler led six trips. She adapted rigging methods originally developed for emergency rescue operations. "We perfected the high-line haul system that we used to pull appliances up and out of sinkholes and steep drops," she recalled in 2019. "You used to climb down through the skeletons of old appliances to get into the cave. With six cleanups, we removed about sixteen tons of material out of Rocky River."

Using the haul system and a large group of volunteers, Handler was able to pull tons of trash not only from cave entrances, but also from watersheds affecting the caves. Her daily record was nine tons removed from the Blue Spring watershed. One the biggest cleanups that the task force did focused on the watershed of Russell Cave National Monument in Alabama.

"Over a six-year period we removed over one hundred pounds of debris and trash and over four hundred tires," Handler said. "We've probably done seventy to eighty different cleanup sites, some of them multiple times." The task force received a group conservation award from the National Speleological Society in 2009 for their work.

As he recalled in a 2009 article, "Jim Wilbanks Shaves His Head for the SCCi and Breast Cancer Awareness," Handler once helped get him to shave his head for cave conservation. It began with a group of friends at the annual TAG Fall Cave-In who had shaved their heads in support of a woman undergoing chemotherapy for breast cancer.

"All my life I have had a school or occupation which required having my hair cut and shaving," Wilbanks wrote. "When I retired, I resolved to never cut my hair or shave again. I really liked my hair long." But someone in the conversation at TAG asked him what it would take to get him to shave his head.

"I'd do it for a thousand dollar contribution the SCCi," Wilbanks replied.

Meanwhile, a series of announcements had begun over the event PA system. Handler, who had led the Borbollón expedition in Mexico two decades earlier, took the microphone to discuss an upcoming SERA business meeting. First she announced that she was contributing a hundred dollars toward Wilbanks' haircut. Another caver, Dan Barnick, said that he would add $500 if the target $1000 was raised. As the evening progressed, Wilbanks began to get anxious. "Women were running their hands through my hair and bemoaning their loss," he joked. He discussed maybe just cutting off his lengthy ponytail instead.

Meanwhile, Handler walked through the crowd "with a fistful of cash," raising money. She grabbed the mic to announce that she had $800 and needed "ten more twenty dollar bills." The number was soon reached. Then she asked over the PA system, "How much for the beard?"

"Two hundred dollars," Wilbanks immediately answered. When another caver covered that, he wished he had said $500. Oddly enough, one of the attendees at the TAG event had brought along an electric clipper with a full set of accessories. The shearing was soon accomplished, and SCCi had raised a total of $1700.

In 2019, Handler and Wilbanks, along with caver Troy Fuqua, still led the SERA Karst Task Force in work with SCCi and other organizations, cleaning up karst areas and also educating the public on the importance of clean caves to clean groundwater.

SCCi first became more than an idea with the 1991 donation of Howard's Waterfall Cave by Charles B. "Chuck" Henson of Ringgold, Georgia, who died in 2013 at the age of sixty-seven. Almost twenty-five years later, SCCi received more than 2,300 acres in northwest Georgia from an anonymous donor, along with additional acreage from the Georgia-Alabama Land Trust, Inc. The donation covered an area called Johnson's Crook, home to a classic TAG cave of the same name, along with thirty additional known caves. The tract had belonged to a failed real estate development that landed two men in jail in 2014 for money laundering and wire fraud—luckily for the caves, only a few lots in the scheme ever saw actual construction. The undeveloped land holds potential for new cave discovery and serves as habitat for native wildlife, hardwood forests, and miles of ecological diversity. It was named the Charles B. Henson Preserve at Johnson's Crook in honor of Henson's key role in cave conservation.

While conservation groups have protected caves and kept them open to exploration, caving—especially vertical caving—will always be dangerous. The classic pits managed by SCCi require advance permitting, a minimum group size, and other evidence of preparation, but that can't change the reality that rigging a pit involves inherent risk. In 2019, both Stephens Gap and Valhalla saw fatalities. In one case, an inexperienced and unpermitted caver snuck onto the property and fell off a ledge. In another case, a highly experienced rock climber joined a permitted college group, but apparently attempted to cross a knot near the rig point—a tricky caving maneuver that rock climbers seldom need to learn—and fell to his death.

In such cases, private owners would inevitably close a cave permanently. Potentially avoidable tragedies like these have instead caused

SCCi and other conservancies to temporarily close sites. The managers study the incidents and examine whether any change in management policies might save lives in the future. But in the end, the responsibility for safe caving will always lie with the individual. Climbing, scuba diving, hang gliding, motocross racing, driving on the interstate, hustling pool, jaywalking a city street—like caving, all these things are inherently dangerous. Those who learn to minimize the dangers of caving, to treat each trip as if it might be their last, find overcoming the risk rewarding in ways difficult to express to others, ways that nonetheless change their lives for the better.

In the early heyday of TAG exploration, the remote mountains and gulfs hid pits and caves that locals considered wild curiosities, if they thought of them at all. Roads were bad and trails were faint. Except for the occasional logging operation or well-guarded moonshine still, the vast limestone landscape was generally open to anyone with the gumption to explore. That world has largely vanished. Today only careful conservation and management can keep wild places open to new discovery, research, and recreation. Luckily cavers have proven themselves up to the task.

SOCIAL INTERLUDE

FROM: Taylor, Michael   Wed, Jul 30, 2014, 10:54 AM
TO: Taylor, Kathryn L.
SUBJECT: Classic Lee caving trip

Last night I hiked over 7 miles on a mountain looking for a cave. Now I am at parts store with Lee to get a new thermostat for his car. Classic Lee and Sharon trip!

FROM: Taylor, Kathryn L.   Wed, Jul 30, 2014, 11:14 AM
TO: Taylor, Michael
SUBJECT: RE: Classic Lee caving trip

I bet you did not find the cave last night either.

FROM: Taylor, Michael   Wed, Jul 30, 2014, 12:02 PM
TO: Taylor, Kathryn L.
SUBJECT: RE: Classic Lee caving trip

No comment.

FROM: Taylor, Michael   Wed, Jul 30, 2014, 12:06 PM
TO: Taylor, Kathryn L.
SUBJECT: RE: Classic Lee caving trip

However, we did find two great leads near Rumbling Falls, one of which the landowner took us to on a wild 4-wheeler ride with me and Lee hanging on for dear life.

FROM: Taylor, Kathryn L.   Wed, Jul 30, 2014, 12:12 PM

TO: Taylor, Michael

SUBJECT: RE: Classic Lee caving trip

I hear dueling banjos in the background. You did see the movie, right?

Chapter 15

SLOW GOING

Most caves change negligibly in a million years, while most cavers have an annoying tendency to start aging noticeably after about thirty. They may be active underground, but if you run into the same folks at enough gatherings you will notice the arrival of gray hair, wrinkles, and the occasional pronounced limp.

Some, like Karen Witte, former president of the FSCC and the first person to wriggle into the large chambers of Boyer's Discovery, blow out their knees and quit caving altogether. After years of hardcore Mexico trips, she hung up her helmet to become a commercial airline pilot and elk rancher, with only a few cave photos on the wall as evidence of her youthful obsession. On assignment to *National Geographic* in 1981, she and the late caver Ernie Garza mapped the Mayan cave Naj Tunich in Guatemala. He and I took a detour from the 1996 NSS convention in Salida, Colorado, to visit her comfortable ranch in the mountains. We helped feed her elk.

Other cavers keep plugging along, although you overhear them in the convention hot tub swapping stories of knee and shoulder replacements, heart conditions, chemotherapy, obscure tropical diseases picked up on third-world expeditions, and just general wear and tear. So it was with Lee and me.

His first indication of a potential problem came during the 2007 NSS convention, held that year in Indiana. I had reserved a large double hotel room for the event, which I offered to share with Lee and Sharon for the last three days since they did not want to spend a full week camping in southern Indiana in July. (Kathy, home with the kids, had no interest in Indiana at all.) The more fun place to stay at any cave convention is the campground. I was, however, traveling with guitars, amps, and other sound equipment best not left in the heat. Starting with the 1991 NSS convention in Schoharie, New York, I had become a bass player for the all-caver rock band Terminal Syphons. We had scheduled a four-hour show for the Wednesday night campground party. The convention was only one stop on the Pearsons' summer vacation to various points west.

For most of its 981 miles, the Ohio River borders hilly karst lands. The geography of Midwestern states like Ohio, Indiana, and Illinois comprises vast tracts of flat farmland, yet these states' southern extremities resemble the cave-and-sinkhole-riddled forests of Kentucky and West Virginia. The Indiana convention guidebook described many caves (mostly small) and pits (mostly under one hundred feet deep) in Crawford and Harrison counties. Lee and I planned to spend Thursday hitting these old school: just the two of us, with our TAG-tested Mitchell and rope-walker climbing systems. I considered the cave day something of a reward for making it through a hectic Monday, Tuesday, and Wednesday.

At almost every NSS convention since 1985, Dr. Albert Ogden opens and closes the Wednesday night campground party by saying, "Thanks for coming to our annual practice." In reality, the Terminal Syphons typically spend hours on Monday or Tuesday (and some years both) practicing a list of forty or so songs, with brief breaks whenever a band member has to present a convention session or sit on a panel actually related to caving. Then we spend much of Wednesday setting up the campground sound system, stage lights, and so on for a dance party that lasts long into the night (except for a few years when we've been shut down early by a nearby residential neighborhood). Albert typically sells out of Syphons T-shirts and ball caps.

In 2007 Bill Stone, a noted inventor, engineer, and explorer, played with the Syphons. The month before convention, he had given a widely popular TED talk comparing the exploration of deep caves in Mexico to the human exploration of Mars. Bill is something of a rock star in the caving world and plays guitar well enough to be one on stage, so we had an extra set of new songs to practice around Bill's tight schedule. The convention staff had lined up an excellent sound engineer, and the police did not shut us down early. Cavers danced and sang along like no audience on Earth, beards, braids and tie-dyed shirts whirling through the night. Come Thursday morning I was tired with blisters on my fingers, and I was more than ready for some caving with Lee.

We started with a small, decorated cavern uncovered by highway construction in the 1970s. Entry was via a permanent steel ladder, thirty-seven feet long, installed in a vertical concrete culvert next to the roadside. Its steel gate had been left open for the convention, and Lee and I enjoyed an hour or so of looking for leads off the cave's single large room. We then climbed out and drove to first one then another nearby pit, both easy drops in the seventy-five-foot range.

Lee Pearson, sporting a rare beard at the 2007 NSS Convention, prepares to rappel into an Indiana pit. Note the TAG-style rack, more suited to a descent of 750 feet than 75.

I was huffing and puffing on the climb out of our second drop for all the usual reasons: not enough exercise, too much weight, generally out of shape. But uncharacteristically, Lee was also red-faced and fatigued at the top of the pit. He said he felt weak, with a "sick headache." A few times over the years, reaching back to our earliest caving trips together in Cookeville, Lee had felt a "sick headache" coming on, which always meant that the day's caving was done. We took it easy Friday, attending convention sessions in advance of the closing awards banquet. It was held that year in an old limestone quarry commercially transformed into a massive climate-controlled storage facility. Buses drove us nearly a mile beneath a hillside to the improvised underground ballroom hosting the banquet, where I was honored to be among cavers chosen that year as fellows of the NSS.

After Lee and Sharon returned home to Florida, where they had moved to be close to aging parents, his sick headaches kept popping up. Always an addicted runner, he noticed his times inexplicably falling off. He felt unusually tired and began avoiding caving trips altogether. Finally, just over a year after the Indiana convention, Lee went to see a doctor, who suggested checking his heart with a stress test. The test had barely begun when doctor interrupted it to rush him to an emergency quadruple bypass operation. His heart function was so reduced, the doctor later said, that only Lee's constant exercise and good physical shape had kept him alive to the age of fifty-four. Upon release from the hospital, he was weak as a kitten. Doctors cautioned that he might not ever run or cave again. Yet within a few months, he was once more doing both with gusto. He told me he felt he had more energy than ever before.

After recovering from surgery in 2009, Lee moved back to Cookeville, where he quickly became involved in many projects with the Upper Cumberland Grotto. Kathy and I visited him and Sharon there several times over the next two years, until they returned to Florida to be near their aging parents and grown children. After that, our caving trips together dropped to about once every other year or so, when we could coordinate travel plans. Our own children were graduating high school and taking off for college, and we stayed busy.

. . . .

In July 2014, Lee and I met for three days of caving in Tennessee. I was driving back from a writing workshop in Kentucky and had talked Sharon and him into meeting at a nice cabin in a Tennessee state park. On the first day, we went with Cookeville caver Uriah Prior to a well-known but seldom visited cave with a great deal of passage. Part of the ungated cave contained Native American pictographs, so it was one of those listed as an "Unnamed Cave" with a number in all official publications. The next day, we poked around several smaller Cookeville caves, then drove south toward the Plateau. Lee wanted to show me some new vacation cabins at a perfect location for future caving trips.

The bright green fields of the lush valley reached toward forested ridges on three sides. I recognized the spot from an afternoon I had spent with Marion Smith back when I was writing about Rumbling Falls for *Sports Illustrated.* He had driven me around to several springs that had been shown through dye tracing to connect with the river in the cave, along with a large spring closer to the cave that had no hydrologic connection. The main bulk of the Rumbling River appeared to exit six miles north of the point where water vanished into a gravel-filled sump. Dye tracing had confirmed that most of it flowed into a cave called Swamp River and a lesser amount wound up in a cave called Thunder Run. Thunder Run had large rooms and a borehole, but both caves were wet, difficult to enter, and prone to flooding. More important to exploration was a missing segment of passage between the furthest downstream point of Rumbling Falls and the furthest upstream points of Swamp River.

It was possible that somewhere near this valley was a connection to Rumbling Falls itself, perhaps the missing link that could tie it to one of the two drainage caves. A back door into Rumbling Falls would offer access to large chambers that could then be reached by only the strongest cavers on lengthy, arduous slogs from the Rumble Room. Such a discovery would make a "through trip" possible, where cavers could rappel into the natural entrance and make their way to the Rumble Room, then take a five or six mile downstream hike and exit a mere ten to twelve hours after entering, rather than twenty-four or more.

Lee and I looked at the cabins, all quite pleasant with reasonable rental rates. Since we were just across a county road from a sinkhole that Lee knew contained a short cave, we decided to try to visit it. We stopped at a well-kept farmhouse opposite a field near the sinkhole and rang the bell. A middle-aged woman answered the door, and we asked her whether we could have permission to park there and walk to the cave.

"That actually belongs to my neighbor, Scottie," she said, pointing up the road. "He lives in a trailer on the right, just past that sharp curve. You should ask him."

We thanked her, hopped in the car, and drove off in search of Scottie. We found the trailer but had no luck with knocking on the door. As Lee and I stood in the yard deciding what to do, the owner emerged from a shed around back, followed by an aging Bassett Hound. He greeted us and shook hands, and the dog gave us a good sniff. I took the dog's fierce tail wag to mean we were okay. Scottie, whose last name is omitted here to preserve his privacy, looked to be about forty and wore muddy work boots, with old clothes bearing the signs of someone who spends time with greasy equipment. He spoke frequently to the dog, who wagged his tail further and walked around the yard, all the while looking up at his master with the breed's famously sad eyes. We knew the dog was male from his enormous testicles, which parted the grass as he wandered about.

Lee explained that we were cavers. Scottie asked whether we knew Alfred Crabtree, a neighbor of his a few roads over whom he knew to be a caver. Lee was actually friends with Alfred, who was a very active member of the Upper Cumberland Grotto in Cookeville. Along with a group of younger hard-core cavers, he had recently mapped several new pits and a couple of significant vertical systems in TAG. Alfred was about to start an unusual new job, perfect for a caver, of climbing and repairing gigantic wind turbines around the country. The two compared notes on their mutual friend.

Seemingly satisfied, Scottie said at last, "Well, you can go into the old cave, but I think you guys might want to look at my new sinkhole first."

New sinkhole? Lee and I suppressed grins. Yes, we could do that, we said pretty much in unison.

Scottie explained that he had lost a calf a few weeks earlier. "I kept walking around the field, thinking I had heard her cry," he said, "but I couldn't find her."

Scottie stands next to the small sinkhole on his property where a calf had been trapped. The cave entrance is barely visible after several days of trash removal.

This had gone on for two days. Knowing she was nearby and wouldn't survive much longer, he slowly traversed the area, walking back and forth until he heard a faint bleating from an old trash pile that had been on the farm when he bought it several years earlier. He began pulling logs and other trash from the pile, and realized it was actually a trash-filled sinkhole. The calf had fallen through rotten wood, becoming stuck about ten feet below the surface. Eventually Scottie removed enough trash to reach down and get a rope around the frightened animal. As he lifted her out, he noticed a cool breeze blowing from a hole in the side of the sinkhole.

Lee and I grabbed helmets and gear from our car while Scottie went around back to get his ATV. He suggested that the three of us ride through his fields rather than walk to the sinkhole. The ATV had a basket on the front just big enough for our gear and a rack on the rear not quite big enough for Lee and me. We squeezed together anyway, grabbing the edge of the rack to hang on as Scottie began bouncing down the steep hillside as fast as the machine could carry three men. The dog kept up with us, just the top of his head and, thankfully, nothing else visible in the tall grass. At the base of the hill we turned left and circled a limestone outcrop to the sinkhole, which was no more the ten feet wide. It still appeared to be full of logs and broken boards, perhaps the remains of an old fence.

Lee and I began removing scrap wood, and soon we felt a cool breeze blowing through the pile. We removed several more logs and realized that wind actually came from opposite sides of the sinkhole. There's an old saying among cavers: "If it blows, it goes." With each item we tossed out of the hole, the strength of airflow increased. This definitely seemed the entrance to a large cave system. Lee worked on one side as I worked the other. After pulling a few cobbles and rocks out of my side, the wind increased further. Although it still had air, Lee's side seemed to choke off, so he stepped over the precarious pile of wood still below us to help at my spot. He pulled out a rock that seemed entirely too heavy to lift. Together we shoved it out of the sink. We spent perhaps another twenty minutes pulling trash and debris from that side of the sink, until Lee declared that this was definitely a digging project with potential, but not one we could hope to finish that day—or from our homes in Florida and Arkansas, for that matter.

We agreed to share what we had found with Alfred, since he lived nearby and already knew the landowner. He could put together a strong local digging team, and if they broke into a significant cave we would find a way to return to help map and explore it. We explained this to Scottie, and he seemed as eager as us to learn where the wind came from. It was definitely stronger as we climbed out of the sink than it had been on the way in. We crowded back onto the ATV and bounced through two fields, the dog once more eagerly keeping up with the loud machine.

We skirted woods and another limestone outcrop to reach a much larger sinkhole, perhaps one hundred feet wide and forty feet deep, with enormous hardwoods growing from the sides and bottom. About half-way down the west side of the sink was the entrance to a cave that had been known for over a century and was described in the Tennessee Cave Survey. Scottie borrowed my spare helmet and lamp to show us a spot just inside the entrance where he had found a cache of old mason jars, some of which contained questionable preserved fruit.

Alfred Crabtree, center, with two other cavers removing trash from the blowing sinkhole.

Scottie said we could reach the end of the cave by crawling and stoop-walking for another fifty feet or so, but he had seen it before and didn't feel like crawling. Lee and I checked it out. After a short, easy crawl, the cave opened to a wide chamber perhaps ten feet high at its center. In one alcove were a number of signatures from the early twentieth century. Beyond that was a circular dome that seemed a dead end. A track in the floor indicated the path water occasionally took through the cave. It flowed into a very low space at the base of a wall. We turned and left.

As we climbed from the sinkhole, Scottie told us that the farmer who had sold him the land, whose family had lived there for generations, said that as a boy he had explored "miles and miles" in this cave, once coming out another entrance near a highway in the next valley. The old man had claimed that a storm in the 1950s had plugged a low pathway to the main part of the cave. Lee and I had heard such stories from many rural landowners, usually secondhand, often accompanied by tales of dogs or even cows vanishing underground and reappearing miles away. We'd heard of hidden Confederate gold and of various caves that somehow connected to Mammoth. Not once had such fables led to a significant find. Still, storms could and did wash loose farm soil into sinkholes, so the former owner's tale wasn't entirely impossible.

Scottie bounced us back to our car, and we thanked him again and reiterated that Alfred would be in touch concerning the dig. Then we took a short drive to a gated logging road that entered the property of Fall Creek Falls state park, determined to have one good caving trip before the end of the day. We parked outside the gate and once more grabbed our gear. Lee carried a handheld GPS programed with coordinates of a cave he had long wanted to see, purportedly about a three-mile hike down a trail at the end of this road. It had a Spanish name that translated as "The Beautiful Cave of the Night."

We hiked a half mile down the road, passing the entrance to Camps Gulf—a cave with several large circular chambers similar to those found within Rumbling Falls—and entrances of three smaller caves that we had previously visited. Then the road ended and we followed a well-marked wilderness trail along a ridge beside stunning limestone cliffs and sink-holes. Occasionally we paused to check these for entrances. When we reached Hemlock Falls we knew we were three miles from the spot where we had parked. The path beyond was less traveled. Our chosen cave was supposed to be another a half-mile or so farther along, so we pressed on.

By the time we reached the spot where the GPS unit directed us, the sun had begun to set. The night was coming, but we could see no beautiful cave. We were looking for a fairly large-diameter pit. The GPS suggested we were about 150 feet higher in elevation than we needed to be. The problem was that downhill seemed thick with forest, brambles, and poison ivy. Lee and I struck off parallel to one another, out of sight due to the heavy growth, yet close enough that one could shout to the other if he spotted the cave.

I told Lee I was stopping if I hit a big thicket of poison ivy because I was especially sensitive to it. I think he may have muttered that the stuff didn't bother him. We beat around the hillside for at least an hour, eventually becoming too widely separated to hear each other. No cave. I pulled on my headlamp as darkness descended and hiked alone back up to the trail, knowing that sooner or later I would see or hear Lee.

Eventually I heard the sound of thrashing and cursing about two hundred vertical feet below me. I walked along the trail to a place just above the noise and soon saw Lee's light bobbing uphill. I waited until he reached me, huffing a bit.

"Well, I didn't do it," he said.

"Find the cave?"

"That also. But I didn't stay out of the big thicket of poison ivy. I mean it was everywhere—more than I've ever seen. I'm going to need a good bath tonight."

We realized that we had either bad coordinates or a bad GPS unit, and started back toward the car, with me in the lead. We had walked only about fifty feet when I stopped, turned to Lee, and said, "Well, now we know."

"Know what?" he asked.

"A bear does shit in the woods." I pointed to a round pile glistening with half-digested blackberries. It lay in the center of our path and had not been there when we hiked in.

"I think maybe someone's sending us message," Lee said.

"I think maybe so."

We hiked on. By the time we reached the car we had walked over seven miles and not seen the day's main objective. I was sore and dreading the long drive back to Arkansas. But we had found an exciting new dig, had heard some intriguing cave folklore, and had enjoyed a beautiful day hiking in cave country. Just like old times.

We had taken Sharon's elderly green Chevy for caving that day (I didn't want to muddy up my rental car), and it started running hot as we drove back to our cabin. The next morning, I drove Lee to his old mechanic's shop in Cookeville, where he purchased everything he would need to install a new thermostat, despite traveling with minimal tools. We agreed there was time to hit a short cave or two before returning to the cabin to work on the car.

There are over two hundred caves within the Cookeville city limits and Lee knows most of them. We visited one that he and I had first entered ten or twenty years ago. Normally plugged by trash, heavy rains followed by drought had reopened the entrance. It had had been recently rediscovered by Chuck Sutherland, who gave it the apt name Trash Compactor. Virtually all rainwater that falls within the Cookeville city limits vanishes via sinkholes into caves, so runoff from commercial parking lots, combined with sinkholes used as dumps, had filled many caves in town with garbage. A similar cave called Tires to Spare

lay below an old garage that had disposed of tires there for decades—eventually the landowner had the entrance filled in.

Perhaps the worst of them all was a cave Lee had taken me to right after we met (it may have been literally the day after we met at Xanadu): a well-known cave called Capshaw. It ran four and a half miles beneath Cookeville, its main stream and tributaries carrying much of the runoff from the eastern side of the city. One infeeder near a golf course sinkhole continually shot golf balls into the cave stream. Sewage from an aging city pump station routinely leaked into the cave, to the degree that it smelled like a toilet. When Lee first took me and some Florida friends to Capshaw in 1980, cavers called it "Crapshaw." A long environmental battle had finally cleaned it up, I had heard. We avoided Crapshaw and checked out smaller locations, including a newly discovered cave near a private school with a nice-sized room at the back.

The little green car was fixed and Lee and Sharon set off early the next morning for Colorado while I set off for Arkansas. I was not nearly as sore as I expected to be. A few days later, Sharon called Kathy to report that the poison ivy had kicked in "big time" as they were on the road, and it was bad enough that Lee had sought relief at a veteran's hospital near St. Louis. The doctor who treated him agreed he'd never seen such a nasty case. Lee lumped this into his list of reasons not to go caving. But steroids made the rash more bearable, and several days later he successfully soloed the summit of Long's Peak. He sent me a selfie in which he grins from ear to ear on the peak.

. . . .

Clinton Elmore drills a hole for a small charge in order to create a path for the haul system that would remove rock and dirt from the small passage at the base of the sinkhole.

On the day he messaged me the summit photo, Lee and I were invited to join a secret Facebook group dedicated to Scottie's dig, where Alfred Crabtree, Marion Smith, Joel Buckner, Clinton Elmore, Jim Fox, Kristen Bobo, and one or two others were now working regularly. According to group messages, first they had rigged a hoist to remove loose trash and rocks from the sinkhole that had trapped Scottie's calf, then they began to excavate along the path of the wind. I managed to take a Friday off in September so that I could drive out and help on Saturday. I was amazed at the progress they had made. Most of the trash had

As Marion Smith and the owner's dog look on, the dig crew haul rocks from the sink and gains another few feet of passage.

been removed from the sinkhole, revealing a narrow chimney about fifteen feet deep.

Alfred and crew had rigged an efficient pulley system to remove buckets of rubble as they followed the wind, enlarging the narrow channel as needed with rock hammers and a technique called micro-shaving, a method of drilling small holes in limestone, filling them with old-fashioned black powder, and setting off tiny blasts to remove a few pounds of rock. It is a slow but minimally damaging way of making a tight crawl passable to humans. Upon arrival I found Joel Buckner and Jim Fox working at the dig, setting off one small charge after another. Jim invited me down into the hole to observe the process. With a battery-powered drill, he made a finger-sized hole in a boulder that protruded into the crawlway. He filled the hole with a small preset charge of black powder and attached a detonator, checking with Joel outside before connecting a wire from the charge to another wire snaking up to a pickup parked beside the sinkhole. Jim and I climbed out to where Joel waited.

I pulled out my cell phone and filmed as Joel touched the wire lead to the car battery. A loud pop like a muffled gunshot emanated from the hole. We climbed down through smoke and began hauling out buckets of rubble. We repeated this process several times over the course of the day: fire a small shot, then remove detritus. Marion stopped by for a while to see how the dig was going. He was itching for us to succeed, but not enough to stay long. He headed off to do some ridgewalking. Gradually we turned from vertical to horizontal as we followed the course of the wind another ten feet beyond where we had started. The overhead boulders seemed loose and dicey in this horizontal tunnel, so Joel spent considerable time bracing them with scrap lumber that I pulled from the sinkhole and fed down to him. This dig would be slow going.

As I made the eight-hour drive home the next morning, sore from repeatedly hauling buckets of rock up a twenty-foot line, I was excited about a chance to find a back door to Rumbling Falls, but also glad I lived too far away to work the dig every weekend. I stopped for a break at the Johnny Cash Memorial Rest Area, and it took me several minutes to stand up straight once I managed to get out of the car.

SOCIAL INTERLUDE

I went out today expecting to do some housekeeping. I am going out of town tomorrow and thought we wouldn't do much today. Loaded a couple of shots, and wouldn't you know it got through the entire column, after some shaving some of the ceiling boulders past where we were last dropped into the passage and were summarily dismissed with two more shaves. Greer and Allyn were on hand, and we moved everything into the void created by our last efforts with you, Michael. The shoring was from the trip with Michael and Joel.

Once through into cave, a low crawl led to a crack where the air was coming through. That was hammered on and two shaves opened it. The balance of the cave, ~450 ft. was as we found it except for a couple of places Kristen and I had to dig through to get to the bottom. The air was not as strong today due to the temp being in the fifties, so sniffing out the way through all the breakdown will take time. I want to return in two or three weeks with Clinton, Lavender, whoever else wants to push. We might find more stuff!

ALFRED CRABTREE | Post to SUB Dudes, secret Facebook group, October 5, 2014

ALFRED CRABTREE: Fellow SUBS, I'd like to give a good college push to Scottie's hole up there next to Swamp River. I believe we can get somewhere and just try to make a connection to wherever that air is flowing. MOS might be down for Sunday, but I'd like to get all who have helped in the least invited and get a date we can all or most join. The BSC thing is big, but not many are going to make that slog back there. I am, so I wanna push once more, then hand Scotties project off to Kristen so it will get written up and named properly. Cool? Dates anyone this weekend maybe! PLEASE!

KRISTEN BOBO: I may be able to come Sunday to push harder, though you may prefer someone else with you on that. I would like to get a few photos of the chert passage though. It would be great if you could get MOS to push.

JIM FOX: I could prob not get there until 2:00, but I will come hear how it went!

JOEL BUCKNER: I can't Sunday, not sure about Sat. Have been trying to get a dig crew together Sat for the "best" lead in TN but most of my old crew are getting too decrepit, too domesticated, too into football, or pulling out the old "recovering from surgery" excuse. ;)

Conversation on SUB Dudes, secret Facebook group, November 11, 2014

Chapter 16

BACK DOOR

Cavers who hope to find virgin passage soon become adept at digging. In my case it happened a little over a year after my first visit to Xanadu. At twenty-one, I had become familiar the caves of Pelham Ridge, a long, narrow band of limestone wrinkling across southern Georgia. On a day when I was supposedly composing a research paper on Milton, I sat in Strozier Library of Florida State University and cracked open a small, dusty bulletin of the Georgia Geological Survey. I was soon onto something.

Forty years later I no longer recall the title of the article, but the gist was that in the early 1950s the author had investigated and catalogued limestone outcrops in the vicinity of Cairo, Georgia. Many of the outcrops listed were sinkhole entrances to familiar caves: Waterfall, Glory Hole, Climax, and several smaller, nastier places my friends and I had spent happy hours wriggling through. But among them was a location that was new to me. The author described a dry creek bed leading to steep-walled sink lined by cream-colored limestone, with "a small, blowing cave entrance visible at the base."

I carried the journal to the library's map room and found the appropriate topographic quadrant. The sinkhole lay very near a familiar dirt road, across from a building (or what had been a building when the topo was made). I memorized the location so I could transfer it to my own map at home. That night I asked Allen Moser—then as now the caver most knowledgeable about South Georgia karst—if he had heard of this particular named sinkhole. He hadn't.

The following weekend, Allen and I drove to the map coordinates and found the sink, a wide spot ringed by hardwoods in the middle of a pasture, just downstream from a cattle pond. A small brick house stood across the road, the name painted on its rural mailbox matching the name of the sinkhole given in the geological journal. I knocked, and a large man of about fifty, dressed in overalls and a white T-shirt, answered the door. Allen and I introduced ourselves and explained about the article. We asked whether he owned the sinkhole across the street, and, if so, whether we could take a look at it.

"Well, no, I don't own that parcel," he said. "It sold a while back. But I don't think the owner would mind you looking, long as you close that cattle gate behind you."

I had already stepped eagerly from the porch, shouting thanks over my shoulder, when the big man added, "Course, that big cave ain't down there no more."

Slowly I turned.

"Naw," he said, "they ain't nothing but mud in that hole now."

"How's that?" I asked, hopes sinking.

In the rural South, when it becomes clear that a speaker has captured a listener's undivided attention, local etiquette dictates that the speaker pause, spit in the dirt, and launch into a tale. This farmer adhered to procedure.

"I grew up in this house right here," he said. "And when I was a boy, I played all over these fields and woods. Ever little nook and cranny. Oh, I had to work the fields, too. Hard work. Out in heat that would suck the breath right out of you. So whenever it got too hot, I'd sneak down into that sinkhole. Let the breeze coming out of the cave cool me off. Ooh-wee that felt good. Back when I was real little, my mama would pack me lunch in a handkerchief, and I'd carry it down by the cave to eat."

The man paused his narrative to pull a much-used handkerchief from his back pocket. He fluttered it before us. "After I ate my piece of chicken and biscuit, I'd wave my hanky over the cave and let that wind blow it up into the air. It would shoot way up over my head, and then I'd catch it and do it all over again. Well, naturally enough, pretty soon I got curious about what was down in there blowing so hard. Eventually, I got hold of a flashlight and went looking. You had to crawl in, then kind of climb down some over some rocks to where you could stand up."

I hung on every word. "Where you could stand up" was a magical phrase.

"There were three main rooms. They weren't huge or nothing like Carlsbad Caverns, but they were pretty big." The farmer looked around. "I guess the biggest was about the size of that barn over yonder. Bigger than the house, anyway. We had a water well in the backyard, and I found the pipe from it going right down through the middle of that room. There was some little tunnels leading off in the back, but I never tried to crawl into those. They looked like good places for snakes or bats."

By this point in his story, I may have been salivating. But I could tell the point was coming, and I guessed that it was going to be pretty. It wasn't.

"It was my dad that first started throwing trash down in the sinkhole. Old washing machines and bailing wire and such. And then we sold that field to a man who kept cattle—we had always planted it in corn and soy beans."

The new owner had taken advantage of the intermittent stream leading to the sink and built a cattle pond above it. He had continued the practice of using the sink for a trash dump, discarding appliances and even a junked car into it.

"Maybe twenty, twenty-five years ago a hurricane come through here. Or the remains of one, it was. It rained hard for three days, and that little creek turnt into a river. The dam was just clay shoved up with a dozer, and all that water flushed down into the hole. It shoved clay around all that trash, and the whole thing filled in. You couldn't even see the rocks no more."

He spit again. "Been that way ever since. Used to be fifty feet deep, now I bet it's not more than fifteen. They fixed the cattle pond, and I guess the overflow still gets down in the ground somehow, but after a big rain it backs up for a day or two. You can't see nothing but mud and a little trash down in there now." He spit once more, signaling an end to the story. "You welcome to go have a look."

We did and saw exactly what had been described: A shallow depression, crisscrossed by a few dry channels from the intermittent stream. Although in July no water flowed, I could see that the runoff from past rains had sunk into the red clay in several fist-sized holes along one edge of the sink.

Allen went to one of these and reached down into it, pulling out a couple of muddy lumps. "Hey Mike, come here and put your hand over this hole," he said.

I did, once more a small boy with his arm in the sandbox. A faint but unmistakable coolness rose into my palm: a whisper of cave air.

Allen said what I was thinking. "Looks like we got us a digging project."

For much of the following year, excavating the "lost" cave consumed my time, energy, and scant resources. Using an old roll of fencing to shore up the tunnel, I enlisted a bucket brigade that spent one weekend after another working its way past the washing machine, alongside the Chevrolet, and beyond a buried limestone ledge in search of the cool breeze that grew ever steadier. Digging fever took over.

Before long, a friend of a friend named Jimmy arrived from Alabama, driving a white Corvette, its small trunk packed with caving gear and a (legally purchased) case of dynamite and detonation cord. As the owner and a crowd of cavers looked on from beyond the cattle pond dam, Jimmy unrolled wire from our dig tunnel, hooked it to a detonator, and threw the switch. We felt, rather than heard, the explosive whump as toxic smoke shot from the hole. Itching to see what had been accomplished, we sprang toward the entrance—only to be told we had to wait at least thirty minutes for the fumes to clear.

The wait was unbearable. We had to know, had to know now.

There was nothing unusual in our actions: if you want to find a significant new cave anywhere in the United States, you pretty much have to dig for it. In the early days of TAG, cavers could still find huge open-air pits that had never been explored. But over time the big entrances were found, even in the most remote locations. Cavers increasingly became miners, finding likely spots—both above and below ground—to attack with shovels, picks, and occasionally even heavy equipment and explosives, all in hopes of revealing new cave. The results have sometimes been extraordinary, sometimes unremarkable, and often controversial, blurring the boundary between conservation and exploitation, between appreciating nature and reshaping it to fit one's desires.

What many cavers would regard as the most wildly successful dig of all time was the opening of Lechuguilla Cave in Carlsbad Caverns National Park. As with most long digging projects, that a cave was there was indisputable: wind howled from a breakdown pile at the base of a pit, in an area of known significant caves. Spurred on by caver Dave Allred—who had often used digging techniques to open little finds in the Northeast—teams had been attacking the breakdown pile for years when the breakthrough finally occurred over Memorial Day weekend in 1986. Since then, the cave has yielded over 150 miles of wonderfully decorated passage with no sign of ending for decades to come. But it has also been the subject of contentious management battles, early conservation missteps, and a rethinking of policies for digging into caves on public lands.

"You can't manage a resource if you don't know it's there," Jim Goodbar, a senior cave specialist for the US Bureau of Land Management, once told me. "Digging in caves is thus a viable means of exploration."

Val Hildreth-Werker and Jim Werker, longtime conservation advocates within the National Speleological Society, agree that well-planned digging in caves can be a powerful tool for conservation and study. "People are surprised that we do both digging and conservation," Val, who edits the annual *NSS News* conservation issue, has said. "But we could not pursue conservation prototypes if we hadn't dug into truly unexplored caves. The baseline data a dig provides leads to new opportunities for conservation."

"The important thing with any dig is to go slow," Jim added. "Measure the airflow before you start digging, so that you can later construct an airlock to maintain the original flow. Take photographs before you set foot in a new cave, and use photographic monitoring to track the effects of exploration on the passages." After a highly successful digging project in New Mexico, Jim placed special sleeves into a formation-lined area to accept a camera stand, so that a particular section could be photo-monitored throughout years of exploration. Jim and Val have also advocated allowing biologists and microbiologists to be the first to enter a cave after a digging breakthrough, in order to take baseline biology measurements.

None of these excellent ideas were, of course, anywhere near my mind on that morning in 1981 as dynamite fumes finally cleared. Since it was "my" dig, I was allowed to be first into the hole. I snaked my way through the role of fencing, past the Chevy, around the refrigerator, and to the limestone wall. There at the bottom was new space, allowing me, for the first time, to move below the cliff face and into what appeared the upper portion of a cave entrance. An entrance, I quickly saw, that was choked with just as much breakdown, trash, and clay fill as the sinkhole above it had been.

The breeze still beckoned, but we remained a long way from mapping a cave. Over the following weeks most of my Florida State digging crew mutinied, drawn away by going passage in nearby Climax Cave and by an even more tantalizing dig in Malloy's Waterfall Cave (that other dig, called "The Grim Triangle of Death," eventually yielded one of the state's most heavily decorated chambers). So the sinkhole remained unexplored. Our original tunnel once more filled up with runoff and trash. As far I know it sits there still in South Georgia, awaiting some future youngster to contract a case of digging fever.

In the end, our dig at Scottie's was also a bust. The back of the small cave was dangerously unstable. "That is a nasty place," Alfred said, and he knew nasty. Moreover, the strong wind vanished somewhere within the loose boulders comprising the ceiling—following it was simply too risky.

"That cave is SCARY," Marion later wrote. "In spite of the wind, it will tend to be unstable." By May 2015 Alfred's crew had added a bit over five hundred feet of new cave to the Tennessee Cave Survey. It was the perfect location for an entrance, but not the key to Rumbling Falls.

I tried unsuccessfully to interest someone from the crew in starting a new dig within Scottie's other cave. They were already busy pushing other sinkholes, not to mention finding new actual caves to survey.

Despite the story of the previous landowner, the small cave with signatures in the back looked like exactly that: a small cave. We had all
learned over the years that old farmers in cave country can tell enticing
stories.

Not everyone, however, had given up on a finding a back door.

On May 4, 2015, Marion Smith took Troy Fuqua to another blowing hole he had found within the general area above the lower portions
of Rumbling Falls. Fuqua (pronounced "FYOO-kwuh"), was originally
from Nashville and now lived in Madison, Alabama, where he worked
as an electrical engineering consultant. He had developed a reputation
for digging caves in TAG by improving microshaving techniques and
constructing creative devices for hauling rubble. Marion and Troy hiked
up a difficult four-hundred-foot climb to a hole no larger than a bowling
ball in a dry wash. It blew a constant, forceful wind. Fuqua carried a
small bag of tools, and did five "shots" of microshaving that suggested
the dig looked promising. They returned on June 3 and found that as
they widened and deepened the narrow passage, removing rock became
exponentially more difficult. Marion recovered an old five-gallon bucket
and saw a few drill marks where someone had previously tried to dig at
the hole and evidently given up. (Much later, he learned that this was
Hal Love, circa 2001.)

After gaining permission from the landowner and arranging easier
access to the site across his property, Fuqua began the first of what
would become increasingly long camps at the remote location over the
next two years. He recruited others to work with him and Marion at
the site. In August he designed a custom-made track and trolley system
to haul rubble from dozens of small blasts. Someone sitting outside the
cave could pull the trolley with a long piece of webbing and dump it,
and it would return itself to the rock face.

At Scottie's dig, we had run ordinary speaker wire to a convenient
truck battery to fire the shots to bust the rocks, but Fuqua would have
none of that. He found the perfect gauge of wire on a Chinese version
of eBay to make a firing system that required nothing more than a common drill battery. He ordered additional parts for the shaving process
from around the world, and fabricated those he could not find, testing
new methods on boulders in a field near his home. After three days in

August had proved his new methods sound, he left the dig for the winter, vowing to return in the spring.

In October 2015, I knew nothing about this dig, but I couldn't stop thinking about Scottie's other cave, now that his dig had been declared complete. I went to Nashville to host a session at the Southern Festival of Books and built an extra day into my trip for a trial dig. I booked one of the tidy cabins that Lee and I had looked at the year before and went to see Scottie. I couldn't stop thinking about his story of the man who spent "long days" exploring the cave as a boy. I would have dismissed it except for the old signatures in the round room at the back. Most caves I had seen with a signature room were large enough for people carrying lanterns to spend at least a few hours exploring and cooling off on a summer day, long before the age of air conditioning. This one was much too short.

Before leaving for Tennessee, I called Scottie and persuaded him to call the former landowner, who was in his seventies and retired in Alabama. (He is not named here both for his own privacy and because his name is closely associated with the cave name, which I prefer to omit. Same goes for Scottie's last name, for that matter.) The retired farmer stood by his story. He said he would "duck under" into the main passage from the signature room. While he could not estimate distances, it felt to him like he had to travel "about a mile" to reach a second entrance that put him out in a sink near a highway.

I wondered whether such a cave, if it existed, might be either a more stable part of the same system as Scottie's other sink where Alfred had dug, or perhaps an easy way into Swamp River, or maybe something entirely new. The original owner claimed that a storm had blocked most of the cave many years ago. He said that if someone dug "on the right where the water goes," they would likely reach the "main part." Scottie gave me the man's number and I tried to call him myself twice before I got to Tennessee. I got only voice mail and no return calls.

I drove over from Nashville in the morning. With Scottie's permission I spent the afternoon digging "where the water goes." Kristen Bobo had said she had tried a short dig in a dome room beside the signature area, but that had offered little promise. The spot where the water vanished, however, was closer to the short entrance crawl. The soil there was loose clay and seemed to have been deposited in two layers. I poked my hoe, back end first, into the little stream channel and reached longer than the handle, so I turned it around and started pulling out dirt. The deposits appeared very old, with a dried crust on top, but within them I soon removed the little blue bottle, proving a modern flood had washed in this dirt and debris.

I thought I felt a small breeze, but I couldn't be certain. After two hours, I had pulled out a good wheelbarrow-load of dirt. From this effort I had only extended my ability to reach into hole by a few feet. On the cabin porch at sunset, I realized that I had a couple of bars of cell signal, so I composed a Facebook message to Alfred's digging group. "I am sharing this with all you guys," I wrote, "because it will take work to chase what may be a pipe dream, but it's the kind of thing you could do with a couple spare hours after a cave or float trip, and who knows?"

I encouraged anyone interested to dig in the spot where I had started and suggested that maybe Lee and I could put together a group effort at Thanksgiving or Christmas. I reiterated that Scottie believed the man who had sold him the property. What I didn't realize was that Marion and Troy were already in the process of getting easier access to what would begin a major digging project. What I also didn't realize that fall and winter of 2015 was that I would be taking most of 2016 off from caving, even as Fuqua inched ever closer to Rumbling Falls.

It started with an expired prescription for blood pressure medication. My Arkadelphia doctor usually renewed prescriptions with a phone call. His approach to maladies was akin to that of the typical high school football coach: shake it off and quit your whining. I got on well with this approach. But my regular doctor had taken a long-term leave to battle an illness of his own, temporarily turning his patients over to an uncomfortably thorough nurse practitioner named Denise. Years had passed since my last routine visit, Denise explained over the phone, so there would be no Lisinopril until I came by the office to give up a few ounces of blood and be otherwise poked and prodded.

So I did. A few days later I received by phone a comprehensive list of all the reasons that nothing good comes from a routine doctor visit: My blood sugar was high, so Denise signed me up for a ten-week nutrition course to keep me from turning into a card-carrying diabetic. Bad cholesterol was up and good was down, so she put me on a daily statin. I had gained weight and needed to exercise. (Okay, this one was no surprise, considering my last few caving trips. I vowed to get in shape.) My blood pressure was too high, so she switched medications. Finally, she added that my PSA was high, so she had scheduled me an appointment with a urologist.

I wished I had let her call go to voice mail.

After agreeing to future appointments and hanging up, I realized that the only term she used that was utterly foreign to me was PSA. Like anyone with a medical question, I consulted Dr. Google. The answers were somewhat alarming, if also reassuring. High levels of prostate-specific antigen—PSA—could be a warning sign of prostate cancer, I read, but it was not a foolproof test. Some websites condemned it heartily, saying high numbers could be caused by all sorts of minor problems down there that were not cancer, and anyway, prostate cancer tended to be extremely slow growing.

Cancer? Yes, I read on, cancer. "Prostate cancer is the most common non-skin cancer among American men," declared the Centers for Disease Control website. "Most prostate cancers grow slowly and don't cause any health problems in men who have them." Whew.

Long story short, after weeks of highly uncomfortable tests by the urologist, I learned that my cancer was *not* the slow-growing kind, and a surgeon put his hand on my shoulder and said, "You want that sucker out of there." I was scheduled for robotic laparoscopic surgery late in the spring. Basically the surgeon sat across the room from me with what looked like an elaborate video game controller as six robotic tentacles reached into my abdomen, removed my prostate, and sewed everything back together. Eight weeks after the surgery, I was allowed to begin taking walks. By the end of the summer, I was kayaking and traveling to conventions. I was almost back to normal (which was not always the outcome of prostate surgery, I had learned, so in that regard I was quite lucky). I was cancer free and ready to go caving, but as with every other August a new semester was underway. Digging at Scottie's place would have to wait.

. . . .

When Marion and Troy Fuqua returned on June 20, 2016, they found that a pack rat living in the dug passage had eaten all their webbing and a plastic bucket, but they soon had the haul system up and running again for several dig trips. By July, Troy's ever-growing tunnel had entered a narrow canyon. Marion attended nearly all of several push trips that seemed to be getting closer to actual walking passage (skipping one for the NSS convention). Yet each time they rounded a corner, there would be more digging, blasting, and hauling to be done. Troy enlisted cavers Brandon Crane, Jon Mnich, and Derek Reneer to set up bucket chains to the surface. They installed additional lengths of rail for the trolley, and brought in additional buckets. By Halloween, Troy and Marion were belly-crawling against a fierce wind a distance of twenty feet over rough cobbles, blasting another rock, then belly-crawling twenty feet back with buckets of debris for a crew who would take them out of the dig. Still they pushed forward. By December 2, they had gained only forty feet, and still the wind blew fiercely.

That October, my elderly mother was evacuated from a hurricane that did considerable damage to her Florida home, then shortly after being allowed to return home she was attacked by a vicious loose dog that had been traumatized by the storm. She saved herself by climbing onto a picnic table and screaming until a neighbor called the police. When she was released from the hospital with a severe leg wound, she came to live with us. As she recuperated, Kathy and I realized that she would not be able to return to living alone in Florida. Chris had finished college and was taking a year off before grad school, so he and I began making regular drives together to Florida to clean out the family home and get it ready for sale. Twice we hauled family keepsakes back to Arkansas by way of Tennessee, pausing to hike to waterfalls and visit caves, both wild and commercial. For the first time since I was six years old, I saw Ruby Falls. It was exactly as I had remembered it, gaudy lights and all.

. . . .

In the summer of 2017, Troy set up a lengthy camp near the dig. At first the landowner was reluctant to agree because there was no electricity at the site. After Troy finished laughing, he assured him no electricity was no problem. The team hauled in a generator to charge drills and lights. With a strong crew carrying in lengths of lightweight, bendable pipe by hand, Troy was able to extend the rock-removal trolley all the way from the cave entrance to the current site of digging. The group camped at the same site for five days over the July Fourth holiday. On July 5, the last day, a massive thunderstorm moved through the area, destroying much of their camp. Changes in barometric pressure caused the dig to suck air with as much force as it normally blew. On August 2, they blasted into a tight squeeze to an offset pit fifteen feet deep that was, for the first time in over two years of work at the site, passable without additional blasting.

Tory set a bolt. A small rope was rigged and Smith, Crane, and Reneer descended. The only way forward was crawl four inches high, with strong wind. On August 16, Marion got Alfred Crabtree to break up a large boulder blocking entry to the crawl, then Alfred returned alone August 30 to dig about two or three feet of the crawl open. Two weeks later, he and Jim Fox spent over five hours pushing the crawl until both were exhausted. On September 21, Troy and Jim returned to push the small but growing passage.

That was also the day Marion was released from the hospital in Chattanooga after receiving a serious skull fracture in a pit. Two hours after he got home, Troy and Jim stopped by the house with some good news. On September 24 he was able to celebrate his seventy-fifth birthday with friends at his favorite Mexican restaurant. Six days later, he could barely walk, but he attended the fall meeting of the Tennessee Cave Survey, where the news began to spread.

"It was brutal," Troy told an enraptured crowd at the following spring meeting of the Tennessee Cave Survey, held in Sewanee on April 21, 2018. "But I went around the little corner, and I popped out right here."

. . . .

He spoke in a lecture hall on the campus of Tennessee Technical University, giving a talk that had been described on the agenda as a "report on a digging project," with no cave specifically mentioned. On the large screen flashed a slide depicting sizable walking passage beneath the end of the crawlway.

"I looked on the floor, and there were footprints. And then beautiful passage. Survey stations. We took lots of pictures." He flashed through shots of enormous chambers.

The audience erupted in applause that became a standing ovation.

"Any questions?" Troy asked.

Several people yelled out in unison, "What cave were you in?"

Chris and I were sitting in the audience.

In answer to the question, Troy clicked to reveal a map of Rumbling Falls cave. Near the end of a large chamber called Division Hall, about four miles downriver from the Rumble Room, a red arrow pointed toward what Troy said would be known from that moment forward as the Blasted Goat Entrance of Rumbling Falls Cave. More applause followed.

A caver stands near the rope in the Rumble Room in 2018, illuminated by custom-made flash guns firing No. 50 bulbs. Note fog creeping in on the right side—the chamber is so large that it creates its own weather.

Troy finished his talk, showing how his crew had enlarged and stabilized the dig to make it friendlier to what might become hordes of cavers. They built an improvised ladder for the down-climb from the crawlway. He showed photos of a twelve-hour through-trip on November 4—the first from the upper entrance to Blasted Goat.

The spot where they had popped in from the dig, he said, was the place where, during the original survey twenty years earlier, Marion, Swartz, and Chambers had seen a live cave rat and also a bat. These animals had gotten into a point many miles and huge pits away from the only known entrance, so they began considering another way in. They named the passage Rat's Dream. Marion had thought many times over the ensuing years about trying to explore outward from that area in search of a back door. A five-hundred-foot borehole called Division Hall connected Rat's Dream to a maze they called Saturday Nightmare. Near the end of Division Hall was a fifty-foot dome, with old surface debris at its base. A Virginia caver named Aaron Moss successfully climbed the dome in 2010, finding nothing at the top. The climb took place only two hundred feet from the spot where Troy's dig finally connected.

"It's been Marion's dream to get in from that spot," Troy said as he closed his speech. "I was so glad to help him see that dream."

SOCIAL INTERLUDE

LEE: So, I was running the workout with (behind) the kids yesterday. It sounded easy enough, 2 400s, 3 200s and then 4 100s. Well, I completed the workout, but then, I think because of my medication, my blood pressure tanked. I felt so faint, frail, and old. All but one coach left, and I think he was afraid I might die. Anyway, I managed to drive home, and when I got home I checked my blood pressure and it was $^{82}/_{53}$. Dang, no wonder I felt so light-headed. Curse you Red Baron and your blood pressure and heart rev limiter drugs. Can't an old man get in a decent workout? Anyway, feeling fine today. I was sick most of last week, and one of my kids changed my nickname to Couch Lee instead of Coach Lee. Know that hurts.

ME: Damn. And you can't even get real BC powder anymore. This Colorado hike is starting to sound a little scary.

LEE: Right! But it will be fun, right up until we die.

ME: Exactly! That's my thought on caving too . . .

LEE: One of the kids said, Coach, age is only a number. I said, yes, and in my case a very big number. Still, I love them and they seem to like me, so it's great.

ME: Tell it to MOS. He keeps giving old cavers a role model for tough.

LEE: Yes, Marion is doing well, but he seems to be looking a little frailer than say 10 years ago. Hey, we each do the best we can with what we have.

April 24, 2019, exchange on Facebook Messenger, about 8:30 p.m.

Chapter 17

CRAPSHAW

In May 2018, Lee, Sharon, Kathy and I rented a vacation apartment in downtown Cookeville for a week. Kathy hired someone we knew to sit with my mom and Kathy's dad so that we could have a fun break with a fun couple. As usual, most days Lee and I went caving while Sharon and Kathy went shopping. In the evenings the four of us would find a nice restaurant and talk long into the night. For the first time in many years, Lee and I returned to Capshaw Cave, where he took me through virtually the entire four miles of mapped passages, including a little-known formation area that few ever see.

The main Capshaw entrance lies in a sinkhole beside a busy suburban street. We approached the closest house for permission to park on the road before entering the cave. The resident we spoke to was Sharon Martin, a retired biologist for the US Fish and Wildlife Service. She had lived at the same location back in the bad old Crapshaw days. As we stood on her porch she described the long battle in the 1980s to get city officials to admit that they were inadvertently pumping raw sewage from a lift station directly into the cave. After years of denial the city had finally given in, building a new lift station at another location. Capshaw had slowly cleaned itself out with years of surface runoff.

Cavers relax on a recreational trip through Capshaw Cave.

"I'm sure there's still coliform and strep bacteria in there," Martin added. "Don't get any cuts while you're in the cave."

We got no cuts, although Lee did blow out one of the old tennis shoes he had chosen to wear that day—right at the deepest point in the cave, of course. We wrapped some webbing around it to hold it together on the slog out. The cave stream smelled better than it had nearly forty years ago, but I tried to keep its water away from my mouth when we splashed through deeper pools. There were some dry stretches, actually pleasant walking, and in one of these Lee told me he had decided he was becoming less interested in caving. He was really enjoying working as a volunteer high school track coach in Florida, and still enjoyed his own running. The previous spring, I had driven to Birmingham to watch him compete in the national Senior Olympics in three categories—opportunities he had won by finishing as the best in Florida in his age bracket.

Lee said that due to his surgery in 2008, he been through so many scans that he worried about the additional radiation he subjected himself to every time he went caving. The amount of free radon within caves varies by location and geology, but it was safe to say that our walk through Capshaw was giving us an exposure equivalent to two or

An ancient Native American pictograph depicting the Floating Warrior on the wall of an unnamed Tennessee cave.

three chest x-rays. We both knew cavers over the years who had died of cancer, and such deaths had begun to make Lee think more about radon and caving.

"I've probably done enough caving," he said. "I'd rather run and go climbing."

I was on sabbatical then and had been doing what felt like a lot of caving, at least for me. At that moment I felt closer to caves and cavers than I had in years. As we followed the cobbled stream, I didn't try so much to win Lee back to the underground as to simply share some of what I had done recently. The walking was slow with his barely held-together shoe, and I had plenty to share.

While staying at Rivendell Writers Colony, situated at that time on the edge of the Cumberland Plateau in Sewanee, I had taken a couple of other writers into some interesting caves that I described to Lee. I added that while there I had also participated in several WNS-related surveys, including a visit to the Georgia railroad tunnel.

I told how after months of pestering, I had finally talked Alan Cressler and Jan Simek into letting me accompany them on a research trip to

Dr. Jan Simek of the University of Tennessee examines what may or may not be an ancient Native American pictograph depicting a turkey on the wall of a well-known Tennessee cave.

examine what might be a new-found pictograph. We went to a Tennessee location that has operated for decades as a public tour cave and is loaded with nineteenth century historic signatures. Despite this heavy human traffic, it had only been in recent years that the cave had been shown to be also loaded with Mississippian-age petroglyphs (figures scratched into the rock) and pictographs (figures painted on the rock).

One large pictograph depicted a common mystical figure that Simek called Hatchet Nose because he has a blade where his nose should be. Whenever that figure was drawn reclining near a body of water, as in this cave, it usually indicated a place where one might pass from the physical to the spiritual world.

"We think they believed the spirit world is underground," Simek said. "It is just like the surface world, but everything is backward and upside down."

I had immediately thought of the Upside Down in the television show *Stranger Things* (which I had been watching occasionally when Kathy wasn't home, because it creeped her out). I wasn't sure about backward and upside down part, but I understood how ancient people thought caves could connect them to the spiritual world. That was something all TAG cavers knew.

The image that I had gone into the cave to examine with Simek and Cressler was purported to be a native depiction of a turkey that lay beneath layers of historic signatures. Once we reached it and the painted shape was pointed out, it did indeed look like a turkey or other bird in flight, to me at least. I described the figure to Lee. Cressler had explained how they would do careful analysis of the photos he took, using a technique called iDStretch, a specialized app created by researchers who study rock art. This involved creating false color images and other manipulations to help determine whether the bird was really on top of or beneath the old signatures. Even if it predated the early signatures, Simek had cautioned that it might have been drawn by an early nineteenth- rather than a thirteenth-century visitor.

I described to Lee my recent signature-hunting trip to Mammoth Cave with Marion, Joe, Kristen, and Chris. I also told him how Chris and I had spent a sunny day nerdholing with Marion and Gerald in an area of sandstone caves near Sparta. Most of the sandstone caves we found were barely two body-lengths long, but a couple had been of sufficient size to list among the ten thousand in the Tennessee Cave Survey. It was surprisingly fun to listen to the two famous cavers squabble on the mountain all afternoon. Chris and I were eager to poke into the little holes they spotted. One I dropped into was only slightly greater than the width of my body and about the height of a phone booth, although I knew that size estimate would mean nothing to Chris. I could stand up in it and just wave my extended fingers at the three outside.

Chris and I had also spent a wet day ridgewalking in a different sandstone area with Chuck Sutherland. Lee had gotten to know Chuck during his last Cookeville sojourn, and we agreed that we both admired the younger caver's passion for collecting data and sharing it with the largest possible audience. I mentioned that like Chuck, Alan Cressler believed there was too much secrecy in caving these days.

Recently Chuck had been checking out potential cave areas using LIDAR data from satellites. LIDAR is an acronym for light detection and ranging, a remote sensing tool which has produced amazingly sharp contours of cave country. Unlike old aerial photographs, LIDAR cuts through trees and underbrush, and unlike old topographic maps, every surface feature was located exactly where an image said it would be.

"It's become a very, very powerful tool for understanding the way that the world works around us," he said. "We just drill right through the tree canopy. It'll even drill through leaf litter. I've seen sinkholes on the surface that are a foot deep, and if you get into them and dig through them, you'll have maybe three or four feet deep of leaves. The LIDAR will drill through that. It's amazing. It's black magic. It's so cool."

Cavers could take a known cave map and place it accurately beneath a three-dimensional LIDAR map of the surface in order to produce a video animation showing the relationship between the two. You could rotate the image, moving above and below ground, to look for clues as to places where new passage might lie. Hal Love had done that exactly that with Secret Squirrel, creating amazing videos that suggested several possible spots where the cave might be extended with future exploration.

Unfortunately, while LIDAR was great at finding large sinkholes no caver had ever examined, the vast majority of these finds still had no easily entered caves at their bottoms. The mountain Chris and I split with Chuck and one other caver had shown some very "cavy" features on the LIDAR set, but in person in the rain they had turned out to be miserable crawlways and rock shelters. Even so, wildflowers were in bloom and it was a scenic walk amid spring showers.

As we stopped to re-tie the webbing on Lee's bad shoe, I described a current project I was working on with a team from my university, making a series of short educational films about research to stop or at least slow the continued spread of WNS across the US. We had set up a trip with our old friend Allen Mosler to film bat research in a South Georgia cave familiar from my Florida State days, where Pete Pattavina was monitoring the health of a large colony (thus far) beyond the reach of WNS.

The sinkhole entrance had changed in nearly four decades, reshaped by hurricane floods to the point where we could no longer free-climb down as I had done in college. Instead a cable ladder was rigged next to the sinkhole's signature waterfall, so that we climbed it twenty or so feet

Allen Mosler, the author, and Pete Pattavina at the parking area for Waterfall Cave, nearly forty years after Mosler first took Taylor to the entrance sinkhole.

down to the entrance area. Pete had not liked the ladder on the way in, and instead as we left he free-climbed out directly in the cascading falls, using a safety line with a single ascender to struggle upward through the pouring water.

It had been over thirty years since I had last set foot on a cable ladder, and when it was my turn, I saw that no one had rigged a traditional safety belay for climbers on the ladder. Instead, a local caver (the daughter of a caving couple I had known back in college) tossed Pete's rope, climbing harness, and ascender for the rest of to use as a safety while on the wobbly ladder. The result was that after I climbed just a few feet off the floor, the ascender held me too tightly to the ladder for me to make the next step—or to step back down to remove it. I struggled in place, getting soaked from the spray of the waterfall and wearing myself out before an audience of seasoned cavers and my own students. After ten or fifteen minutes of such buffoonery, Allen Mosler, behind me in the line to exit, took pity and used his pocketknife to cut the safety line, so I could get back onto the floor of the sinkhole. He then climbed the ladder to the top and rigged a traditional belay to help me reach the lip.

Despite embarrassing myself in front of the students I had brought along to help with the filming, we spent the next two days shooting in Tennessee caves with Cory Holliday. I explained to Lee that over next year we planned to shoot ongoing bat research in Arkansas, Georgia, Tennessee, Texas, and South Dakota. And I described the microbial research Chris and I had done in Secret Squirrel. We had arranged a second collection trip in hopes of collecting actual tarballs and also in hopes of avoiding some of the human contamination that had marred samples in our previous effort. Later analysis of our first samples had yielded a complex ecosystem containing six different archaea commonly associated with mid-ocean thermal springs.

At last we reached the eleven-foot climb to the surface from Capshaw. We had enjoyed a good day, checking out several sinkholes and small caves in addition to the long ramble here. That night Lee, Sharon, Kathy, and I ate out, talking and laughing as we always did until late in the evening. Yet Lee definitely sounded serious about stepping away from caving.

He seemed even more serious the week after our trip to Cookeville. Lee had picked up some sort of bad infection, probably from Capshaw. His doctors had put him on powerful antibiotics and he was hoping to stay out of the hospital. He sounded miserable on the phone.

"Caves just don't like me anymore," he said. "This is just like the poison ivy last year."

I could see his point and tried to give him some space. As I had told him, I had plenty of trips planned related to bat filming. I was still acting out a scientific fantasy, dabbling in cave microbiology. My sabbatical had ended and I would be juggling these trips around an academic schedule. Chris was starting his graduate program in the fall and was making time for another Secret Squirrel collection only because he had gotten as hooked as I was by the petroleum-based ecosystem that seemed to be living there.

As the academic year progressed, Sharon and Kathy talked weekly by phone, and Lee and I talked once a month or so on Facebook Messenger, but I didn't start bugging him about caving again until the

Students Chris Taylor and Quincy Gragg collect samples from iron-rich calcite deposits in a wall above the tarball area.

spring. I was going to the Cookeville NSS Convention in June 2019, so lodging was sure to fill up in town fast. In March I tried to get Lee and Sharon to agree to stay in the same downtown vacation rental we had used before.

"You don't even have to go caving," I promised. "There's loads to do at convention without going caving."

"There's no way I'd go to an NSS convention and *not* go caving."

"That works too."

"But I don't want to go caving," he said. "Why don't you go climbing in Colorado with me instead?"

I didn't really want to go climbing. We left it there. I still went ahead and reserved the Cookeville rental for the week of convention, just in case. I agreed to talk about mountain climbing with him, maybe even go to Colorado with him, if he didn't mind me talking about caving. Later that month, Lee was out for a few weeks getting his gallbladder removed. I became hard to reach because I had been talked into taking an older role—the Prince—for a college production of *Romeo and Juliet*.

Early in May, Sharon called Kathy in the middle of a Monday night. Kathy waved me over and turned the phone on speaker. I could tell from her face—not to mention the time—that it was serious. "Repeat what you just said so Mike can hear," she said.

"Okay," Sharon said, "the important thing is that Lee is stable and the doctors think he's going to be all right, but Lee basically died earlier tonight."

She explained Lee had jogged a mile to the Sebring YMCA where he planned to work out. Just before he got there, he collapsed on a sidewalk near some city baseball fields.

"If he had fallen thirty seconds earlier, he would landed in a ditch and no one would have seen him. A woman was driving by at just the right moment to see him fall." Sharon said the woman, whose name she had not yet learned, screeched to a dramatic stop at the entrance to the parking and ran over to him, dialing 911 as she went.

"If she had kept driving he'd be dead," she said.

As the woman spoke with the emergency dispatcher, an off-duty sheriff on his way to Home Depot saw a crowd standing around a fallen man. He pulled over and started chest compressions. A nurse at the ballfields noticed the commotion and ran over to start mouth-to-mouth resuscitation as the sheriff continued CPR.

"Her last name is Angel, I kid you not," Sharon said. "She did mouth-to-mouth on Lee while the other woman did compressions. She's gorgeous, and Lee didn't get to enjoy it. She wasn't even going to go to her kid's ballgame and changed her mind at the last minute. Lee had no pulse at all, no breathing. The paramedics said they probably could have revived him, but he would have been brain damaged if not for those two keeping oxygen in his brain."

Sharon said Lee normally runs with no ID. "It was around 10 p.m. when I started getting worried," she said. "I called both city hospitals, asking if Lee Pearson had been admitted. When they said no I started driving around town." She eventually returned home and called the hospitals a second time. Finally she called 911. This dispatcher sent her to Sebring police station, where an officer told her a man wearing a purple Fitbit was listed as John Doe at Highlands Regional Hospital. She had found him. After midnight, she actually saw Lee in the intensive care unit, and sometime during the night she called us.

Sharon said that Lee had not had a heart attack per se, but an electrical malfunction in his heart. They were going to put in a combination pacemaker/defibrillator, and the doctor had told her there was good chance he could lead a normal life with that. She said the local newspaper was coming out to do a story about the two women who saved his life.

Lee and I had been running over scary bridges since we were too young and foolish to know better. The act of caving seemed to have made us young and foolish for life. This struck me as marvelous. Caving—belonging to the larger caving community, personally knowing TAG explorers who were every bit as daring as Magellan or Hillary or Armstrong, personally finding places no light had ever touched nor eye ever seen—these experiences tied us to a natural world unknown to most who live in a make-believe one of screens and media. We knew our own mortality intimately, in ways that might or might not have been healthy, but that at least let us laugh with ease about the fact that we would not get off this rock alive.

Later that night I opened Messenger and wrote to Lee, "So did you do it? I heard you were getting in shape today!"

Three weeks later, when he was home with a new electrical device sewn into his chest and the energy to check his Facebook messages, he texted back, "Man, I've got to get in shape."

Then he texted me a training video of a woman running—full tilt running—to the summit of Long's Peak. That started a conversation where we basically picked up where we had left off before his untimely and very temporary death:

> **ME:** I'll be waving and wishing you good luck when I wimp out after an hour . . .
> **LEE:** Don't say that, Brother. We can do it. It's just one step at a time.

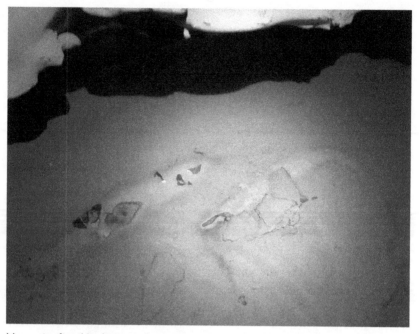

Moments after this photograph was taken, the larger gray patch spit out dozens of tarballs that fizzed like bubbles in champagne, spreading a strong petroleum odor throughout the passage.

ME: Said Marion to Gerald.
LEE: Said Lee to Mike.
ME: That lady in the video has me breathing hard already.
LEE: Yes, me too. If only it were that easy!

I realized I was probably going to have to climb a mountain in Colorado.

On Memorial Day weekend before the NSS convention, Chris and I were finally able to return to Secret Squirrel. Hal Love was going to lead a convention trip there, so as we worked our way to the Petroleum Passage, he could check out the hike, the gate, and main route to make sure they were ready for company. This time we brought along one of James Engman's research assistants, a pre-med undergraduate who had just done a research internship at Vanderbilt Medical Center's nephrology lab, where Hal also worked.

The tarballs did not disappoint. As Chris poked a sampling swab into one of the dark patches on the floor of the Petroleum Passage, dozens of black tarballs erupted like an effervescent volcano spewing from the floor. They popped to the surface, releasing a petroleum stench that nearly chased us out of the chamber. I managed to get the whole eruption on video. We collected a complete tarball for chemical and microbial analysis, along with dozens of fresh swabs from that part of the cave. Once again, DNA testing on one of the samples revealed *Methanopyrus kandleri*, and James Engman emailed me another definition he found, calling the it "a species of hyperthermophilic, halotolerant, methanogenic archaeon, originally isolated from sediments associated with undersea, hydrothermal, vent fields."

"How did they get to our cave?" he asked me in the email. "You think if you go deep enough, everything is connected?"

I emailed back, "Yep."

Shortly after the trip, I sent Lee a link to my tarball video. He answered with advice on choosing the best hiking shoes for Long's Peak.

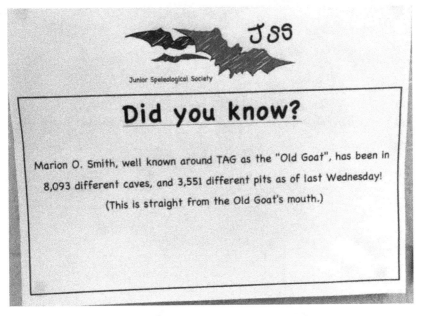

Junior Speleological Society

Did you know?

Marion O. Smith, well known around TAG as the "Old Goat", has been in 8,093 different caves, and 3,551 different pits as of last Wednesday! (This is straight from the Old Goat's mouth.)

Sign seen on the wall at the 2019 NSS Convention in Cookeville, Tennessee. JSS is the Junior Speleological Society. Goat was seen in the halls as well.

MICHAEL TAYLOR | Facebook post, June 18, 2019

Marion suggested calling this photo Bloat and Goat. I countered with Fatso and Ratso.

MICHAEL TAYLOR | Facebook post, June 21, 2019

Chapter 18

CONVENTION

"Boss Bitch," reads the nametag hanging on a purple convention lanyard worn by Maureen Handler. The director of any NSS annual convention has about a million jobs, but right now she is helping Sharon Jones, the significant other of Marion O. Smith, set out trash-bag-sized containers of fresh popcorn on tables in a barn-like structure at the Putnam County Fairgrounds in Cookeville, Tennessee.

Somewhere in the crowd outside, Frank Bogle wears a nametag proclaiming him "Boss Bitch Assistant." More than half of the 1,100 convention attendees occupy a colorful nylon city spread over the grounds. The summer sun is nowhere near setting, but both beer trucks are already open for business, as is the Cavern Tavern, a tent lounge serving free cocktails next door.

Midway through the 2019 NSS convention, the Terminal Syphons are onstage, getting in a 6 p.m. sound check before dinner and the traditional Wednesday night campground party. John Wilson, our drummer, fiddles with his complicated electric kit as Keith Goggin jumps into the instantly familiar guitar intro of "Mr. Breeze," a song not on tonight's playlist and thus perfect for sound check. The band joins in. I see the Old Goat himself moving to the beat in the corner, all bones and beard, feet doing a relaxed shuffle of the sort one might see in a Ma and Pa Kettle film circa 1949.

Hosting the NSS convention in Cookeville was Maureen's idea. It was a good one.

Earlier today, Ben Miller gave a talk called "Finding a Nice Cave in the Kingdom of Horror Holes," in which he revealed a new Tennessee cave depth record for Jewett III, a complex system of miserable crawls and wet pits. On the convention's opening day, at a special session called "Tennessee: Land of 10,000 Caves," over a dozen speakers told great Tennessee stories. TAG legend Bill Walter spoke of thirty years and forty-one miles of exploration in Blue Springs. Troy Fuqua repeated his slide show on opening the back door to Rumbling Falls. Joel Buckner gave a stunning presentation, "Discoveries in Tennessee since the 1970s," which included some of the latest Lechuguilla-like images from Secret Squirrel taken by Bob Biddix. On Tuesday, Hal Love led eight convention attendees on a limited tour of the cave and all had gone well.

In the process of deciding what sessions to attend when not at band practice, I've worn creases into my convention program. Naturally enough, its cover bears Chuck Sutherland's Tennessee cave density map. Each day has been marked by tales of discovery and accomplishment. More active cavers are doing interesting things than could ever fit within a single convention—or within a single book, for that matter. Judging by what I've seen so far, caving's golden age of discovery is far from over. I've been fortunate to personally know just a fraction of the many people making the discoveries, to have visited just a fraction of the places they have found.

The previous NSS convention held in Tennessee took place in 1998 in Sewanee on the campus of the University of the South. Coincidentally, I was finishing up my second cave-related book, *Dark Life*, on the search for microbes in Lechuguilla Cave, beneath assorted volcanoes and ice sheets, and on Mars and the moons of Jupiter. As Keith digs those Georgia peaches into the microphone, I suddenly recall that I used the Wednesday night campground party for the final scene of *Dark Life*. The Syphons end our sound check, and I realize that I feel a powerful inclination to repeat myself in 2019.

Night falls and we play our usual mix of classic rock, blues, caver originals, and obscure covers of contemporary Southern bands. About an hour into the show, a massive thunderstorm chases a surge of cavers into the barn. Most stick with us to the bitter end, which will come sometime after 1 a.m. The rain gradually lessens. I see a few of same faces I saw at the last Tennessee convention, two decades older and still in TAG. I think momentarily of cavers lost since then—but I notice with some relief that our crowd is now populated by more than old farts: I see cavers in their twenties sporting nose rings and glowing necklaces. They dance with enthusiasm, their skinny frames built for crawlways. One has brought in an assortment of Hula-Hoops, and they've cleared a corner of the hall for musical Hula-Hooping as we play on.

Dave Bunnell, a fine cave photographer and the long-time editor of the *NSS News*, looks as though he might throw out a hip, but he demonstrates some skillful hula moves with the younger set. Elsewhere I see Jim Fox, Clinton Elmore, and other strong cavers who Facebook assures me are at the height of their exploratory prowess. There's Bill Steele, leader of the annual PESH expeditions to Huautla in Mexico, talking with John Lyles, leader of the Gypsum Karst Project and a principal Lechuguilla explorer.

Cory Holliday and Pete Pattavina are both at the convention to give bat talks. Cory is leading a bat flight viewing tomorrow, and he told me that Pete is taking a vertical training course (understandable after our adventure at Waterfall Cave). While WNS continues to decimate some Southern species, the endangered gray has flourished—this species may be among the dark shadows whirling now at moths near the fairground light posts.

A summer breeze brings a whiff of refreshment to the hot barn. I look out through wraparound windows paned with chicken wire instead of glass. Lightning flares behind distant hills to the west, shimmering in puddles that dot the soaked campground. Somewhere out there, rain surges into sinkholes, rushing downward through falls and streams into a hidden world. Here in town, Capshaw must be a raging whitewater river about now.

Thirty miles south, rainwater flows into the river of Rumbling Falls and in smaller amounts splashes over the Blasted Goat Exit, Scottie's sinkhole, and my own digging project. They await my return. With Troy's engineering success, the race for a back door is over. Yet I am certain passage exists beyond the century-old plug from which I extracted a blue bottle nearly three years ago. It will keep. Out there lie vast boreholes and tiny crawlways awaiting a first human encounter, one that may never arrive. To the caves, it's all the same. But to the caver, it sometimes seems that the boreholes diminish and the crawlways multiply. There may or may not be borehole or some strange new life form beyond the next turn in a crawlway. The point is the search for hidden nature, which will continue long after I cease to dig.

We shift from "Stray Cat Strut" to "Stormy Monday." In a couple of hours there'll be cheers and whistles when Albert launches the final song with the line, "Thank you all for coming to our annual practice." A week after convention, Dave Bunnell will post on Facebook striking images of a Rumbling Falls through-trip with many of the cavers now in the room. By then I'll be at a different caver gathering in South Dakota, celebrating two hundred miles of discovery at Jewel Cave National Monument. Dr. Hazel Barton, the keynote speaker, will describe some amazing microbial projects her lab is undertaking. In a free moment she'll offer me some advice and encouragement on our Tennessee tarball project.

While I'm out there, I'll post images of the Jewel Cave event on Facebook, which will prompt another Messenger conversation with Lee. We've made reservations for Colorado the second week in July. Kathy and I will visit my sister and her family in Boulder before heading up to meet Lee and Sharon in the mountains.

> **LEE:** Looks like you're having a great time. I've had two days now of some easy running and I feel good. Of course with this thing in my chest, I give new meaning to the phrase running scared.
>
> **ME:** I had to climb about 200 feet on a trail near Jewel, elevation about 3500, and I sure was breathing heavy.
>
> **LEE:** We'll just do the best we can. That's all we can do. Just a reminder, your sister has made it.
>
> **ME:** She's lived in the mountains for about 40 years now.
>
> **LEE:** Well we've been underground now for at least that long. That has to count for something.

ME: True. I'll start with you, but I can't promise to finish with you.

LEE: We'll just give it the ole college try. Heck, we might not even make it out of the parking lot. But, I'm hoping for at least the Gremlin Forest.

A week after this conversation, the four of us stay in a comfortable YMCA cabin near Estes Park. I never did talk Lee into coming to the convention, but I feel a need to climb Long's Peak with him. I mean, he played the death card and all.

Starting at 3 a.m. with headlamps, we pass the Gremlin Forest in minutes. We hike miles under a bright full moon and then under an empty blue Colorado sky. Hours later we make it all the way to the Keyhole. The presence of sloppy ice in the Trough (coupled with the fact that we've had only two days to acclimatize to the altitude) keeps us from the summit. Lee's new pacemaker works fine, and he doesn't keel over. Neither do I, although I walk very slowly coming down. My Fitbit awards 42,000 steps and 371 floors of vertical.

Sign at the base of the Keyhole on the summit hike to Long's Peak, Colorado.

On the trail Lee is faster and stronger than me, a true pace maker like old times. When we first reach the base of the short slope up to the Keyhole, Lee runs up the rocks to scout the route. I stay below. While waiting for his return, I snap a photo of a warning sign meant for climbers. It could apply equally to cavers seeking discovery. It could apply equally to life itself.

Back in my office in Arkansas, I keep an old blue bottle on a corner of my desk. It smells of the cave, which I know is the smell of actinomycetes. James Engman and his students have been presenting posters on our work in Secret Squirrel at various state conferences, and were one of sixty student groups selected to present at a national conference called "Posters on the Hill," to be held in Washington, DC. I'm sure a paper is in the works. We have more collection trips planned to examine the ways insects, salamanders, and other fauna interact with the tarball ecosystem. Beyond TAG, National Park managers at both Wind Cave and Lechuguilla Cave have planned celebrations recognizing that each of these caves has reached a mapped length of 150 miles.

"The torch in TAG caving has been passed to a new generation that includes Mike A. Green, Kyle Lassiter, Matt Tomlinson, Clinton Elmore, John Zetterberg, Zeke McKee, Justin Huffman, and many others," Marion writes to me on Christmas Eve, 2019. "The old geezers, such as me, can only hope to hear about their successes and make suggestions for additional things to try."

Forty years ago I walked into a grotto meeting in Tallahassee and realized I had stumbled into a golden age of cave exploration. It's still going strong as new explorers take charge. Even so, I plan to lure Lee back to Tennessee to help me dig, maybe next winter.

I hope the cave goes. I hope we all do.

Group shot after emerging from the lower entrance of Rumbling Falls.
Photo: Dave Bunnell

Now that Convention is over, we are starting up our work on the NSS HQ again. We will be having a work weekend August 17. I'll be down on the 16 to start removing the old fence along Pulaski Pike. It was severely damaged by a dump truck. The plan is to remove all the fence before the contractor (a caver!) comes in Monday the 19th to start the replacement. We can use any and all hands on Friday afternoon and all day Saturday. I'll be camping out (indoors) Friday night. Come join the fun!

MAUREEN HANDLER | Facebook post, August 2, 2019

With Marion O Smith, age 77 and crawling.

JEFF DILCHER This reminds me of Marion at Baby Hog Horror Hole. I wondered why he was handing me a ball of mud, till I saw the ends of his glasses sticking out of it!

MICHAEL TAYLOR Was there perhaps some colorful commentary during this crawl?

JIM FOX | Facebook post, October 5, 2019

Shawn Wyatt in his new sandstone cave discovery, Rothwell Tomato Spring Cave. Marion O. Smith for scale. Good work ridgewalking Shawn, thanks for the invite!!

WARREN WYATT Very nice find, man

SHAWN WYATT Warren Wyatt thanks it's all about the caves

MICHAEL TAYLOR What number was that for the goat?

ALFRED CRABTREE Michael Taylor It was #1 for Wednesday lol

ALFRED CRABTREE | Facebook post, August 1, 2019

297

IF YOU WANT TO GO CAVING . . .

The only safe way to begin caving is to go with someone experienced. An excellent introduction to the underground wilderness is to take one of the "wild" or "spelunking" tours offered at many of the national parks, national monuments, and state parks that feature caves, as well at many commercial tour caves. You can also meet an experienced guide through one of the grottos of the National Speleological Society. You can find a local grotto and learn much about safe caving techniques from the NSS website, caves.org.

Although most spelunking tours and grottos with beginner trips will lend you a helmet, lamp, and other necessary gear for your first trip, you should bring sturdy but flexible clothing and lug-soled boots that provide some ankle support. You should carry a small back-up flashlight and batteries, water, and perhaps a light snack. Also bring a complete change of clothes (including shoes and underwear) for after the cave trip, along with a garbage bag for your muddy clothes—which will never look quite the same again. Be sure to learn any WNS decontamination requirements for your chosen cave—these vary by state and are listed at www.whitenosesyndrome.org/static-page/decontamination-information.

Keep in mind that most caves are on private land and that many landowners have closed their caves to all exploration because of an inconsiderate act by a single caver. Always obtain permission from the landowner before setting foot on private property, and always thank the landowner when such permission is granted. If a landowner or guide requests that you sign a liability waiver, be willing to do so without hesitation—or don't go caving. Leave farm gates as you find them, whether open or closed. Never camp on cave property without permission and never disturb a locked cave gate. (Many gated caves may be entered legally by going through proper channels; often a contact number for a particular cave is posted within sight of the entrance. Simply call the number and follow established procedure.)

A final note about the cavers you meet: They may seem a bit wary at first, even cold. Don't worry. It's only natural that cavers exercise caution in introducing new practitioners to their special places. Even if you are a highly experienced climber or hiker, your guides will (or should) spend a great deal of time talking to you about safety and conservation before they take you underground. They will want to see a certain determination and self-reliance in your thinking, to be sure that you won't get weird in a tight spot. Indulge them. Even after you join a grotto, it may take a year or two before you are taken to any of a group's biggest or best caves (often kept secret). You may have to pass the grotto's vertical training program before you get to see your first pit. Be patient. Every caver I know who has taken the time to learn with an experienced group has made friends for life and has found a truly life-changing way of looking at the world's hidden nature.

NOTES

CHAPTER ONE

1   *more caves per square mile:* see Chuck Sutherland, "KTAG—Cave Density Map."

3   *been decimated by white-nose syndrome:* For the latest US spread map of the disease and information on current research, see whitenosesyndrome. org, the website of the interagency White-Nose Response Team, which is coordinated by the US Fish and Wildlife Service.

3   *As recently as sixty thousand years ago:* While many studies of the Y chromosome published since 2010 support this relatively recent "out of Africa" date, others have found small African populations with much earlier common male ancestors, some going as far back as 338,000 years. See Fernando L. Mendez et al., "An African American Paternal Lineage."

5   *similar microorganisms may exist today:* While new studies suggesting possibilities for extant microbial life beneath the surfaces of Mars and various moons of Jupiter and Saturn seem to pop up almost daily (see Sylvain Piqueux et al., "Widespread Shallow Water Ice on Mars"), the basic scientific principles that make such extraterrestrial life likely have been around for decades, as discussed in my 1999 book *Dark Life*. See also C. Allen, "Microscopic Physical Biomarkers."

CHAPTER TWO

20   *Florida State Cave Club:* From 1968 to 1992, the club was both an
      official grotto of the National Speleological Society and an official
      student organization of Florida State University. That year the two
      sponsors parted ways and the club became the Flint River Grotto of the
      NSS. A history of the grotto (and also the Florida Cave Protection Act)
      appears in the guidebook to the 2016 Florida Cave Crawl, *Caving by
      the Coon Bottom*, which can be found online at www.flintrivergrotto.
      org/2016-Cave-Crawl.pdf.

21   *"spelunker" was a term of derision:* See the definition for "spelunker"
      at *Merriam-Webster,* www.merriam-webster.com/dictionary/spelunker.
      Clay Perry was the New England author and explorer who popularized
      the word in the 1940s, when "cavers" had been "caving" for decades.

CHAPTER THREE

29   *Monteagle grade:* John C. Glennon, "Monteagle Mountain," Crash-
      Forensics.com, accessed September 2018, www.crashforensics.com/
      monteaglemountain.cfm; also "White-Knuckle Roads," *Overdrive Mag-
      azine,* May 7, 2008, www.overdriveonline.com/white-knuckle-roads.

32   *how it reached the US remains a hotly debated topic:* "I don't think
      we yet know whether Pd is native to Europe or Asia," Cory Holliday
      wrote to the author in early 2020. "If anyone knows, it would be Joe
      Hoyt who published the [first] paper about the fungus in Asia." See
      Joseph R. Hoyt et al., "Widespread Bat White-Nose Syndrome Fungus,
      Northeastern China."

32   *billions of dollars every year:* See Justin G. Boyles et al., "Economic
      Importance of Bats in Agriculture."

33   *Our gear had to be clean:* Updated WNS decontamination protocols
      for cavers can be found on the White-Nose Syndrome Response Team
      website (accessed February 3, 2020): www.whitenosesyndrome.org/
      static-page/decontamination-information.

34   *had written a letter:* The full letter, dated February 15, 2018, can be
      found online at the website of the National Speleological Society, caves.
      org/WNS/wns%20letter%20to%20feds%202018.pdf.

35   *although similar in appearance to actual pipistrelles:* See Steven R.
      Hoofer and Ronald A. Van Den Bussche, "Molecular Phylogenetics,"

2003, and also Darren Naish (tetrapodzoology), "Putting the 'Perimy-otines' Well Away from Pips Proper."

38   *had sprayed an antifungal agent:* See Emma Hiolski, "Battling a Deadly Bat Fungus."

CHAPTER FIVE

58   *"warm little pond":* the full letter can be read online at the University of Cambridge's Darwin Correspondence Project, "To J. D. Hooker, 1 February [1871]," www.darwinproject.ac.uk/letter/DCP-LETT-7471.xml.

59   *greatest mass of life on Earth:* There have been many articles and studies on the deep biosphere in recent decades, but one of the most comprehensive clearing houses for current information on the hidden realm that harbors (by mass) most of the planet's life is the website of the Deep Carbon Observatory, an international scientific consortium: deepcarbon.net.

59   *with three "domains":* see C. R. Woese and G. E. Fox, "Phylogenetic Structure of the Prokaryotic Domain."

63   *hypogene speleogenesis:* See Aleksandr Borisovič Klimčuk, *Hypogene Speleogenesis.*

65   *Lower Kane Cave:* see Annette Summers Engel et al., "Bacterial Diversity and Ecosystem Function"; and Annette Summers Engel, Libby A. Stern, and Philip C. Bennett, "Microbial Contributions to Cave Formation."

CHAPTER SIX

77   *permanently preserve it from encroaching development:* See "Hollow Ridge Cave Preserve" on the Southeastern Cave Conservancy website (accessed February 4, 2020), www.scci.org/preserves/hollow-ridge.

78   *article for the NSS News:* See Charles Clark et al, "Xanadu."

CHAPTER SEVEN

95   *Marion Smith grew up:* Most of my information on Smith's childhood and early years of caving came from articles and interviews in the NSS convention guidebooks by Bill Putnam (*Caves and Caving in TAG*) and Geary M. Schindel and John L. Hickman (*Journeys through TAG*) and also the special issue of the *NSS News* devoted to Smith in 2012, on the occasion of his seventieth birthday. Some additional information came

from interviews with Smith and Jim Wilbanks, and from the *"TAG, You're It!"* (Benjamin von Cramon, dir.) video referenced in Chapter 12.

101   *an article focusing on her and Marion Smith:* See Mark Jenkins and Stephen Alvarez, "Deep South."

104   *Smith had left his walking stick:* A photograph posted on Facebook in February 2020 showed Marion pointing out an interesting signature with his walking stick. An observant caver commented that it seemed to be a different stick than the one he had carried for several years. Another caver replied that the previous stick—the one my son had retrieved—had served as a temporary splint during a cave rescue. The night of January 17, 2020, Jim Fox was with Marion and a caver named Justin Huffman exploring a lead in a multi-drop cave above a 107-foot-deep pit when a large boulder gave way and landed on Fox, trapping him above the narrow pit and causing a complex fracture of his femur. As Fox described the moment in a written narrative of the accident and rescue, Huffman made a difficult traverse and rolled the boulder off of him, helping to pull him from the pit's edge and stabilize him as best as possible before leaving the cave to alert rescuers. To quote Fox's account, which he posted on Facebook, "Marion O. Smith was still maybe twenty feet above us at our last bolt on a ledge. Before Justin left us, he came down and stayed with me, later gave me his coat and hat. A little later Marion went for water and Advil, having to rappel down the 107, climb a sixty-foot pit, then rappel the sixty and climb the 107 to get back to me, and he had not eaten. I appreciated this greatly. Marion then told me stories and kept my mind off of the pain for the next three hours until the rescue teams could reach me. Many of them drove from Chattanooga, Huntsville, West Virginia, and Knoxville." The walking stick became a splint that protruded from the Sked stretcher used to negotiate the injured man through pits and tight squeezes. Rescuers kept saying, "don't touch the popsicle stick." After a difficult extraction from the cave and complex surgery on his shattered leg, Jim was on the mend and looking forward to an eventual return underground, while Marion was soon pointing a new stick at newfound cave signatures. TAG cavers are tough.

105   *Smith told a reporter:* see David Cobb, "Getting Stuck."

CHAPTER EIGHT

114   *As I was learning vertical techniques: On Rope* by Bruce Smith and Allen Padgett had not yet been written, but after its publication in 1989 and more recent updates, it would become the safety starting point for those studying vertical caving methods.

122   *Bogle had been on the fourth trip:* Most of the story that follows came from a phone interview with Frank Bogle in April 2019 as well as published accident reports.

125   *It was finally descended in 1971:* While my descriptions of Farris and Stamps pits are drawn from memory, historical details concerning both locations came from an unpublished oral history paper (H. Lee Pearson, III. "Cave Lore of the Upper Cumberland." Cookeville, TN: 1984. Unpublished article in author's possession.) and from comments Marion O. Smith wrote in the margins of an early version of this book's manuscript.

CHAPTER TEN

158   *intriguing definitions he had pulled off the Internet:* Jamie did exactly what he and I have long told our students *not* to do, but when in a hurry we all do it anyway: He consulted Wikipedia. These definitions come from en.wikipedia.org/wiki/Euryarchaeota and en.wikipedia.org/wiki/Methanopyrales.

CHAPTER ELEVEN

164   *The caver who pulled the separate threads together:* Most of the Schreiber background information comes articles and interviews in the NSS convention guidebooks by Bill Putnam (*Caves and Caving in TAG*) and Geary M. Schindel and John L. Hickman (*Journeys through TAG*), and also the *NSS News* article on him by Marion O. Smith.

CHAPTER TWELVE

166   *Cole theorized that the brake-bar method:* See David W. Hughes, "An Interview with John Cole."

167   *recalls in a video:* See Benjamin von Cramon, *"TAG, You're It!"*

CHAPTER THIRTEEN

198   *a cookie shaped like a hand:* In a private communication with the author, Marion Smith writes that he never ate the award, and when it got very dry he threw it away. Only later did he learn that the cookie had been laced with marijuana.

199   *As I type these words:* After completing the first draft of this book, I sent the manuscript to several well-known cavers and several writer friends for review. After receiving and entering their corrections, I nervously printed out and sent the manuscript to MOS. He read the book twice, immediately catching grammatical gaffs such as mixing up "farther" and "further," and writing dozens of clarifications and corrections in tiny printed lines of pen and pencil. He described some of the corrections over the phone and mailed me the heavily marked manuscript. As I incorporated (most of) these suggestions during the first week of 2020, I doubtless introduced new errors that Marion will catch in the published book. One can always hope for a second edition.

200   *more claustrophobic aspects of caving:* The *Destination Discovery* article was later reprinted as the chapter "Tight Spot" in *Cave Passages.*

CHAPTER FOURTEEN

222   *boldly exclaimed:* See Michael Ray Taylor, "Spelean Spotlight: Albert Ogden."

222   *Tom Miller and Pete Shifflett:* This story is told in detail in *Cave Passages.*

CHAPTER EIGHTEEN

292   *a national conference called "Posters on the Hill":* I had no way of knowing then that the April 22 conference in Washington, DC, would be cancelled by a worldwide pandemic, one that evidently originated from bats in China (see Kristian G. Andersen et al., "The Proximal Origin of SARS-CoV-2"). The novel coronavirus also nixed my plans to present scientific discoveries at Secret Squirrel at the spring 2020 meeting of the Tennessee Cave Survey. As this book goes to press, the students and I hope these events may be rescheduled for some future date. By the time you read these words, I also hope that notions of traveling and attending conferences once more seem normal. While

caving may never have been perceived as an entirely normal activity, it is also my fervent wish that the cavers in this book, young and old, will soon venture once more beneath TAG, that the current pause will become only a short blip in the ongoing golden age of cave discovery.

BIBLIOGRAPHY

Allen, C. "Microscopic Physical Biomarkers in Carbonate Hot Springs: Implications in the Search for Life on Mars." *Icarus* 147, no. 1 (2000): 49–67. doi.org/10.1006/icar.2000.6435.

Andersen, Kristian G., Andrew Rambaut, W. Ian Lipkin, Edward C. Holmes, and Robert F. Garry. "The Proximal Origin of SARS-CoV-2." *Nature Medicine*, March 17, 2020. doi.org/10.1038/s41591-020-08.

Barr, Thomas C. *Caves of Tennessee.* Bulletin 64. Nashville: State of Tennessee, Dept. of Environment & Conservation, Div. of Geology, 1961.

Barton, Hazel A., Michael R. Taylor, and Norman R. Pace. "Molecular Phylogenetic Analysis of a Bacterial Community in an Oligotrophic Cave Environment." *Geomicrobiology Journal* 21, no. 1 (2004): 11–20. doi.org/10.1080/01490450490253428.

Boyles, Justin G., Paul M. Cryan, Gary F. McCracken, and Thomas H. Kunz. "Economic Importance of Bats in Agriculture." *Science* 332, no. 6025 (April 1, 2011): 41–42. doi.org/10.1126/science.1201366.

Brucker, Roger W., and Richard A. Watson. *The Longest Cave.* New York: Alfred A. Knopf, 1976.

Clark, Charles, Ray Lewis, Jeff Sims, and Martha Clark. "Xanadu," *NSS News* 39, no. 8 (1981): 168–75.

Cobb, David. "Getting Stuck in Van Buren County Cave Doesn't Stop 71-Year-Old Spelunker." *Chattanooga (TN) Times-Free Press*, February 4, 2014.

Diaz-Granados, Carol, James Richard Duncan, and F. Kent Reilly. *Picture Cave: Unraveling the Mysteries of the Mississippian Cosmos.* Austin: University of Texas Press, 2015.

Engel, Annette Summers, Megan L. Porter, Libby A. Stern, Sarah Quinlan, and Philip C. Bennett. "Bacterial Diversity and Ecosystem Function of Filamentous Microbial Mats from Aphotic (Cave) Sulfidic Springs Dominated by Chemolithoautotrophic '*Epsilonproteobacteria.*'" *FEMS Microbiology Ecology* 51, no. 1 (December 2004): 31–53. doi.org/10.1016/j.femsec.2004.07.004.

Engel, Annette Summers, Libby A. Stern, and Philip C. Bennett. "Microbial Contributions to Cave Formation: New Insights into Sulfuric Acid Speleogenesis." *Geology* 32, no. 5 (May 2004): 369. doi.org/10.1130/g20288.1.

"Georgia Underground." *Dogwood City Grotto Newsletter* 6, no. 3 (September–October 1969). Special issue on Ellison's Cave.

Hiolski, Emma. "Battling a Deadly Bat Fungus." *Chemical & Engineering News* 96, no. 15 (April 10, 2018). cen.acs.org/biological-chemistry/infectious-disease/Battling-deadly-bat-fungus/96/i15.

Hoofer, Steven R., and Ronald A. Van Den Bussche. "Molecular Phylogenetics of the Chiropteran Family Vespertilionidae." *Acta Chiropterologica* 5, suppl. (January 1, 2003): 1–63. doi.org/10.3161/001.005.s101.

Hug, L., Baker, B., Anantharaman, K. et al. "A New View of the Tree of Life." *Nature Microbiology* 1, no. 5 (May 2016): article no. 16048. doi.org/10.1038/nmicrobiol.2016.48.

Hughes, David W. "An Interview with John Cole." *NSS News* 39 no. 7 (1981): 145–47, 158.

———. *Vertical Bill: The Story of Bill Cuddington and the Development of Vertical Caving in America.* Huntsville, AL: National Speleological Society, 2007.

Hoyt, J. R., K. Sun, K. L. Parise, G. Lu, K. E. Langwig, T. Jiang, et al. (2016). "Widespread Bat White-Nose Syndrome Fungus, Northeastern China." *Emerging Infectious Diseases* 22, no. 1, 140–42. doi.org/10.3201/eid2201.151314.

Jenkins, Mark, and Stephen Alvarez. "Deep South." *National Geographic*, June 2009. www.nationalgeographic.com/magazine/2009/06/tag-caves.

Klimčuk, Aleksandr Borisovič. *Hypogene Speleogenesis: Hydrogeological and Morphogenetic Perspective.* Carlsbad, NM: National Cave and Karst Research Institute, 2007.

Matthews, Larry E. *Big Bone Cave.* Huntsville, AL: National Speleological Society, 2006.

———. *Caves of Chattanooga.* Huntsville, AL: National Speleological Society, 2007.

———. *Caves of Grassy Cove.* Huntsville, AL: National Speleological Society, 2014.

———. *Cumberland Caverns,* 2nd ed. Cloverdale, IN: Greyhound Press, 2005.

———. *Descriptions of Tennessee Caves.* Bulletin 69. Nashville: State of Tennessee, Dept. of Environment & Conservation, Div. of Geology, 1973.

———. *Dunbar Cave: The Showplace of the South.* Huntsville, AL: National Speleological Society, 2005.

Matthews, Larry E., and Bob Biddix. *Caves of the Highland Rim.* Huntsville, AL: National Speleological Society, 2019.

Matthews, Larry E., and G. Thomas Rea. *Caves of Knoxville and the Great Smokey Mountains.* Huntsville, AL: National Speleological Society, 2008.

Matthews, Larry E., and Bill Walter. *Blue Spring Cave.* Huntsville, AL: National Speleological Society, 2010.

Mendez, Fernando L., Thomas Krahn, Bonnie Schrack, Astrid-Maria Krahn, Krishna R. Veeramah, August E. Woerner, et al. "An African American Paternal Lineage Adds an Extremely Ancient Root to the Human Y Chromosome Phylogenetic Tree." *American Journal of Human Genetics* 92, no. 3 (March 7, 2013): 454–59. www.ncbi.nlm.nih.gov/pmc/articles/PMC3591855.

Muir, John. *A Thousand-Mile Walk to the Gulf.* Cambridge, MA: Houghton-Mifflin, 1916. (The Sierra Club maintains a free digitized version at vault. sierraclub.org/john_muir_exhibit/writings/a_thousand_mile_walk_to_the_gulf.)

Naish, Darren (writing as tetrapodzoology). "Putting the 'Perimyotines' Well Away from Pips Proper (Vesper Bats Part XII)," ScienceBlogs, April 11, 2011. scienceblogs.com/tetrapodzoology/2011/04/12/placing-perimyotines.

Pace, N. R. "Time for a Change." *Nature* 441, no. 289 (2006). doi. org/10.1038/441289a

———. "A Molecular View of Microbial Diversity and the Biosphere." *Science* 276, no. 5313 (May 2, 1997):734–40. www.ncbi.nlm.nih.gov/pubmed/9115194.

Piqueux, Sylvain, Jennifer Buz, Christopher S. Edwards, Joshua L. Band-field, Armin Kleinböhl, David M. Kass, and Paul O. Hayne. "Widespread Shallow Water Ice on Mars at High and Mid Latitudes." *Geophysical Research Letters* 46, no. 24 (December 10, 2019): 14,290–98. doi. org/10.1029/2019GL083947.

Putnam, Bill, ed. *Caves and Caving in TAG: A Guidebook for the 1989 Convention of the National Speleological Society.* Huntsville, AL: National Speleological Society, 1998.

Raines, Terry, ed. *Sótano de las Golondrinas.* Bulletin 2. Austin, TX: Association for Mexican Cave Studies, 1968.

Schindel, Geary M., and John L. Hickman, eds., *Journeys through TAG: 1998 National Speleological Society Convention Guidebook.* Huntsville, AL: National Speleological Society, 1998.

Smith, Bruce, and Allen Padgett. *On Rope: North American Vertical Rope Techniques for Caving, Search and Rescue, Mountaineering.* Huntsville, AL.: Vertical Section, National Speleological Society, 1989.

Smith, Marion O. *The Discovery and Exploration of Rumbling Falls Cave.* 2017 (limited edition private printing).

———. *The Exploration & Survey of Ellison's Cave.* 1977 (limited edition private printing).

———. "The Story of a Caver: Richard Walter Schreiber." *NSS News* 48, no. 4 (1990): 97–100.

"Special Issue: MOS." *NSS News* 70, no. 10 (October 2012) (special issue on Marion O. Smith).

Sutherland, Chuck. "KTAG—Cave Density Map." *Chuck Sutherland: A Tennessee Naturalist's Photography, Maps, and Projects* (blog), October 23, 2017. chuck-sutherland.blogspot.com/2017/10/ktag-cave-density-map. html.

Sutherland, Chuck, and Caralynn Strand, eds. *Land of 10,000 Caves: 2019 NSS Convention.* Huntsville, AL: National Speleological Society, 2019.

Taylor, Michael Ray. *Cave Passages: Roaming the Underground Wilderness.* New York: Scribner, 1996.

———. *Caves: Exploring Hidden Realms.* Washington, DC: National Geographic Books, 2000.

———. *Dark Life: Martian Nanobacteria, Rock-Eating Cave Bugs, and Other Extreme Organisms of Inner Earth and Outer Space.* New York: Scribner, 1996.

———. "Dig It." *American Caves,* Summer/Fall 2003.

———. "Fighting to Save America's Bats." *New York Times,* April 13, 2018.

———. "Going Deep," *Sports Illustrated*, March 3, 2003.

———. "Hidden River Cave: A Karst Reclamation Success Story," in *Cave Conservation and Restoration*, edited by Val Hildreth Werker and Jim C. Werker, 331–32. Huntsville, AL: National Speleological Society, 2006.

———. "Journey into Lechuguilla Cave." September 30, 2002, on The Mysterious Life of Caves, a website to accompany *Nova: The Mysterious Life of Caves*, aired Oct. 1, 2002, on PBS, written, produced, and directed by Sarah Holt. www.pbs.org/wgbh/nova/caves/journey.html.

———. "Spelean Spotlight: Albert Ogden." *NSS News* 77, no. 5 (2019): 22–23.

———. "Spelean Spotlight: Diana Northup." *NSS News* 74, no. 4 (2016): 24–26.

———. "Spelean Spotlight: Maureen Handler." *NSS News* 77, no. 8 (2019): 28–29.

Taylor, Michael Ray, and D. J. Stoddard. "The Terminal Syphons." *NSS News* 71, no. 1 (2013): 18–22.

von Cramon, Benjamin, dir. *"TAG, You're It!"—TAG Caving*. Produced by the National Speleological Society. YouTube, October 9, 2017. www.youtube.com/watch?v=Co_IPai6Peo. (This 52-minute video includes extensive interviews with Marion O. Smith, Jim Wilbanks, and other early TAG explorers, along with segments on recently discovered caves.)

Watson, Patty Jo, Mary C. Kennedy, P. Willey, Louise M. Robbins, and Ronald C. Wilson. "Prehistoric Footprints in Jaguar Cave, Tennessee." *Journal of Field Archaeology* 30, no. 1 (2005): 25–43. doi. org/10.1179/009346905791072440.

Watson, Traci. "The Trickster Microbes That Are Shaking Up the Tree of Life." *Nature* 569 (May 16, 2019): 322–24. doi.org/10.1038/d41586-019-01496-w.

Widmer, Urs, and Michael Ray Taylor, eds. *Lechuguilla: Jewel of the Underground*. Schoharie, NY: Speleo Projects, 1991.

Willey, P., Judy Stolen, George Crothers, and Patty Jo Watson. "Preservation of Prehistoric Footprints in Jaguar Cave, Tennessee." *Journal of Cave and Karst Studies* 67, no. 1 (April 2005): 61–68.

———. *The Mammoth Cave*. Vincennes, IN: Harvey, Mason & Co., 1858.

Woese, C. R., and G. E. Fox. "Phylogenetic Structure of the Prokaryotic Domain: The Primary Kingdoms." *Proceedings of the National Academy of Sciences of the United States of America* 74, no. 11 (November 1977): 5088–90. www.ncbi.nlm.nih.gov/pmc/articles/PMC432104.

Wright, Charles W. *A Guide Manual to the Mammoth Cave of Kentucky*. Louisville, KY: Bradley & Gilbert, 1860.

PHOTOGRAPHY & ILLUSTRATION CREDITS

151, Bob Biddix
153, Bob Biddix
157, Bob Biddix
160, Bob Biddix
161, Peter Sprouse
170, Dave Bunnell
175, Bob Cohen
176, Maureen Handler
179, Alan Cressler
185, Ryan Maurer
190, courtesy of Maureen Handler
191, Maureen Handler
195, courtesy of the National
   Speleological Society
198, Chris Anderson
201, Chris Anderson
206, Chris Anderson
213, Chris Anderson
216, Chris Anderson
219, Chuck Sutherland
222, Chuck Sutherland
226, Ryan Maurer

229, Chuck Sutherland
232, Maureen Handler
241, Michael Ray Taylor
245, Michael Ray Taylor
247, Alfred Crabtree
250, Lee Pearson
251, Jim Fox
252, Jim Fox
269, Brian Mayfield
274, Chuck Sutherland
275, Chuck Sutherland
276, Michael Ray Taylor
279, courtesy of Michael Ray Taylor
281, Michael Ray Taylor
284, Michael Ray Taylor
287, Michael Ray Taylor
288, Michael Ray Taylor
293, Michael Ray Taylor
295, Dave Bunnell
296, Jim Fox
297, Alfred Crabtree

ACKNOWLEDGMENTS

When I wrote *Cave Passages* twenty-five years ago, I was surprised at how serendipity helped the book along: A key caving source that I hadn't been able to find through other means popped up at a poker game with graduate literature students in South Carolina. As I wrote about the life and death of Sheck Exley, I learned that Lee Pearson had been eyewitness to a key traumatic event in the famed cave diver's past. And so on. Providential coincidence became a running theme, tying the chapters together. The same serendipity was at play in *Hidden Nature*, nudged along by various friends to whom I remain forever grateful.

In the summer of 2015, after returning from a Tennessee visit, I created a file of notes on caving trips I had taken with Lee over the years. I typed a few lines about Xanadu, listed a dozen assorted pits, and described our recent rendezvous involving a farmer, a sinkhole, and a well-endowed Basset Hound. I wasn't sure where I was going with it, but I sensed a story in the ways that friendship and caving shape lives. I labeled this file "Notes in search of an outline." Over the next few months I added occasional memories and Facebook exchanges. In the summer of 2016, I spent several weeks housebound, recovering from surgery. Like me, the cave file grew fatter that summer. I put it into a folder labeled "Cave Buds," where I started adding old photos and recent Facebook posts. But I don't think the folder would have led to this book but for a random conversation between Margaret Renkl and Beth Kressel-Itkin.

Margaret, who writes beautifully about nature and the South for the *New York Times*, was for many years the editor of Chapter 16, a Nashville-based website promoting books and literature in Tennessee. In May 2017 she gave me an assignment to interview a personal hero, the singer and songwriter John Prine, for the site. The morning after Margaret edited the piece, she had coffee with Beth, who was then acquisitions editor for Vanderbilt University Press. Beth told Margaret that she wished the press would publish more books on nature, especially books aimed at a general, as opposed to academic, audience. I'm sure she was angling for something from Margaret, who—luckily for me—was already deep into writing *Late Migrations*, a beautiful book on nature and loss. Rather than discuss her own project, Margaret deflected Beth's comment, suggesting that what she really wanted was a book on Tennessee caves, and Margaret knew someone who could write it. By 10 a.m., Beth had emailed me. I told her I had a file in hand that seemed a perfect start for a proposal. I thus owe enormous thanks to Margaret Renkl for suggesting the idea and to Beth Kressel-Itkin for listening.

Before submitting my proposal to Vanderbilt, I drove to Tennessee to attend a meeting of the Tennessee Cave Survey. While there I hand-delivered a very early list of possible chapters to one Marion O. Smith, who made a great many useful suggestions on TAG cavers worthy of including in such a book. In the end I only managed to include a small part of this group, but I remain grateful to Marion for his continued willingness to offer helpful suggestions, from the inception of the book to its finish. Any errors that remain are due to my own thick-headedness despite periodic advice from the world's most experienced—and factually precise—caver.

As I wrote the book, Margaret moved on from Chapter 16 to devote more time to her weekly *Times* column and book writing, while Beth moved on to Texas, yet both remained supporters and helped encourage me toward the finish line. When Zack Gresham took over Beth's spot at Vanderbilt, he ensured a smooth editorial transition and became a champion of the project with the press's new management, for which I remain grateful. I also wish to thank Joell Smith-Borne, Betsy Phillips, and the rest of the Vanderbilt team for their superb editing, design, and marketing efforts.

Many cavers and researchers graciously granted interviews, allowed me to horn in on expeditions, and otherwise provided assistance in the course of this book. While I am especially grateful to Lee Pearson and Marion Smith, I also remain indebted to Maureen Handler, Chuck Sutherland, Alan Cressler, Allen Mosler, Joel Buckner, Hal Love, Clinton Elmore, Anne Elmore, Jim Fox, Jan Simek, Albert Ogden, Joe Douglas, Kristen Bobo, Alfred Crabtree, Frank Bogle, Lou Simpson, Bill Steele, and many others in the caving world.

In the bat world I am indebted to Pete Pattavina, Cory Holliday, Chris Cornelison, Catherine Hibbard, Shawn Thomas, Winifred Frick, Jo Schaper, Michelle Verant, Kelly Lutsch, Melissa Meierhofer, Amy Turner, Merlin Tuttle, and many other warriors in the fight against white-nose syndrome who were willing to answer my (often confused) questions.

Among early readers I am especially thankful for members of the faculty writers group at Henderson State University, especially Angela Boswell and Travis Langley, who would meet for one of my chapters in the summer when they both had better things to do, and also to Jennifer Dawes, Trudi Sabaj, Mary-Jane Dunn-White, Brian George, Nydia Jeffers, Andrew Burt, David Sesser, Matthew Bowman, and Constanze Weise. I am also grateful to the Ellis College of Arts and Sciences at Henderson for travel grants that supported trips to the 2019 NSS convention and to take students to "Secret Squirrel" cave. Some early chapters were influenced by my wonderful companions at the late, great Rivendell Writers Colony: Ginger Eager, Liz Latty, Brian Fairchild, and Rita Bourland.

Useful insights and suggestions were offered by Ronal Kerbo, Dan O'Rourke, Lou Simpson, Jim Wilbanks, Allen Mosler, Allen Padgett, Hal Love, Joel Buckner, and of course Marion O. Smith and Lee and Sharon Person. I appreciate those cavers who allowed me to quote snippets of their social media posts throughout the book, and I am awed by the willingness of so many talented photographers to share images: Chris Anderson, Frank Bogel, Joel Buckner, Dave Bunnell, Bob Biddix, Kristen Bobo, Curt Buettner, Alfred Crabtree, Alan Cressler, Jim Fox, Maureen Handler, Jim Honaker, Kenneth Ingham, Ryan Maurer, Brian Mayfield, Chuck Sutherland, and Dustin Thames, along with the many others who assisted them amid the unimaginable drudgery of a cave photo trip.

Portions of this book were previously published in somewhat altered form in *Sports Illustrated* and the *New York Times*. I have also previously written on related topics for the *NSS News* and other caver-specific journals. I am grateful to the editors of these publications who helped shape stories that led to chapters, especially Chris Hunt of *SI*, one of the most talented editors I have ever known.

Writing a memoir that spans decades and complex topics becomes more about what you leave out than what you include: For every caving story used, I know dozens as good or better. For every bit of history from sixty years of TAG exploration, I've ignored hundreds of other bits and countless wonderful cavers. In other words, this work is a personal and eclectic endeavor, and I apologize in advance to the caving pioneers and heroes omitted who probably deserved mention. One example: a good book could be built around Chuck Mangelsdorf, the Nashville caver and lawyer who tirelessly fought to stop the Spencer, Tennessee, sewage plan long before he was aware of Rumbling Falls Cave, even though some of his closest friends were among those keeping its existence secret from him and his environmental advocacy group. And yet as the Rumbling Falls chapter expanded, I cut the Chuck section entirely. Time and space—nothing at all to the cave, but enemies to cavers and writers.

I wish I had included more. No doubt I left out other important stuff and important people. This book is one caver's personal love letter to TAG, a region that shaped his life. All I can say in defense of omissions or errors is that it is a letter from the heart. Finally, speaking of heart, I will be forever grateful for the unflagging patience and support of my wife Kathy, my sons Alex, Ken, and Chris, and my extended family.

INDEX

Page numbers in **bold** refer to illustrations.

CPSIA information can be obtained
at www.ICGtesting.com
Printed in the USA
LVHW030233260821
696068LV00009B/313

9 780826 501028